Abiding by the Sermon on the Mount

A Dispensational Approach for Interpretation and Application

JIM OLIVER

Copyright © Jim Oliver 2015

All Rights Reserved

Revision 11/24/2016

Keizer, Oregon

ISBN-13:
978-1514186640

ISBN-10:
1514186640

DEDICATION
and
ACKNOWLEDGEMENTS

To my wife, Kara, and children for their support in this endeavor. They have sat through many hours of being read to and have me given many insights.

I would like to acknowledge my debt to the many pastors and authors from whom I have gained doctrinal principles of God's Word. Particularly, I thank Col. RB Thieme Jr. who through many years of diligent study of God's Word provided me with a foundational understanding of it. I would not have been able to accomplish this endeavor without his teaching.

My gratitude also goes out to Vivian Walters and Rick Breen who have taken a great deal of time and effort to read this manuscript and have made invaluable suggestions to make it much more coherent and readable

Jim Oliver

CONTENTS

Preface	**2**
Forward: The Dispensational Perspective	**4**
Part 1: Introduction—Matthew 5:1-2	**6**

A. The Overall Context of the Sermon
B. The Organization of the Sermon
C. The Biblical Introduction: The Occasion of the Sermon—Matthew 5:1-2

Part II: The Beatitudes—Matthew 5:3-12 — **14**

A Introduction: Blessed
B. Matthew 5:3—The Beatitude of Salvation
  The Kingdom
D. Matthew 5:4—The Beatitude of Comfort
E. Matthew 5:5—The Beatitude of Covenant Qualification
F. Matthew 5:6—The Beatitude of the Desire for Doctrine
G. Matthew 5:7—The Beatitude of Giving and Receiving Grace
H. Matthew 5:8—The Beatitude of Spirituality
I. Matthew 5:9—The Beatitude of Witnessing
J. Matthew 5:10-11—The Beatitudes of Persecution
K. A Review of the Beatitudes
L. Matthew 5:12—Inner Happiness Produces Outer Happiness

Part III: Impact of the Mature Believer—Matthew 5:13-16 — **46**

A Matthew 5:13—Salt of the Earth
B Matthew 5:14-16—Light of the World

Part IV: The Lord's Relationship to the Law—Matthew 5:17-20 — **57**

A. Matthew 5:17—Fulfilling the Law
B. Matthew 5:18—Continuing the 'Fulfillment' Concept
C. Matthew 5:19—Jesus Stresses the Importance of the Law
D. Matthew 5:20—Superseding Religious Righteousness

Part V: Jesus Reframes the Mosaic Law —Matthew5:21-48 — **70**

A. Introduction
B. Matthew 5:21-22—Murder and Anger
C. Matthew 5:23-26—Reconciliation
D. Matthew 5:27-28—From Overt to Mental Adultery
E. Matthew 5:29-30—Self-Judgment
F. Matthew 5:31-32—The Case of Immoral Divorce
G. Matthew 5:33-37—The Issue of Oaths or Swearing
H. Matthew 5:38-42—The Case for Revenge
I. Matthew 5:43-48—Virtue Love Commanded and Illustrated

Part VI: A Warning against Pharisaic Hypocrisy—Matthew 6:1-18   109
A   Matthew 6:1—The Principle of the Warning
B   Matthew 6:2-4—Application: Charity
C   Matthew 6:5-13—Application: Prayer
D   Matthew 6:14-15—Commentary on Forgiveness
E   Matthew 6:16-18—Application: Fasting

Part VII: Priorities for Spiritual Living—Matthew 6:19-24   143
A.   Matthew 6:19-21—A Scale of Values
B.   Matthew 6:22-23—Understanding the Possibility of Failure
C.   Matthew 6:24—The Exclusivity of Divine Power

Part VIII: The Logistical Grace Rationale—Matthew 6:25-34   158
A.   Matthew 6:25—The Application and Principle of Logistical Grace
B.   Matthew 6:26-34—Illustrations of Logistical Grace

Part IX: A Warning, a Reminder and an Offer—Matthew 7:1-12   169
A   Matthew 7:1-6—Stop Judging
B   Matthew 7:7-10—Reminder of Spiritual Life Functions
C.   Matthew 7:11—Offer of the Holy Spirit to the Disciples
D.   Matthew 7:12—The Golden Rule: The Limits of the Mosaic Law

Part X: Entering the Gate of Salvation—Matthew 7:13-14   190
A   Matthew 7:13—The Narrow Gate
B   Matthew 7:14—The Small Gate

Part XI: False Prophets—Matthew 7:15-23   194
A   Matthew 7:15-20—Warnings of False Prophets
B   Matthew 7:21-23—The Condemnation of the False Prophet

Part XII: Illustration Comparing Believers with Unbelievers—Matthew 7:24-27   204

Part XIII: Conclusion—Matthew 7:28-29   206

About the Author

Links to Further Studies

End Notes

Jim Oliver

PROLOGUE

Jesus Christ delivered the Sermon on the Mount to His disciples over 2,000 years ago, yet today people quote it so often that it has become idiomatic in our language. These quotes include, "Turn the other cheek," "Blessed are the poor," "the salt of the earth," "the light of the world," "judge not that you not be judged" and others. Often, those who quote these lines take them completely out of context, misapplying them. An incident I experienced recently provided an extreme example of just such a misapplication. A man struck me on the cheek, just hard enough to smart a bit, and then lifted his other hand to strike my other cheek, while yelling, "Turn the other cheek! Turn the other cheek!" I rejected that notion which seemed to diffuse the situation!

This book explores these statements as well as the entire sermon from the perspective of the sociology of Jesus's era, the Greek vocabulary Matthew and Luke used to quote our Lord as well as grammar and syntax. My task has been to discover the meaning behind all of the words Jesus Christ spoke to His disciples in the Sermon and to find out how we can apply them in today's world.

PREFACE

So often in this life, we become preoccupied with pet causes and priorities. We may become involved in political movements, spending time crusading against what we perceive as inequities in life. Nevertheless, all of these things pale in comparison to the fact that the Lord of the Universe, the Son of God, died for each one of us.

For God so loved the world, that He gave His only begotten Son, that whoever believes in Him shall not perish, but have eternal life. John 3:16

No person's ministry stands alone. I have gained the principles written here because many teachers of the Word and theologians have studied under the ministry of God the Holy Spirit, taught, and then have chosen to commit their conclusions to the written word. For these many people I am very grateful. I am particularly grateful to R. B. Thieme, Jr. who served as my pastor for 20 years. One particular principle he taught was the necessity of taking accurate Bible teaching and "making it your own." I have taken this to heart, therefore, I have also undertaken my own Biblical research to confirm and in many cases to expand upon his teachings. Therefore, I apologize in advance if I have quoted him and not given specific credit.

I am also grateful for the ability to access the work of many other theological writers and Biblical language tools through the Logos Bible Software library system. Where, in the past, I would have had to spend many hours in seminary libraries, I have many of these resources readily available, with the ability to access documents instantly.

Another reason I enjoy this digital library system is its vastness of resources. Ordinarily, in a library, I have to be very selective in my choice of resources. Because of time constraints, I invariably choose those writings that already align with my thinking. However, with such a number of varied resources, I try to read as many of them as possible. Often, when reading about viewpoints differing from my own, I pick up statements that challenge my thinking, leading me to a tangent of thought I would never have explored. Therefore, I urge you, my reader, even if your foundation of understanding the Scripture differs from mine, to read this book as a challenge to expand your horizons of Biblical thinking!

I also have gained from several pastors whose teachings I hear "on the fly," whose insights have certainly taken hold and become incorporated into my thinking. These include Pastor Gary Glenny of Portland Bible Church, Dr. Tom

Cantor and Dr. J Vernon McGee from the radio, Pastor Don Stevens, Pastor Cyrus Rettman, Dr. Leroy Judd and Dan Wray of Keizer Community Church. I probably have not directly quoted from these teachers of the Scripture, but I have certainly gained insights and applications from them.

I have made much use of the original Greek language, noting the meaning of many words, along with their morphology and sentence syntax. I do not think readers of this book need to be experts in the language to gain from what I have written about them. An accurate translation can only be derived from understanding the original languages of the Scripture. Still, people often question certain points. This is why I use the original languages—to present and explain the rationales which are essential to a true understanding.

FORWARD

The Dispensational Perspective

If one were to mention "the Dispensations" to a group of theologians, each may have a different interpretation of the word. Imagine mentioning "the Dispensations" to any other group of people! Because of this—the disparity of dispensational understandings—I need to briefly define the dispensational perspective from which I teach. A dispensation is a period of time, an epoch in human history defined in terms of divine revelation. God has organized and categorized human history into periods of time, each with different divine revelation and resultant differing spiritual lives.

These epochs can be divided into three general categories: the Theocentric Dispensations, the Christological Dispensations, and the Eschatological Dispensations. The Age of the Gentiles (going from Adam to Moses) and the Age of Israel (generally going from Moses to the Birth of Christ) comprise the Theocentric Dispensations. Technically, even though the Age of Israel continued to be the order of the day until the Church Age began, our Lord's teachings—as recorded in the Gospels—become much more easily understood if the thirty years of His walk on earth be considered as a separate dispensation. The next category of dispensations, the Christological, includes the 33 years of our Lord's First Advent and the Church Age. We are currently living in the Church Age. We can separate the Church Age into the early Church Age, characterized by the living apostles, and the latter Church Age, the present day. The Eschatological Dispensations have not yet occurred. These include the Great Tribulation and the 1000 year Millennial Rule of our Lord, His Second Advent. The glorious Eternal State follows His Millennial Rule.

These distinctions highly influence how dispensational theologians both interpret the Scripture and offer applications to believer's lives. The principle becomes a central issue when interpreting the Sermon on the Mount. On one hand, as we will discuss in more detail, our Lord was offering an immediate fulfillment of the Unconditional Covenants to Israel. He would immediately fulfill all of the Old Testament prophecies concerning Him if Israel believed in Him, believed that His was the Messiah. However, Israel—primarily the religious hierarchy whom most followed—rejected Him. Upon that rejection, He began to focus His ministry on the coming Church Age. By the time of the events leading up to and including to Matthew 12, the Jewish establishment had made its rejection of our Lord obvious, so He began, through the parables, to look toward the Church Age.

This interpretation of the Sermon on the Mount takes into consideration that it was foundational to our Lord's presentation of Himself to Israel as her long-awaited Messiah. The application portion of this discussion on the Sermon takes into consideration that the Church Age, with its many unique features, was not yet in view. Therefore, our application of this Sermon—as Church Age believers—may differ from the disciples' application. That difference becomes a central issue in this presentation.

There is one dispensational distinction in this book I have blurred that may confuse the reader. Church Age believers, when filled with and empowered by the Holy Spirit, are said to be "spiritual" and living the "spiritual life" God has designed for them. When referring to the lives Jews lived, who lived in the Age of Israel adhering to the dictates of the correctly interpreted Mosaic Law, I call this their "spiritual lives" as well. Technically, I should refer to that life using different nomenclature. Because our Lord did not give the Spirit until after Pentecost, Jews living in the Age of Israel did not have "spiritual lives," but orthodox religious lives. But the term religious often refers to any religion these days. So please understand that when I use the term "spiritual" when describing those in the Age of Israel, I mean that they were living lives that pleased God because they were following the dictates of the Mosaic Law as our Lord had given it to Moses.

Any errors, misinterpretations, shortcomings in this book are solely mine. If the reader has any comments or questions, feel free to communicate with me through my blog or e-mail.

PART I

Introduction

A. The Overall Context of the Sermon

Even though Jesus during His thirty-three years on earth was the God-Man, He chose to limit His ability to communicate with Israel. As God, He could have spoken to as many people as He chose. However, He, as a human being, could only speak to so many people at one time. This is one application of the Doctrine of Kenosis. It teaches that our Lord voluntarily restricted the use of certain functions of His deity as per the Father's plan for His Incarnation. Therefore, He would be sending His disciples out into Israel to announce His Advent in His stead. This is discussed in Mark 6:6-13 and Matthew 10.

Jesus chose His disciples to go out into Israel for two general reasons. First, they were to announce His advent and second, to communicate to Israel the spiritual life. Not only did they go out to announce His arrival but also everything related to it. His advent was the central and most important aspect of the unconditional covenants God made with Israel. These covenants also included His perfect millennial rule and the restoration of the Earth to its original state, as our Lord created it. That glorious age that the prophets wrote about was just around the corner; Israel only needed to embrace and believe in her Messiah. In order to embrace Him, however, the Jews needed to have the capacity to recognize Him. That capacity required that they be living the life dictated by the Mosaic Law. Adherence to it paved the way for both faith in Christ as it revealed Him prior to His incarnation and for recognizing Him when He arrived.

The Pharisaic spiritual life, under which they were living, completely distorted the life prescribed by the Mosaic Law; it was steeped in legalism. This necessitated corrective communication because people bound by legalism cannot respond to the wonder of their Messiah's arrival. Also, prior to this Sermon, the disciples—also steeped in legalism—knew no Biblical truth to impart, so these words fulfilled their own knowledge deficit. Today, legalism is often misconstrued to be enforcement of differing cultural practices. In reality, it is the enforcement of false systems of thought and behavior upon the less educated by religious authorities. Legalistic people take Biblical principles and add to them, thinking they improve upon them. Adam's wife added touching to our Lord's prohibition of eating of the Tree of the Knowledge of Good and Evil. The Pharisees added myriads of additional regulations to the Mosaic Law. The Judaizers insisted that Gentile believers adhere to the Mosaic Law, to include circumcision, as a part of the Church Age spiritual life. Modern examples of legalism also abound!

This following example of legalism is quite prevalent in churches today. Many churches teach against imbibing alcoholic beverage in any form or of any quantity. There are reasons to avoid alcohol such as having an uncontrollable alcoholic tendency or when it becomes an obstacle to another believer's spiritual life. However, it is a distortion of the Bible to teach authoritatively that a person who enjoys an occasional drink of wine with a meal is sinful. To teach against any form of alcohol consumption as evil dogmatically, then to enforce that policy as a requirement of Christian spirituality is legalism. Our Lord, who turned that water into the best wine at the marriage at Cana, did not condemn those who drank it!

Not only did our Lord's teaching address the disciples own lack of Biblical knowledge but in turn gave them Biblical truths to teach Israel. It also corrected their own spiritual lives, providing the framework for their service to our Lord. The function of every believer's spiritual life in every generation, in every dispensation, is service to our Lord. We must base our desire to serve upon our knowledge and appreciation of Him and His work for us; we must predicate our motivation on spiritual growth, resulting in the correct motivation to serve.

Before we approach this study, we must remember to interpret every passage in the Scripture within the context of its time of presentation. This involves both the broad dispensational perspective as well as the local and immediate framework. As to the broad dispensational context, while our Lord presented it during His First Advent, much of this sermon is relevant to every dispensation. As to the immediate and local context, He presented it specifically for His disciples.

R. B. Thieme Jr. separated this short 33-year period of our Lord's walk on earth into its own dispensation, calling it the Dispensation of the Hypostatic Union. This distinction is an important one to remember as we study our Lord's teachings. It is especially important in the study of this sermon because our Lord's ministry was not only the fulfillment of the entire content of Old Testament prophecy but also the setting of the stage for future dispensations. Human history revolves around both our Lord's life and His multi-faceted ministries. Since He was the fulfillment of all prophecy, Jesus Christ not only pointed this out by His many miracles but also by His teachings. Because the Jews mostly rejected Him, He turned His ministry toward the future. His crucifixion, substitutionary death, physical death, resurrection, and ascension actually inaugurated this glorious Church Age.

B. The Organization of the Sermon

This sermon can be broken down into twelve general parts. A brief description of each section follows.

1. Matthew 5:1-2—The Introduction

Matthew began our Lord's sermon by a description of its location and intended recipients.

2. Matthew 5:3-12—The Beatitudes

The first part of this sermon, the Beatitudes, does not specifically delineate the Christian way of life—that is, the spiritual life of the Church Age believer—nor does it specifically address the spiritual life of those living in our Lord's dispensation. Neither Church Age believers nor those living in the Age of Israel can apply these beatitudes, and then assume that they are living the spiritual life of their dispensation. The principles, however, in a general way, apply to the spiritual life in every generation, every dispensation. Through these verses, our Lord taught the process or path of spiritual growth, starting with the realization of the need for salvation, progressing to belief in Him, then to the development of the advanced faith rest life. These principles apply to every generation of believers, no matter which dispensation he finds himself living in!

The first 13 verses present spiritual progression. Each beatitude builds upon the preceding one, leading one to inner happiness. The first begins with the realization of the need for salvation, and then finally peaks with potential of spiritual maturity in the last one. Understand that believers never arrive at a point in their spiritual growth when they need grow no more. The temporal process of spiritual growth should only end at the end of our physical lives. Even in eternity, will we ever have a complete knowledge of our God?

Many theologians understand this entire Sermon, especially the Beatitudes, as a platform for our Lord's millennial rule. In a sense, this is accurate because had the Jews believed in Him, He would have ushered in the Millennium, with His perfect rule. However, for our purposes in this Church Age, we are better off understanding it as the means our Lord used to train His disciples to announce His arrival. Therefore, we will interpret this Sermon in that manner. However, we need to realize that we, in this Church Age, can apply many of these lessons today as well. Paragraph 5, below, explains this in more detail.

3. The Impact of the Mature Believer on the World—Matthew 5:13-16

In this section of the sermon, our Lord presents the impact of the maturing believer to those around him or her using the analogy of salt. As salt preserves and enhances food, so the believer influences those both within his sphere of influence and outside of it, to include one's entire country.

4. Matthew 5:17-20—The Lord's Relationship to the Law

In the four verses that comprise this section, our Lord clarifies His mission as the God-Man to the human race. Misconceptions and wrong ideas were pervasive in that day, just as they are now. Our Lord needed to arm His disciples with correct information to evangelize Israel effectively.

5. Matthew 5:21-48—Jesus Reframes the Mosaic Law

In the next part of this sermon, our Lord reframed the Mosaic Law. By reframing various aspects of the Law, He did not introduce anything new, but demonstrated how the Law, as far as its intents and purposes were, was perfect. These lessons sounded new to believers in Jesus' day, because since Moses received the Law, it had been much distorted. Our Lord grounded His disciples with accurate applications of the Law.

As we study these passages, understand that these principles apply to every generation, not only to the Jews in Jesus' day and not only to Church Age believers.

Jesus, up to the time He taught this sermon, had not yet prophesied the coming of the Church Age. He had not yet revealed the mysteries of the mighty age to come. How then, in light of these facts, are we—believers of this Church Age—to understand the many lessons in this sermon? As we will note from passage to passage, Jesus delineated many principles of grace that carry over to our Age of Grace, though these principles are often not directly or mechanically applicable to our spiritual life. Often, for specific interpretations and applications of these principles, we need to go to Church Age mystery doctrines as taught by the apostles Paul, John, Peter, and James.

To the 80 disciples our Lord was sending out to Israel, through whom He was offering the Kingdom, this sermon served as their formal training. He taught them the dynamics of the Kingdom He offered to Israel. Because of her rejection of Him, He would delay the reality of His rule until after the Church Age and Tribulation. To other Jews within earshot, this message also shocked them out of their complacent legalism in order to open them up to our Lord's grace message. To Church Age believers, these serve as guidelines and instructions regarding grace.

6. Matthew 6:1-18—Warnings against Pharisaic Hypocrisy

In this collection of verses, Jesus teaches against the Pharisaic displays of so-called spirituality. The Pharisees were at the top of the religious hierarchy at that time, so the general populace emulated them. In these verses, Jesus addresses some of their practices and gives correctional admonishments.

7. Matthew 6:19-24—Priorities of Spiritual Living

In this section, our Lord taught His disciples about setting spiritual priorities and life values. Focus and value must be set toward Heaven. He also addressed the possibility of failure in the spiritual life when believers allow an area of carnality to control their lives. He addressed the exclusivity of divine power, how it alone must control the believer's life.

8. Matthew 6:25-34—The Logistical Grace Rationale

If mastered by every believer, understanding and believing the issue of divine logistical support should help him avoid areas of sin and stress. Militarily, logistical support includes beans and bullets, everything necessary to support the soldier for combat. God supports every believer in like manner.

9. Matthew 7:1-12—A Warning, a Reminder and an Offer

In this section, Jesus warns the disciples of a pitfall. He was giving them the great responsibility of announcing His arrival. That pitfall was, and continues to be for many believers, judging other people. Jesus then reminded the disciples of the basic functions of the spiritual life, and then offered them the filling of the Holy Spirit, with His empowering ministry.

10. Matthew 7:13-14—Entering the Gate of Salvation

One may ask why our Lord used this venue to present the Gospel. After all, He aimed this message at His disciples, considered believers. All were believers in Him, except for Judas, who was most likely present at that time. Presumably, others, possibly other unbelievers, were also present.

11. Matthew 7:15-23—False Prophets

Those who claimed to be teaching the truth constantly challenged Jesus. We must heed the warnings He gave His disciples because false teachers constantly lead modern believers astray.

12. Matthew 7:24-27—An Illustration Contrasting Believers with Unbelievers

Couched in an illustration, Jesus contrasts believers with unbelievers. Church Age believers can also take this illustration to motivate further spiritual growth.

13. Matthew 7:28-29—Conclusion

Matthew concludes the Sermon by describing the crowd's response to our Lord's teaching.

C. Matthew 5:1-2—The Biblical Introduction: The Occasion of the Sermon

The first two verses of Chapter 5 reveal the occasion of the Sermon. It is always important that we start the study of Scripture by looking at the original languages to see if the words or the sentence structures carry implications not immediately evident in the English translation.

1. Matthew 5:1

When Jesus saw the crowds, He went up on the mountain; and after He sat down, His disciples came to Him. Matthew 5:1

When Jesus saw the crowds ...
Ἰδὼν δὲ τοὺς ὄχλους ...

The first word in the verse is the aorist active participle from the verb EIDON (εἶδον). The meaning of this root or lemma is "to see," or "to pay attention to." As a participle, this verb can have the characteristics of a noun, verb, or even an adjective. In this case, it acts as a verb, translated, "seeing." An aorist participle's action precedes the next action. He saw the crowds, and then proceeded with the next action.

The postpositive conjunction DE (δὲ) translated, "when," "but," "then," or "and" follows. Though it falls as the second word in the Greek word order, in English, it makes sense to begin the sentence with it. The next word is the articular accusative plural masculine noun OCHLOS (ὄχλος), translated "crowd," or "horde." The translation can read as "But having seen the crowds ..."

... He went up on the mountain
... ἀνέβη εἰς τὸ ὄρος

The next phrase, "He went up on the mountain," does not offer any exegetical surprises that would change its translation. It begins with the verb ANABAINO (ἀναβαίνω) in the aorist active indicative. The preposition EIS (εἰς) translated, "on," "onto" or "into" continues the phrase. The articular accusative noun, OROS (ὄρος), translated "mountain" completes the phrase. The definite article indicates that this was not just any mountain, but the mountain nearby, the Mount of Olives.

When Jesus saw the large crowd of people that His teachings and miracles attracted, He assessed the situation. He did not start to teach them as we often assume He did. Instead, He did something that no modern preacher or evangelist would do. He left the crowd, going up on the mountain where the crowd would not follow Him. He had an agenda at that moment, beyond presenting Himself to that particular group of people. He needed to orient His disciples to the realities of His ministry and message.[i]

First, He was not prepared to manage such a mass of people alone. He needed an organization. The disciples served as that system of organization. Second, He needed to orient the disciples to the Kingdom of God for their personal spiritual growth and spiritual application. Third, He needed to prepare them to offer the Kingdom to Israel. This was going to be an abbreviated crash course. They did not have four years to go through management courses and seminary! He needed to bring them up to speed quickly in order to make the issue clear for their own edification and for Israel's, to whom He was to send them.

It is important to note that Jesus taught during the Age of the Law, to those who kept the Mosaic Law for their spiritual lives. One purpose of the Law was to demonstrate the inability of humans to attain to God's righteousness, therefore their need for salvation through grace. If people lived according to the Law, they would be set up to believe in Christ, as the Levitical offerings revealed Him. Therefore, we could say that accurately observing the Law resulted in individual salvation, and then it could lead to spiritual growth. Where many followed this pattern, it led to national prosperity. However, the Law had been grossly misinterpreted, becoming a system of legalism. Principles of grace and sanctification delineated by the correct interpretation and application of the Law should have governed their spiritual life, not the harsh legalism of the day. So, much of Jesus' teaching in this sermon was corrective.

... and after He sat down ...
... καὶ καθίσαντος ...

This phrase, "and after He sat down ..." begins with the conjunction, KAI (καί), not unexpectedly translated, "and." Next is the verb KATHIZO (καθίζω) in the aorist active participle, genitive masculine singular. Because the participle functions as a verb, "he sat down" translates it accurately. As was the custom of the day, Jesus sat down to teach. Teachers always sat in front of their congregations instead of standing up as most do today. His seating Himself was a signal that He was going to start teaching. Today, we usually stand in front of our congregants and if necessary, clear our throats! I like the idea of taking a seat then starting to teach!

... His disciples came to Him.
... αὐτοῦ προσῆλθαν αὐτῷ οἱ μαθηταὶ αὐτοῦ.

When Jesus had seated Himself, His disciples went to Him and began to listen to Him. Though He focused this sermon particularly at His disciples, undoubtedly, others from the crowd found Him and listened.

2. Matthew 5:2

And he opened His mouth and taught them, saying ...
καὶ ἀνοίξας τὸ στόμα αὐτοῦ ἐδίδασκεν αὐτοὺς λέγων

Verse 2 is important because the phrase "He opened His mouth and began teaching them," emphasizes every word He spoke. The verb, the imperfect active indicative of DIDASKO (διδάσκω) translated as "teaching," indicates that He kept on teaching them. The imperfect tense also indicates that He began to teach them, introducing a speech or a body of content that He was preparing to communicate. Just as with believers today, these disciples needed to learn in an academic setting. They needed verbal communication to learn about our Lord's plan for them. They could not follow Him from a distance, continually observing Him to discover the personal plan that He had for them. He needed to teach them academically about the temporal spiritual life that He offered them. Being far beyond a simple philosophy of life, they needed to learn it academically and then learn how to apply it.

The same holds true for believers today. Every believer needs to learn what the Scripture says while sitting down in an academic environment. No one can go out into nature, allegedly communing with God, to gain an understanding of the mechanics of the Church Age spiritual life. No one can read and fully understand the Scripture without the interpretive and communication gifted pastor. The unique life our Lord has bequeathed to us Church Age believers involves great power that we must handle with a thorough understanding of the nuances of the Word. The importance of gaining technical knowledge of Scripture cannot be over-emphasized!

Later on, God would introduce through Paul a radical change for the Church Age believer's ability to learn. God the Holy Spirit actually teaches Church Age believers; this is something He never did for people in any other dispensation. However, the Spirit only teaches believers what *"He hears."*

But when He, the Spirit of truth, comes, He will guide you into all the truth; for He will not speak on His own initiative, but whatever He hears, He will speak; and He will disclose to you what is to come.
John 16:13

He only teaches you through the mechanics that a prepared pastor-teacher or Bible teacher has mastered. No believer can read the Scripture for himself and gain the technical knowledge that the Spirit communicates through those supernaturally gifted to teach. The Church Age spiritual life is technical, requiring academically learned skills.

Church Age pastors need to understand that the Spirit teaches them through their disciplined study of the Scripture to teach their congregations in order to bring about spiritual growth. No believer should ever stop growing spiritually. Therefore, pastors today need to follow this pattern of doctrinal communication. They should continually teach until congregations understand the doctrinal content of the Word. Repetition is paramount! A congregation should hear the teachings until they cannot forget them!

PART II

THE BEATITUDES
MATTHEW 5:3-12

A. Introduction: Blessed

This section of the Sermon on the Mount presents the Beatitudes. The word 'beatitude' comes from the Latin word, "beaut," spelled "BEAT" which means "blessing." "BEAT" should not be pronounced as "beat" as in "beatnik:" the 'a' should have a short 'u' sound as in "beaut."

Interestingly enough, author Jack Kerouac in a conversation with author John Cleelon Holmes coined the concept of the "Beat Generation" as a misinterpretation of this. A National Public Radio commentary presented this, then other on-line articles and the publication, *American Catholic Arts and Fictions: Culture, Ideology, Aesthetics* corroborated this. Holmes considered his generation, "sympathetic," his interpretation of "blessed." He evidently expected his readers to pronounce the word as "beaut" phonetically, not "beat!" Since the word was written then pronounced as 'beat,' instead of "beaut," the media applied the term to the Dobie Gillis bongo-beating subculture! Novelist Jack Kerouac and other "Beat Generation" authors helped bring in that blur of meanings.[ii]

Theologians call these passages "The Blessings," because every paragraph or verse in it begins with the phrase, "blessed are…" Certainly, that phrase caught the attention of everyone within earshot of our Lord. After all, who does not want to be "blessed?" Especially, if you have any control over it!

The Mosaic Law carried within it a system of both blessings and curses. To the person who fulfilled various aspects of the Law, God blessed; yet to those who failed, cursing was the order of the day. Every person in the Old Testament demonstrated this principle because believers received either blessing or cursing by virtue of their relationship with Him. The same principle applies today: God blesses every believer who fulfills His plan, while believers who fail suffer from not only consequences from their bad decisions but divine discipline as well.

By His teaching, the Messiah more clearly defined and interpreted those blessings. In addition, our Lord gave immediacy and force to these blessings by His physical presence. He was actually present and offering the long awaited Millennial Kingdom to Israel. If Israel had accepted Him by faith then progressed spiritually, they would have qualified for these blessings. Our Lord would have carried out His salvation work on the Cross, and then God would have resurrected Him. Then, He would have, after having fulfilled the end times as per Daniel, ushered in His Millennial Kingdom. Israel and the entire world would have experienced the full imputation and realization of these blessings. The reality of these millennial blessings then was imminent; Israel was on the verge of entering the Millennium!

Again, we call this first section the Beatitudes after the Latin word transliterated as "beaut" or "beat." The Latin "beat" came from the Greek word MAKARIOS (μακάριος) most often translated as "blessed." It is a very old word, coming from Homer's day. In that early day, it described the exalted state of the Greek pantheon of gods as being above the plight of suffering and laboring humanity. Its root, MAKAR (μακάρ) referred primarily to the gods. When used describing people, it denoted the state of possessing the exalted state of the gods; namely those prosperous and rich, being above earthly work and concerns! It came to describe the state of those who were successful, wealthy, and seemingly favored by the various deities.

MAKARIOS is often translated "happy" in many New Testament verses. Specifically, in this series of passages, our Lord used it to describe the happiness and fulfillment resulting from one's relationship with God and from adhering to His divine plan. This happiness, as we have described in other studies[iii] can be a permanent and enduring inner happiness from the source of the Father Himself. For you to gain the best understanding of this concept as it relates to your Church Age spiritual life, please see the linked studies in the appendix.

Many verses from the sermon appear in both Matthew and Luke. Matthew was evidently present while Luke wrote from extensive interviews. It is possible that our Lord taught these same principles on a number of different occasions fulfilling the principle of inculcation. We really do not know, nor is it an important issue. We know that our Lord taught these things and that under the ministry of God the Holy Spirit, both Matthew and Luke recorded what the Spirit led them to write. Because of this, whenever both disciples' writings overlap, this author will present both, and then look at the syntactical issues of Matthew and, if relevant, of Luke. We may gain some insight from the differences.

B. Matthew 5:3—The Beatitude of Salvation

Blessed are the poor in spirit, for theirs is the Kingdom of Heaven.

And turning His gaze toward His disciples, He began to say, "Blessed are you who are poor, for yours is the kingdom of God."
Luke 6:20

Blessed are the poor ...
Μακάριοι οἱ πτωχοὶ ...

To insure that we correctly understand these verses, we need to look at both the Greek vocabulary and syntax. Note at this point, before we delve into the construction of the Greek, that it is not so important that we produce a concise word for word translation, but that we understand the meaning of the words and their relationship to each other. Once we understand the meanings, then we can translate our understanding of their relationships in various ways. This writer's goal is to insure that you understand the words and their relationship to each other so that you fully understand what our Lord meant.

We have already established the meaning of the first word of Matthew 5:3, MAKARIOS, (μακάριος) as inner happiness from the source of God. It appears here as an adjective in the nominative, masculine plural. The second important word is PTOCHOS (πτωχός), translated "poor," appearing also as a nominative masculine plural adjective. That they agree in number, person and case is important because it is the key to their grammatical relationship. The definite article HOI (οἱ), also in the nominative, masculine plural precedes PTOCHOS, "poor." This makes "poor" act as a substantive, as a noun. Therefore, now we know that "poor" is the subject of the sentence.

Note that there is no verb between the two words, as in the English translation, only the definite article. This verbless clause, a common Greek syntactical structure, appears regularly in Scripture. Greek readers understood the words' predicate relationship because all three words concur grammatically and appear in this certain order. These three words conceptually encompass the subject and verb. PTOCHOS, "poor," the second adjective used substantively acts as the subject of the verse. To be technical: the first adjective, blessed, is in the second predicate position relative to the second adjective, poor, which means that the subject is predicated or acted upon by the characteristic defined by that first adjective. Therefore, the poor are acted upon by happiness. We, then arrive at the translation, "Blessed, or filled with inner happiness, are the PTOCHOS "the poor."

The Greeks were free to place words in whatever position they wished, to put emphasis on them. Because the word, MAKARIOS, happy or blessed appears first, it receives the greatest emphasis, even though it modifies the second word, "poor." We will clarify that next word, the substantival adjective, PTOCHOS, translated, "poor" in a moment. The verse so far reads as "Blessed are the poor..." and then continues with:

... in spirit ...
... τῷ πνεύματι ...

In Matthew, the noun PNEUMATI (πνεύματι) in the neuter dative singular follows the substantival adjective, PTOCHOS. PNEUMATI, "in spirit," describes these poor. Being a dative noun, it serves as the object of the predicate. Luke does not use this noun to describe them. This illustrates the importance of comparing scripture with scripture. Matthew defines these poor whereas Luke does not. Though Luke mentions the poor, we have to go to Matthew to find out to what poor our Lord referred. So, who are these people, the PTOCHOS PNEUMATI, the poor in spirit? PNEUMATI, translated "in spirit" is a locative of sphere, defining these people as poor in the sphere of spirit, not necessarily financially poor. Though the NASB and other translators define PTOCHOS as poor, a more exact translation is valid and communicates more effectively. These poor people are destitute—spiritually destitute—having no spiritual assets at all. This poverty or destitution is spiritual, not financial! If you read Luke only, you may be tempted to assume that He was referring to the financially poor. Who are these without any spiritual assets, who are spiritually destitute? Every human being is born into this life spiritually dead—spiritually destitute—having an old sin nature, with no hope of gaining any spiritual assets. Paul wrote about this spiritual death in his letter to the Romans.

Therefore, just as through one man sin entered into the world, and death through sin, and so death spread to all men, because all sinned.
Romans 5:12

What are these spiritual assets? Think of an asset as a gift from God that benefits you. God always has your best interest in His thinking. As to what these assets consist of, in some cases, they differ from dispensation to dispensation. Believers in all dispensations, though, gain the most important, the greatest spiritual asset, everlasting life with God in Heaven, upon believing in the person and work of Jesus Christ. Faith and only faith in Christ is the issue. This asset means deliverance from the Lake of Fire and a relationship with God the Father through His Son, Jesus Christ. Another asset God gives to believers in all generations consists of His imputed righteousness. The Apostle Paul wrote about Abraham:

For what does the Scripture say? "Abraham believed God, and it was credited to him as righteousness." Romans 4:3

The Father sees every believer as righteous immediately upon faith in Christ. This righteousness will not come to total fruition for Church Age believers until our Lord transfers the Church to Heaven at the Rapture.

Other assets include the Holy Spirit's spiritual regeneration of believers. Unbelievers consist of two attributes: a body and a soul. Theologians call this state, dichotomy. Upon belief, God bestows a human spirit on each person, that works as an interface between a given person and God. Believers, then, become trichotomous, because the Holy Spirit regenerates within him or her a human spirit.

God also provides a spiritual life for every believer. This life takes on different characteristics during each dispensation. For believing Jews living during the Age of Israel under the Mosaic Law, the spiritual life consisted of following the Law. It involved external rituals designed to teach Christ to the unbeliever for salvation and to teach divine principles to the believer that he or she might become occupied with and reliant upon God. The Father designed the external rituals dictated in the Mosaic Law to make an impact upon one's internal thinking.

For Church Age believers, both Jew and Gentile, God provides an incredible array of power-giving spiritual assets. These assets include the filling of God the Holy Spirit, position in Christ, the indwelling of the entire Trinity, spiritual gifts as well as many others. The Church Age, in terms of the bestowal of divine power, is really the only dispensation to be living in! These internal and invisible assets, unique to the Church Age, when coupled with the believer's volition and further knowledge of the Word should bring the believer to greater and fuller faith in God. That increased faith results in greater appreciation for our Lord, bringing the believer's thinking into line with His.

The translation of Matthew can loosely read, up this point, as "Blessed or filled with inner happiness *are* the spiritually destitute ..." Again, understand that "the destitute" is the subject of the sentence while "blessed" and "spiritually" modify that substantival adjective. While the being verb, "are" does not appear in the Greek, in English we must insert some sort of verb so that it reads smoothly. However, do not read a "present reality" for every human into this, as the verb of being implies. Remember that this verb does not appear in the Greek. If one reads into this a "present reality"—that is "happening now"—one would look for inner happiness in every human being who is poor or, in this context, spiritually destitute! Do you think that the spiritually dead person is really happy or blessed? In fact, many have misinterpreted and misapplied this passage because of its English translation, glorifying the financially poor or downtrodden. The translation using "are" is not erroneous, but it can be misleading, inferring a present reality. The spiritually destitute do not possess happiness or contentedness from the source of the Father! In that respect, they are not happy!

The verse continues with an explanation.

... for theirs is the Kingdom of Heaven.
... ὅτι αὐτῶν ἐστιν ἡ βασιλεία τῶν οὐρανῶν.

The next word, common to both Matthew and Luke, is the adverbial causal conjunction HOTI (ὅτι), with the genitive third person personal pronoun

AUTOS (αὐτός) which can be translated, "because of them" or "for them." Luke made it very personal with, "because of you" whereas, Matthew records, "because of them." The difference here suggests that our Lord taught this on more than one occasion. .Read "for theirs" in the sense of "for them." God provided the Kingdom for them, for their benefit. So, "because of" or "for" the spiritually destitute, God provided a Kingdom.

The Kingdom

"Kingdom," translated from the Greek word BASILEIA (βασιλεία), can refer to one or more different aspects of that over which the Father and Son have authority. It points to a sphere of authority or dominion, not necessarily to a place or to a given amount of property. When you consider the word "kingdom" in this context, think of its source as God the Father. However, He has given His Son authority as well. In order to properly interpret this verse, we need to define the various spheres of authority over which the Father or Son rule. Then we need to determine to which sphere this use of "kingdom" denotes.

Though a detailed and verse-by-verse investigation of "kingdom" is beyond the scope of this study, we will briefly define some spheres of God's authority. First, consider the totality of God's immensity as the first sphere of His authority. This includes the entire universe with its time aspect, the Heavens as both His and the angels' timeless abode and every possible dimension God fills that we do not know about. This entire sphere is subject to God's sovereign rule. The entirety of this sphere is beyond human comprehension!

The Lord has established His throne in the heavens, and His sovereignty rules over all. Psalm 103:19

All of the other spheres of His authority fall within that overall category. One might visualize these subcategories as a multi-sphered Venn diagram, having many overlaps. One subcategory of that sphere is spiritual. Specifically, as this relates to the human race, all those who believe in Jesus Christ form this sphere of authority. Further, we can subdivide it into different dispensations. As examples, regenerate Israel forms one subcategory, while the invisible earthly Church forms another. The pre-flood generations of believers form another with Tribulational saints forming another. Within the invisible Church, both regenerate Jews and regenerate Gentiles form the new man of the Church Age. However, the visible Church contains an overlap of both believers and unbelievers. As a Theocratic Kingdom, Israel contained unbelieving Jews, regenerate Jews and Gentile proselytes. The Millennium, the thousand-year rule of our Lord from Jerusalem, which He brings into being after the 7 years of Tribulation, also forms one of God's Kingdoms or spheres of authority. It begins with believers only but soon, as the population grows, will beget unbelievers.

Though neither John the Baptist nor our Lord specifically defined "the Kingdom" as they spoke, we can assume that both the disciples and the people knew what "the Kingdom" meant. John the Baptist, when paving the way for our Lord, said, "The Kingdom is at hand."

> *Repent, for the kingdom of heaven is at hand. Matthew 3:2*

Our Lord used the same words when He said, "Repent, for the Kingdom of Heaven is at hand."

> *From that time Jesus began to preach and say, "Repent, for the kingdom of heaven is at hand." Matthew 4:17*

He also charged His 80 disciples with the words, "And as you go, preach, saying, 'The Kingdom of Heaven is at hand.'"

> *And as you go, preach, saying, 'The kingdom of heaven is at hand.' Matthew 10:7*

Again, the fact that they did not define it means that they presupposed their recipients' understanding of it. They were not the first to use the phrase "Kingdom of Heaven" or the "Kingdom of God." The Old Testament repeatedly presented the Kingdom to the degree that all Israel waited for it anxiously, as their national and individual destiny:

> *In the days of those kings the God of heaven will set up a kingdom which will never be destroyed, and that kingdom will not be left for another people; it will crush and put an end to all these kingdoms, but it will itself endure forever. Daniel 2:44*

The Kingdom Daniel described is the Millennial Kingdom, beginning when our Lord personally rules over the human race. It is the time of the restoration of Israel and the fulfillment of their unconditional covenants. Israel will again be the nation of our Lord's central focus in history for the last 1000 years. It is a time of perfect environment on the earth. Death, except for capital punishment, will cease. There will be a chicken in every pot! This is the Kingdom our Lord was offering Israel. This was the Kingdom Israel had waited for. Had most of Israel believed in Him, accepting Him as the Messiah, He would have paid for the sins of the world, been resurrected then established His Millennial Kingdom. Ironically, He was offering Israel what they wanted and expected. However, He had to atone for the world's sins, dying spiritually, then die physically and then be resurrected before He could bring His earthly kingdom into being. Because of their lack of faith, our Lord is waiting to bring in that Kingdom until a later time. However, this was only one of two facets of the Kingdom that our Lord was offering to Israel. Those who believed in Him immediately became part of His spiritual kingdom.

> *Jesus answered, "My kingdom is not of this world. If My kingdom were of this world, then My servants would be fighting so that I would not be handed over to the Jews; but as it is, My kingdom is not of this realm." John 18:36*

Matthew wrote "Kingdom of Heaven" while Luke recorded "Kingdom of God." This raises the question, is there any difference between the two phrases? Theologians differ on this issue. Whichever side you may take, remember that God the Holy Spirit supernaturally inspired these two men to write what they did. We are to learn, and gain from that knowledge, the message that each one communicated. Matthew was also an eyewitness to our Lord's ministry whereas Luke, by his own admission, interviewed eyewitnesses to our Lord's ministry. Second, our Lord spoke either Aramaic or Hebrew while both Matthew and Luke wrote in Greek. No language ever translates exactly to another. The translation either gains or discards nuance. Because of the context, these terms appear synonymous. However, interpretively, the phrases meant one thing to the disciples and to those they sought to evangelize, then another to us as an application.

Both interpretation and application involve two issues: entry into the Millennial Kingdom and entry into our Lord's spiritual kingdom. Israel, had they believed, would have entered into our Lord's perfect 1000 year rule and been entered into our Lord's spiritual kingdom upon belief. As it stands, Old Testament saints, to include those believers in our Lord's day who did not live to see the Church Age, entered into His spiritual kingdom. God will resurrect them to see the Millennial Rule of our Lord. Church Age believers having entered into His spiritual kingdom upon salvation will co-rule with our Lord during His Millennial rule. The Kingdom our Lord has prepared, because of His unlimited work of atonement, is for every member of the human race!

Note that in no place do either John or Jesus encourage people to try to bring in the Kingdom. However, through evangelization, the Holy Spirit encourages and even mandates every person to join the Kingdom. In no way is any human able to bring in the Kingdom. That is absolute arrogance, whether it comes in the guise of Phariseeism, Zealotism, Zionism, or any other modern misguided motivation for evangelization. Certainly, the Scripture commands every believer to witness. Furthermore, we are to evangelize. One of the most important spiritual gifts empowers the believer to evangelize, even on a mass scale. Yet, the fulfillment of that spiritual gift requires love for our Lord as motivation and an orientation to grace, not the attempt to "bring in the Kingdom!"

When you believe in Jesus Christ, appropriating His salvation work, then you have become one more person in the Spiritual Kingdom of Heaven. Every human being has the opportunity of being a part of this Kingdom because Jesus Christ died for every human being since the first Adam to the last person born in the Millennium. This Kingdom is eternal. This short discussion presents a small glimpse into the Kingdom.

God, then, has provided something fantastic for every spiritually destitute human being if he will receive the gift of eternal life, becoming a resident of the

Kingdom of Heaven. This fact, in itself, is a fantastic blessing that most never realize.

How does salvation, entry into His spiritual kingdom and entry into the future Millennium, relate to happiness? Many believers in Jesus Christ suffer miserable lives! Possessing salvation does not mean that you are happy, though your understanding of your eternal life should certainly lend itself to the realization of happiness. Everything in your temporal life should pale in importance compared to your salvation. Once you pass into the eternal life phase, having gone through the Evaluation Seat of Christ, you will have eternal happiness! Is temporal happiness available to you as well? Absolutely! You must grow up spiritually to realize this happiness. Start thinking the way Jesus did, then the Father will share His very own happiness with you!

An interpretive translation sounds like this:

> **Inner happiness to the spiritually destitute, for the Kingdom of Heaven is for them. Matthew 5:3**

Apart from the technicalities of the Greek verbless clause, we can liken this statement to a toast! Raise your cup! Inner happiness to the spiritually destitute! Be happy because God has provided a solution to spiritual destitution. Why should we celebrate that the entire human race since the fall begins life spiritually destitute or spiritually dead? This spiritual death qualifies us all for salvation! God has prepared His Kingdom for all of us! However, just because every human being is blessed being born spiritually dead and though God has prepared His Kingdom for the spiritually dead, not every human will realize the resultant happiness. Only those seeking the solution to their spiritual destitution through Jesus Christ will experience the joy that His provided kingdom can bring.

This first beatitude presents the reality of the availability of salvation and the potential of inner happiness to everyone in the human race. The moment you receive your salvation you begin your eternal spiritual life. The next beatitude applies to your spiritual life as a growing believer.

C. Matthew 5:4—The Beatitude of Comfort

> *Blessed are those who mourn, for they shall be comforted. Matthew 5:4*
>
> *Blessed are you who weep now, for you shall laugh. Luke 6:21b*

> *Blessed are those who mourn*
> μακάριοι οἱ πενθοῦντες,

The first thing we note about the first phrase in this verse is the syntactical structure. It repeats the same verbless clause pattern as the previous beatitude. These is a predicate relationship between the adjective, "blessed," and the adjectival participle of the Greek word, PENTHEO (πενθέω). Because we know what the word "blessed" means we can move directly to the category of people Matthew refers to as "the mourning." This participle refers to those in this certain state, to those mourning. These people are in a state of grief, a grief so deep and overwhelming that they cannot conceal it. When it takes hold of a person, it must be expressed, often with tears and wailing. Historically, PENTHO frequently referred to the grief and mourning one had when a loved one has passed away. In this context, mourning refers to the soul response to the realization of spiritual destitution.

Isaiah, in his vision of being in the presence of the Second Person of the Trinity said,

> ***Woe is me, for I am ruined! Because I am a man of unclean lips, and I live among a people of unclean lips; For my eyes have seen the King, the Lord of hosts. Isaiah 6:5***

The Hebrew expresses the soul-wrenching horror he experienced when face-to-face with his corruption, weakness, and spiritual destitution, far better than this English translation!

Instead of "mourning," Luke used the word, KLAIO (κλαίω) in the present active participle, again the substantival use, translated as "weep." Interestingly enough, the various lexicons define this word much the same as PENTHEO, above, though they do not appear as synonyms. In the New Testament, the Greek source word for "weep" appears in two distinct contexts. First, in the present tense, it represents the attitude taken by those who realize their inadequacy when faced with knowledge of God. Second, in the future tense, it refers to the state of those at the end times, who have rejected God's grace, and find their final destination is the Lake of Fire.

God blesses those grieving over their spiritual death because it precedes faith in Christ. This beatitude, then, complements the first by identifying the response to the realization of spiritual destitution. We are all born into the world spiritually dead or destitute.

> ***For all have sinned and fall short of the glory of God ...***
> ***Romans 3:23***

Only through God's grace, do we ever come face to face with that destitution, and seek Him for comfort through salvation and subsequent spiritual growth.

Now we return to Matthew 5:4.

> ***... for they shall be comforted.***
> ***... ὅτι αὐτοὶ παρακληθήσονται.***

"Comfort" is in the future passive. It is important because the Jews to whom our Lord addressed this verse would have immediately recognized this as the "divine passive." This passive voice means that the believer receives, not earns, or deserves this comfort. It always results from divine activity because, ultimately, only God can bring real, total, and continual comfort. No one ever earns or deserves this comfort. You receive it as a grace gift from the Lord.

The future tense does not denote that the comfort comes only in the future but that the comfort is progressive, determined by the amount of our Lord's thinking that circulates in the soul of the individual believer. The reality of this comfort relates directly to the content of the believer's soul. This comfort brings with it the concept of happiness because only through divine comfort can you maintain your contentedness in the face of all adversity. God provides comfort for the believer through knowledge and application of His Word. Instead of being comforted as Matthew recorded, Luke says that they will laugh, as translated from GELAO (γελάω). This laughter of relief reflects the confidence of one who has believed in the Lord, and who has assurance of his status as righteous before Him. Such assurance, like comfort, can only come from spiritual growth.

God, through His word, provides a many facetted comfort, a reason to laugh with relief, sure to apply in any difficult situation. Comfort in the time of grief when a loved one passes away comes from the assurance that death for the believer is a permanent change of station from this temporal life to life face-to-face with our Lord. Therefore, when a loved one passes into God's presence, that one is in the best possible place. Furthermore, He will reunite believers with loved ones in Heaven after their time on earth is complete! Your loss is never permanent. Comfort in times of stress and personal adversity comes from understanding that God provides perfectly for every exigency in your life. Not only has God provided perfectly for these times but also the adversity He allows in your life benefits you. He allows adversity to test and accelerate your spiritual growth. How do we profit from spiritual growth? By means of it you glorify God, provide a witness to people and angels, all the while living a life of great contentment and fulfillment! Note that this is personal comfort. God comforts you when His Spirit activates His Word in your soul. You must understand it, believe it, and then choose to apply it, all through the power of the Spirit.

Therefore, this beatitude provides encouragement for believers in prolonged periods of intense suffering. During the course of spiritual growth, God both tests and accelerates your spiritual growth by means of suffering. The test: do you apply the doctrines you learn to maintain your contentedness? Do you have inner happiness despite the fact that you are living in what the world may call miserable circumstances? One of the by-products of your spiritual maturity is inner happiness and great peace despite your circumstances. To experience this, you, as a Church Age believer, must be empowered by the Holy Spirit, resting in faith as described in the Book of Hebrews and applying other doctrines that relate to sharing God's happiness. This beatitude reminds us that we can possess constant inner happiness regardless of any adverse or undesirable life circumstances we may face as well as tangible grief. A better translation reflects the concept of soul-wrenching grief, expressed outwardly. An interpretive translation then reads this way:

> *Inner happiness to those under soul wrenching agony, for they will receive comfort from God. Matthew 5:4*
>
> *Inner happiness to the weeping because you will laugh. Luke 6:21b*

When you take these first two beatitudes together, they echo Isaiah 61:1-3:

> *The Spirit of the Lord God is upon me, because the Lord has anointed me to bring good news to the afflicted; He has sent me to bind up the brokenhearted, to proclaim liberty to captives and freedom to prisoners; to proclaim the favorable year of the Lord and the day of vengeance of our God; to comfort all who mourn, to grant those who mourn in Zion, giving them a garland instead of ashes, the oil of gladness instead of mourning, the mantle of praise instead of a spirit of fainting. So they will be called oaks of righteousness, the planting of the Lord, that He may be glorified.*
> *Isaiah 61:1-3*

The point of these two beatitudes is that the comfort from the arrival of the Messiah was to be experienced from that precise moment of time. For the Church Age believer, that comfort begins when he or she understands and applies the Gospel by faith, then progresses through spiritual growth to greater faith.

D. Matthew 5:5—The Beatitude of Covenant Qualification

Blessed are the gentle, for they shall inherit the earth. Matthew 5:5

Blessed are the gentle ...
μακάριοι οἱ πραεῖς ...

Again, since we know that MAKARIOS (μακάριος), translated, "blessed," refers to inner happiness, we can move on to the next important word in this phrase, "gentle" PRAUS (πραΰς). Just as in the construction of the first beatitude, this word appears as an adjective used substantively. This word, most often translated as "meek" or "gentle," designates the category of person who is teachable, humble, and therefore blessed because of it. Interpretively, it refers to one who hears the Gospel and responds to it. The ones who respond to the Gospel as the disciples presented it would immediately become qualified to receive the unconditional covenants, as we will see shortly. There is no question that the one who believes is greatly blessed.

We can, by way of application learn more from "gentle," PRAUS, going beyond salvation. This word also describes someone who bears up under life's pressures, such as unjust treatment with calm composure, lacking in bitterness or anger. This is not simple passive submission in the face of unpleasantness but an active, aggressive mental attitude dynamic that deliberately avoids mental attitude sins by applying the appropriate doctrines. For the disciples, this meant strict obedience to the dictates of the Mosaic Law and to what our Lord was teaching them. This resulted in true inner happiness for these believers.

For Church Age believers today, to possess such a mental attitude in this dispensation, one must be fortified with accurate doctrinal rationales and the power of the Holy Spirit. Furthermore, it implies a focus in life upon grace, upon the graciousness God has brought to bear upon the human race through the work of Jesus Christ. Therefore, a better translation of the word in this context deals with humility. Humility for the believer becomes active, aggressive submission to God's will. It includes faith in Christ then learning and applying Jesus' thinking, resulting in continual spiritual maturation. Truly, this grace-oriented person will be full of inner happiness.

The verse continues.

> *... for they shall inherit the earth.*
> *... ὅτι αὐτοὶ κληρονομήσουσιν τὴν γῆν.*

The next phrase speaks of an inheritance designated for this happy humble person. The word, "inherit" is a future active indicative of KLERONOMEO (κληρονομέω). It refers to an allotment given because of a certain qualification. It includes the concept of logical progression. If the believer meets that qualification, then it follows logically, that the Lord will bestow that allotment or inheritance. That allotment, in this case is the land GE (γῆ). We need to go back to the context of this verse. What did "the land" mean to those who heard those words of the Lord? What does "the land" mean to us as Church Age believers?

The Land, to those hearers, was exactly that, the Land of Israel that God had promised to the Jews since the days of Abraham.

The Lord said to Abram, after Lot had separated from him, "Raise your eyes now, and look from the place where you are, northward and southward and eastward and westward; for all the land that you see I will give to you and to your offspring forever." Genesis 13:14-15

On that day the Lord made a covenant with Abram, saying, "To your descendants I give this land, from the river of Egypt to the great river, the river Euphrates ..." Genesis 15:18

The Land included much more territory than even David had conquered. Furthermore, the inherited land symbolized the fulfillment of all of the Unconditional Covenants God promised Israel. These have not yet been fulfilled in their entirety to this day. The coming of the Messiah is one provision in the covenants. God sent the Messiah, as promised, yet they rejected Him. Therefore,

He has delayed His rule until after both the Church Age is complete and the Dispensation of Israel is fulfilled with the seven years of Tribulation.

These disciples, who were going out to spread the news of the Messiah, needed to communicate the means of qualifying for the covenants. Most Jews at that time thought they were already qualified because of their genetic relationship to Abraham and their adherence to the legalistic program promulgated by the Pharisees and Sadducees. Jesus sought to correct this false idea by the principles He taught in this and other sermons.

Our Lord, then, charged the disciples by this beatitude that to be recipients of the unconditional covenants they had to orient to the work of our Lord by faith in Him. Though He had not yet died for the world's sins, the Mosaic Law pointed to that future event. For temporal inner happiness, they needed to build their spiritual life upon that salvation.

Also, note that our Lord brought the Old Testament Scripture into His teaching:

> ***But the humble will inherit the land and will delight themselves in abundant prosperity. Psalm 37:11***

The humble refers to a person who can learn. The Gospel is, after all, spiritual phenomenon, incomprehensible to the spiritually destitute. God the Holy Spirit exerts a certain authority on the unbeliever as well, though in a gentle manner. The humble person will believe the Gospel, accepting the authority of the Spirit, thereby becoming a believer in Jesus Christ.

The humble person would continue to believe what the prophets and priests taught through the ritual of the day, resulting in continual spiritual growth. If a person were not humble, then he, being arrogant, would reject the Gospel message and subsequent doctrinal instruction. The humble person in the time of Christ would have believed in Him and then experienced spiritual growth. Faith in the God of Israel qualified them to participate in the unconditional covenants to Israel. The inheritance of an expanded Israel and eternal life are among the provisions of the unconditional covenants. All regenerate Israel will inherit these. The time of complete fulfillment of the unconditional covenants for every believing Jew is the Kingdom Age, what we know as the Millennium.

An interpretive translation of this beatitude reads this way:

> ***Inner happiness to the spiritual, for they will inherit the unconditional covenants.***

How does this beatitude apply to Church Age believers? We are not specifically a party to the unconditional covenants with Israel, though we benefit greatly from them! We can apply this principle to our lives, however. We stand to inherit much more than Israel ever dreamed. We, in the Church Age, must live our lives in the light of eternity, first, by appropriating the Lord's work by faith in

Him, and then second, by growing in grace and in knowledge of Him to qualify for the full inheritance we have "in Christ." In a nutshell, by virtue of our position in Him, He shares with us His destiny, His life and everything He possesses. Not every Church Age believer qualifies for the full inheritance of participating completely in our Lord's destiny any more than did the believing Exodus generation qualify to enter the Land. The writer of Hebrews expounded on this subject in Hebrews 3-4. Both the doctrines of Positional Truth and Sanctification detail this truth.[iv] Understand that the mechanics for learning these includes the Spirit's teaching ministry to the believer using verbal or written messages presented by one's pastor or other Bible teachers. John taught this in the following verse. The Spirit hears what your pastor or Bible teacher teaches. That content is what the Spirit speaks or teaches you.

But when He, the Spirit of Truth, comes, He will guide you into all the truth; for He will not speak on His own initiative, but whatever He hears, He will speak; and He will disclose to you what is to come. John 16:13

E. Matthew 5:6—The Beatitude of the Desire for Doctrine

Blessed are those who hunger and thirst for righteousness, for they shall be satisfied. Matthew 5:6

Blessed are you who hunger now, for you shall be satisfied. Luke 6:21a

---

Blessed are those who hunger and thirst for righteousness,
μακάριοι οἱ πεινῶντες καὶ διψῶντες τὴν δικαιοσύνην,

As with the last beatitudes we studied, we understand inner happiness, so we can move on to those who qualify for the wonderful happiness God has provided. Two participles that express one concept describe the class of believer, so to speak, who will logically appropriate this inner happiness. We need to understand them idiomatically, understanding that the idiom of the language falls within the literal interpretation model. The first word is the present active participle of PEINAO (πεινάω) translated substantively "you who hunger." We can also translate this as "those who hunger," "hungering ones" or "the hungry." In this context, it refers to a strong, avid desire for something that is a necessity for life. Since the context concerns believers in Jesus Christ, then this is a necessity for the believer. The second participle, also in the present active participle, is DIPSAW (διψάω), translated, thirst; again, this is an idiomatic usage.

Let us explore the literal concepts of hunger and thirst, both representing an intense concept. Today, being hungry and thirsty isn't much of a crisis to middle class Americans who, upon experiencing a hunger pang, can reach into the refrigerator and find any exotic food they've cared to buy, then satisfy that hunger in a matter of seconds. Just yesterday, for example, I prepared in a matter of minutes Thai curry out of ingredients in the 'frig, that was delicious! It did not take but a few minutes! However, if you reached the point of hunger in ancient times, you had to take the time to prepare your meal. By the time you had finished preparing it, you were extremely hungry! Remember when Abraham was visited by angels and offered them food? Genesis 18:6-8 describes this incident. His wife had to bake the bread; his servant slaughtered and prepared a calf, not to mention processing curds and milk to serve. How long did this take? It takes several hours alone to cook up yogurt! By the time you had the food, you would be desperately hungry!

Because the conjunction KAI (καί) connects these two participles, we may assume—based upon Greek grammatical conventions—that they communicate the same desire for the Word of God. The hunger and thirst that represents extreme desire for a relationship with God must be based upon His Word. The object of hunger and thirst is not only the subject of the rest of this verse but both the Prophet Isaiah and David spoke of it as well.[v]

> *Come, everyone who is thirsty, come to the waters; and you without money, come, buy, and eat! Come, buy wine and milk without money and without cost! Isaiah 55:1 HCSB*

> *My soul thirsts for God, for the living God; when shall I come and appear before God? Psalm 42:2*

That both participles are in the active voice is very significant because it emphasizes that this desire comes from one's soul. You choose this. You desire that relationship with God beyond salvation, which involves learning and applying doctrine, because you understand its importance and benefits. To a degree, this hunger and thirst becomes a part of your being because of your salvation. Upon your conversion, did you want to know something of the God who died for you? However, unless you initially heed this desire by learning and applying doctrine, you will squelch it by forming what is tantamount to scar tissue in your soul.[vi] If you are a believer in Jesus Christ and you do not desire the Word, then you have, as the Pharaoh of the Exodus, hardened your heart, having formed what is like scar tissue in your soul. Paul addressed this in Ephesians 4:17-18.

> *So this I say, and affirm together with the Lord, that you walk no longer just as the Gentiles also walk, in the futility of their mind, being darkened in their understanding, excluded from the life of God because of the ignorance that is in them, because of the hardness of their heart; Ephesians 4:17-18*

The believer who lives this way is in danger of ultimately leaving this world under the sin leading to death. The Apostle John addressed this in 1 John 5:16.

> *If anyone sees his brother committing a sin not leading to death, he shall*

ask and God will for him give life to those who commit sin not leading to death. There is a sin leading to death; I do not say that he should make request for this. 1 John 5:16

Once a person has received eternal life from our Lord due to faith in Him, he has the responsibility to bring his thinking into line with His. This is spiritual growth. Many believers reject this concept, never learning and applying the Word. Invariably, these believers live a lifestyle that leads to a shortened life.

A person does not even have to live a life of criminality, living and dying by the sword, to fulfill this concept. One just has to live life controlled by the sin nature, where the Holy Spirit does not restrain. A person can die the sin leading to death by an activity as innocuous as over-eating! If you do not allow the Spirit to control your addictive personality, even obesity can take you from this life earlier than the Lord had planned. Why can you not pray, as per this verse, for someone in this situation? God has already provided the solution for this believer in the form of divine thought coupled with volition and the power of the Spirit. Generally, you cannot pray for the believer who succumbs to his addictive personality in any area of life. That believer's solution lies in making the choice to grow up spiritually. However, because we do not have all the facts in a given case, we can pray that those within this category become aware of the plan God has for them. We can pray for people to understand God's plan for them. God has all the facts and applies His grace accordingly. As a general principle, though, you cannot pray for God to overrule yours or anyone's volition!

Matthew wrote that the object of this hungering and thirsting is righteousness — in the Greek, DIKAIOSUNE (δικαιοσύνη). By definition, this term refers to anything pertaining to the integrity or holiness of God. His righteousness is His perfect standard, while His justice is the application of that perfect standard. For the believer in Jesus' day, it meant adhering to the dictates of the Mosaic Law, leading to spiritual growth.

Pursuit of righteousness also relates to the Church Age believer. Technically, righteousness relates to the three different categories of his or her spiritual life, because this believer has a familial relationship with God. In the first category, positional sanctification, the Father declares every believer justified or righteous because at salvation, both He and the Son have imputed their righteousness to him or her. The second category, to which this verse refers, deals with experiential righteousness and the pursuit of the spiritual life. The third refers to ultimate sanctification, living in the eternal state. This desire, then, does not refer to the desire for salvation but to the desire to conform to God's plan for you. God's desire is for your spirituality and your continual spiritual growth. This only comes if you take the time to avail yourself of the concise systematic teaching of God's Word coupled with the Spirit's empowerment. You experience righteousness when the Spirit fills you; you live by His empowerment. You progress in your sanctification when you learn and apply Bible doctrine. The Apostle John related happiness and blessing to knowledge and application of the

Word:

If you know these things, you are blessed if you do them. John 13:17

James taught a similar message:

But prove yourselves doers of the word, and not merely hearers who delude themselves. James 1:22

... for they shall be satisfied
... ὅτι αὐτοὶ χορτασθήσονται.

The next phrase, "shall be satisfied," comes from the Greek verb, CHORTAZO (χορτάζω), in the future passive indicative. According to Vincent, this is a "... very strong and graphic word, originally applied to the feeding and fattening of animals in a stall."[vii] It means to be satiated. After a good meal, you are full! After a good sermon, you should be spiritually sated. This future tense, a gnomic future, indicates that this is a logical progression. If you desire the Word and the righteousness it provides, then you will be happy and satisfied. The passive voice indicates that this is totally a grace procedure. All you bring is your desire, your use of God's procedure to maintain your empowerment of the Spirit, and God provides everything else in grace. You receive this satisfaction because of God's grace.

An interpretive translation of this beatitude sounds this way:

Inner happiness to those who strongly desire experiential righteousness, for they shall be satisfied.

Or

Inner happiness to those who strongly desire to grow up spiritually, for they will be satisfied.

The phrase "experiential righteousness" refers to the Church Age believer who is living within God's plan for his life on earth. This believer is usually filled with the Holy Spirit and growing spiritually from learning and applying doctrine. Other categories of pertinent righteousness include positional righteousness and ultimate righteousness.

F. Matthew 5:7—The Beatitude of Giving and Receiving Grace

Blessed are the merciful, for they shall receive mercy. Matthew 5:7

Blessed are the merciful ...
μακάριοι οἱ ἐλεήμονες,

Note that with each beatitude, the qualification for happiness progresses to a new level of spiritual growth. The first begins with salvation and works through to the next beatitude by the desire to grow up spiritually. Each presents inner happiness for the believer who continues to progress. As in the previous beatitudes, this one also promises inner happiness, but it has a qualification.

The qualification, according to the Greek nominative plural, masculine adjective, ELEMON (ἐλεήμων) is applying mercy in one's life. Mercy is a mental attitude that considers the welfare and needs of others. You never give mercy because the object of your mercy earns or deserves it, but you predicate extending mercy upon your virtue and integrity. The merciful person will seek out opportunity to demonstrate mercy to others. For the believer in this Church Age, such demonstrations of mercy often relate to one's spiritual gift. Indeed, for the one with the gift of helps, mercy becomes one's lifestyle.

Our Lord and Savior Jesus Christ exemplified mercy to the greatest degree when He went to the Cross and bore the sins of the entire world, for all generations.

What would Jesus' hearers have thought when they heard these words? Would they have matched them up with many Old Testament passages that teach the same thing?

> *Therefore, O king, may my advice be pleasing to you: break away now from your sins by doing righteousness and from your iniquities by showing mercy to the poor, in case there may be a prolonging of your prosperity.*
> *Daniel 4:27*

> *Those who despise their neighbors are sinners, but happy are those who are kind to the poor. Proverbs 14:21*

On the other hand, perhaps the current legalistic teaching had stifled such impulses! The Church Age believer's ability to be merciful toward others relates directly to both spiritual growth and to spirituality. Pure mercy must be a reflection of God's mercy toward you. You can only understand this mercy through God's Word. The Holy Spirit must not only motivate mercy but also empower the believer to apply the pertinent doctrines.

> *... for they shall receive mercy.*
> *... ὅτι αὐτοὶ ἐλεηθήσονται.*

This beatitude continues with a reciprocal aspect. Those who are merciful will receive mercy. The second use of mercy is the future passive indicative of the cognate verb. The translation, then, is accurate. Does this mean that if we show mercy to certain people that we should expect to receive from them the same merciful treatment? Should we predicate our motivation for mercy upon the expectation of receiving mercy? Certainly not! God has already extended to us the ultimate mercy possible. We, who have all been born spiritually dead with no hope of salvation, have been extended the incredibly merciful grace of our Lord by means of His work. Not only that, but He has given us grace upon grace. Not only did He die for us, but has also bestowed upon us His spiritual life by which we can live a life of tremendous happiness and satisfaction, all the while glorifying our Lord! Can He extend to us greater mercy?

Your extending grace to others, then, should be a natural result of your spiritual life whereby you reflect the mercy extended to you. Mercy giving becomes a benchmark of your spiritual growth. To the degree that you show mercy because of your spiritual growth, to that degree, you are growing spiritually.

G. Matthew 5:8—The Beatitude of Spirituality
Blessed are the pure in heart, for they shall see God. Matthew 5:8

Blessed are the pure in heart,
μακάριοι οἱ καθαροὶ τῇ καρδίᾳ,

This beatitude continues to set the standard for happiness. According to the NASB, God reserves this happiness for those characterized as "pure in heart." "The heart" is a literal translation from the Greek word KARDIA (καρδία)—as in cardiac—that refers, in this context, not to the blood-pumping organ but to the seat of thought. Like the physical heart circulating blood throughout the body, the figurative heart circulates thoughts throughout the soul. The pumping dynamic of the physical heart parallels the effort it often takes to apply doctrine. Every believer must "push" recalled doctrines to the forefront of his thinking and apply them, purposely. Applying doctrine takes volitional effort. Just as your heart pumps blood throughout your circulatory system, so you must, by virtue of your choice, pump doctrines the Spirit brings to your thinking throughout your soul so that you can apply them. By way of application, the Spirit only empowers spiritual Church Age believers. Believers in our Lord's day certainly applied the Word but without the Spirit's empowerment.

As an aside here, understand that the thinking that circulates through one's soul influences one's physical heart and other physical attributes. One's thinking influences ones cardiovascular and physiological conditions. Aside from genetic weaknesses and past bad decisions, those whose minds are concentrating upon our Lord and His Word will have a healthy physical heart. God can even override genetics and past decisions, if He wills! These things go hand-in-hand.

Those to whom Jesus spoke would have understood this figurative use of heart because of its use in the Old Testament Scriptures and the then-current Greek vernacular:

Who may ascend into the hill of the Lord? And who may stand in His holy place? He who has clean hands and a pure heart, who has not lifted up his soul to falsehood and has not sworn deceitfully. Psalm 24:3-4

The "heart" also carries other related connotations. Consider that our Lord came to heal the "brokenhearted" as prophesied by the Prophet Isaiah in Isaiah

61:1. This can refer to the entirety of one's being, including volition, emotion, state of soul, and spiritual status.

Purity comes from the Greek adjective, KATHAROS (καθαρός), which means clean or free from adulteration. For the Jew, it referred to ceremonial cleanliness that reflected the believer's state of thinking. The approach to worship in either the Tabernacle or Temple required ceremonial cleansing. The ritual cleansing in itself was not as important as the state of ones' thinking which it represented as he approached worship. Being pure in heart in Jesus' day—and in previous ages—meant that one's thoughts, motives, and actions had to be centered upon God and His instructions, to be free from sin. King David, sometime after his murder of Uriah the Hittite, named his sin to the Father for forgiveness thereby returning to a state of heart purity.

I acknowledged my sin to You, and my iniquity I did not hide; I said, "I will confess my transgressions to the Lord"; And You forgave the guilt of my sin. Selah. Psalm 32:5

For the believer living in this Church Age, heart purity refers to both status and experience. God provides every Church Age believer with mechanics to regain purity of soul after sin. Related to this purity is the empowerment of His Holy Spirit. Only those who appropriate the Father's forgiveness for sins committed after salvation, resulting in "heart purity," qualify for this ministry of the Holy Spirit. The apostle John succinctly presents the mechanics for regaining this purity after sin in 1 John 1:9.

If we confess our sins, He is faithful and righteous to forgive us our sins and to cleanse us from all unrighteousness. 1 John 1:9

The context of this verse clearly indicates that we should confess our sins to the Father, who is faithful, and who forgives our sins. He does so because of our Lord's work on the Cross, where and when He atoned for every sin committed by the human race. Therefore, purity of heart begins for you, Church Age believer, with confessing or naming your sin to the Father by which He cleanses you of sin and any impurity. At this moment, you regain the Spirit's filling and empowerment.

Heart purity has another concept: the experiential. You can never remain in the state of spirituality—of soul purity—without changing your thinking, bringing it into conformity with our Lord's perfect thinking. This process takes your entire life! As you hear the teaching of the Word of God as taught by your pastor, the Spirit teaches you. Because He empowers you, upon your belief in accurate doctrine, you assimilate these spiritual phenomena into your thinking where they become applicable to your life, influencing your thoughts, motives, and actions. By applying His thinking to your life, you become actively and aggressively pure in heart or thought.

Inner happiness logically accompanies your application of divine spiritual phenomena. When you apply the Word of God to your life, you will experience happiness, fulfillment, and great contentedness! It is unavoidable. God rewards you with happiness whenever you choose to apply His word, thereby His power, to your life. This not only glorifies Him but also serves as a witness of His integrity to both people and angels.

The verse continues with this phrase:

> *... for they shall see God.*
> *... ὅτι αὐτοὶ τὸν θεὸν ὄψονται.*

This beatitude continues with a resultant promise attendant to "heart purity." Again, this "heart purity" for Church Age believers refers to spirituality by which we appropriate the Spirit's empowerment and fellowship with the Trinity. The result is that we shall see God. This is most astounding! Can we ever ask for a greater motivation to live the spiritual life than that? The word, "shall see," in the Greek is HORAO (ὁράω), in the future middle indicative. The range of this word's meanings includes actually seeing something or someone, to experiencing, understanding, and perceiving someone or something based upon knowledge. The Greeks had a whole range of verbs dealing with seeing, whereas, only one for hearing.[viii] Hence, one word often contained a nuance not found in another. Matthew, inspired by the Holy Spirit, used this certain verb for the nuance of meaning it contained. The nuance in this verb is much closer to perceiving and understanding than physical seeing with the eye.

The concept of seeing God, even physically, was rooted in the Old Testament Scripture. In those days, men did see visions from God. However, they believed that actually seeing God meant death. They considered this not because God does not want anyone to see Him but because His righteousness and His resultant glory is so much greater than our own. If we were face-to-face with His righteousness, we would burn to a cinder immediately. Our Lord said this to Moses in Exodus 33:20. Did the Old Testament believer, or those to whom Jesus taught, think that they would actually achieve the necessary righteousness to be face-to-face with Him in this life; or was their peak, as the Psalmist wrote, being satisfied with His likeness, as per Psalm 17:15?

> ***As for me, I shall behold Your face in righteousness; I will be satisfied with Your likeness when I awake. Psalm 17:15***

As Church Age believers, if we understand the nuance of HORAO, the verb that Matthew wrote, then we can understand how this directly applies to us. If we maintain our purity, keeping a short account of sin thereby maintaining our spirituality, then through assimilating the Word, we do get to know and understand Him. Therefore, we do see God now, because of learning the Word, by faith, that is.

When we arrive in Heaven, then we shall see the Son and the Father. It is interesting to note that as the disciples looked at Jesus, they were seeing the personal God of Israel in His humanity!

> *... His bond-servants will serve Him; they will see His face, and His name will be on their foreheads. Revelation 22:3-4*

> *They shall see Him as He is. 1 John 3:2*

> *Pursue peace with all men, and the sanctification without which no one will see the Lord. Hebrews 12:14*

H. Matthew 5:9—The Beatitude of Witnessing

Blessed are the peacemakers, for they shall be called sons of God.

Blessed are the peacemakers ...
μακάριοι οἱ εἰρηνοποιοί ...

Superficially, this verse appears to promise happiness to politicians who are trying to reconcile warring factions or countries. However, this, like the previous beatitudes, relates directly to the disciples who were going out to evangelize Israel.

By way of application, this relates to your spiritual life as well. For the disciples, they were to be peacemakers by bringing the Gospel of our Lord's arrival to Israel. We will discuss the mechanics of their peacemaking later in this lesson. However, for the Church Age believer, the application of this verse is more complex.

In this last beatitude, we discussed the importance of purity of heart, referring to both the status of spirituality and experiential spiritual growth. If both of these conditions are present, then it follows logically that you will be a peacemaker. It follows logically because you have grown to a certain point in your spiritual life. Not only are you confident in your own salvation but you have come to understand many facets of the Gospel message. Therefore, you are mature enough to be enthusiastic about the fantastic work our Lord did for us. You have the doctrinal content in your soul to be able to present the Gospel accurately! To fulfill the role of peacemaker you will not have to travel overseas and converse with oppositional political leaders but simply present the gospel to those within your purview.

Between unbelievers and God, there is hostility, enmity, because every human is born into this world as spiritually dead. All unbelievers, then, are antagonistic to God, whether or not they even know it. Unless living under the auspices of divine establishment[ix], every unbeliever lives under Satan's systems of thought and operation. Even those living according to God's establishment principles are vulnerable to arrogance. Satan's systems are fully antagonistic toward God.

When you present the gospel to any unbeliever, you are offering for ratification the peace treaty between God and that person, which is based upon the work of our Lord on the Cross. Although the Gospel is both obscure and incomprehensible being spiritual phenomena to the unbeliever, the Holy Spirit acts as a human spirit, actually teaching the unbeliever accurate Gospel information that he or she hears.

And He, when He comes, will convince the world concerning sin and righteousness and judgment; concerning sin, because they do not believe in Me; John 16:8-9

God commands that every believer be a peacemaker by bringing the message of reconciliation to the unbelievers they encounter. What is this message of reconciliation? God has removed the barrier of sin between humanity and Himself by Jesus' work on the Cross. Being a peacemaker is a part of your spiritual ambassadorship. Paul clearly taught our Lord's ministry of reconciliation. These passages also teach that He has delegated the presentation of reconciliation to us.

Therefore if anyone is in Christ, he is a new creature; the old things passed away; behold, new things have come. Now all these things are from God, who reconciled us to Himself through Christ and gave us the ministry of reconciliation, namely, that God was in Christ reconciling the world to Himself, not counting their trespasses against them, and He has committed to us the word of reconciliation. Therefore, we are ambassadors for Christ, as though God were making an appeal through us; we beg you on behalf of Christ, be reconciled to God. He made Him who knew no sin to be sin on our behalf, so that we might become the righteousness of God in Him.
2 Corinthians 5:17-21

But now in Christ Jesus you who formerly were far off have been brought near by the blood of Christ. For He Himself is our peace, who made both groups into one and broke down the barrier of the dividing wall, by abolishing in His flesh the enmity, which is the Law of commandments contained in ordinances, so that in Himself He might make the two into one new man, thus establishing peace, and might reconcile them both in one body to God through the cross, by it having put to death the enmity. And He came and preached peace to you who were far away, and peace to those who were near; for through Him we both have our access in one Spirit to the Father. Ephesians 2:13-18

... but you will receive power when the Holy Spirit has come upon you; and you shall be My witnesses both in Jerusalem, and in all Judea and Samaria, and even to the remotest part of the earth.
Acts 1:8

But you, be sober in all things, endure hardship,

do the work of an evangelist, fulfill your ministry. 2 Timothy 4:5

An interpretive translation of this first phrase reads this way:

"Happy are those who evangelize ..."

The verse continues:

... for they shall be called sons of God.
... ὅτι αὐτοὶ υἱοὶ θεοῦ κληθήσονται.

This verse continues with a result of being a reconciler: "for they shall be called Sons of God," as per the NASB. The Greek source word for "shall be called" is the future passive of the verb KALEO (καλέω) which the NASB correctly translated as, "will be called." Jesus' hearers would have immediately understood this as an idiom.[x] It refers to a status whereby one person takes on the character of the one whose son he is. The son takes on the character of his "father." This idiom relates to the Greek custom of adoption where the head of the household would choose any younger person to carry on his legacy and to receive the familial inheritance. The adopted son did not need to be related by blood to the father, but took on, by training or by some innate ability, the characteristics of his new "father." In this context, the believer who is mature enough to be presenting the Gospel has matured to the degree that his life reflects and reveals God's integrity and grace. The "sons of God" then refer to the spiritually mature believers.

Who calls this mature believer a son of God? It will not be the one to whom you teach the Gospel. Probably your family or friends will not think to call you God's son either. They may be fixated upon your old sin nature. Even if your dealings with your family and friends reflect your integrity, they probably will not call you a son of God. They may call you honest, however. It will not be those of this world, living in Satan's system of arrogance, who do not even know why they are antagonistic to you! Who is in view here then? God the Father calls you son when you reflect His character; He is the ultimate peacemaker![xi]

Now the God of peace, who brought up from the dead the great Shepherd of the sheep through the blood of the eternal covenant, even Jesus our Lord. Hebrews 13:20

Jesus Christ became the ultimate peacemaker when He died for each one of us on the Cross. God the Father, because of our Lord's substitutionary death, paved the way for the forgiveness of our sins. Because Jesus died for each one of us, He reconciled us to the Father, removing the enmity that exists between those spiritually dead and the Father. We take on the Son's character as we mature because as we study the Word, we assimilate His thinking. Once you reach this state, how can you but share the good news of His work with those with whom you come into contact? Once you reach this point, God will call you His son because you now reflect His grace.

I. Matthew 5:10-11—The Beatitudes of Persecution

Blessed are those who have been persecuted for the sake of righteousness, for theirs is the kingdom of heaven. Blessed are you when people insult you and persecute you, and falsely say all kinds of evil against you because of Me. Matthew 5:10-11

Blessed are you when men hate you, and ostracize you, and insult you, and scorn your name as evil, for the sake of the Son of Man. Luke 6:22

These beatitudes begin with the word "happiness" which refers to inner happiness, as we have established. It is important to remember that inner happiness is progressive. You begin with the understanding of your salvation then your understanding progresses and grows as you mature spiritually. By the time you encounter some persecution you have matured to the degree that you have the capacity for such persecution. You can bear the hostility that persecution brings, having the reality of God's plan in your soul. You understand this to the degree that it is a part of your reality that God has your best interest in His thinking. You know that everything God brings to your life is for your benefit and continued spiritual growth. This is reality, so you do not lose your grace orientation; you do not react and fail spiritually.

Blessed are those who have been persecuted for the sake of righteousness ...
μακάριοι οἱ δεδιωγμένοι ἕνεκεν δικαιοσύνης ...

The word "persecuted" comes from the perfect passive participle of the Greek word, DIOKO (διώκω). The passive indicates that you receive this persecution. You have not asked for it but receive it because those around you have been offended by your righteousness. The persecution may be so bad that it impels you to leave your present abode because you expect personal harm to come to you and your loved ones. By this offending righteousness, this does not refer to the believer who arrogantly and superciliously lords it over those whom he considers inferior or who becomes involved in social activism. Such arrogance is not in view here.

You receive persecution because the world despises divine righteousness. The context demands that this righteousness, from the Greek word DIKAIOSUNE (δικαιοσύνη) belongs to God. Satan initiates this persecution as a part of the angelic conflict. The *Theological Dictionary of the New Testament* defines this righteousness as "...the right conduct of man which follows the will of God and is pleasing to Him, for rectitude of life before God, for uprightness before His judgment."[xii]

How are you—a believer—considered righteous? You are considered righteous in two different ways: one through imputation, and two, because of spiritual growth. First, you believed in Jesus Christ, so you share His righteousness. The Father also imputed His righteousness to you. As a part of justifying you, the Father declared you righteous because of these imputations. Therefore, as a Church Age believer, you have two portions of imputed divine righteousness. Those two categories of righteousness belong to every believer in this Age, so those may not illicit persecution. These imputations of righteousness are real yet often unseen. God considers you to be righteous; therefore, you have eternal life, and you are going to heaven. It is a glorious status.

The second category of righteousness, experiential righteousness, that which you live and experience because you continue to grow up spiritually, may bring persecution to you. Others may observe this righteousness because it results in integrity and witnessing on behalf of our Lord.

This world, because Satan rules it, is antagonistic toward anyone filled with the Spirit and reflecting Christ's character. The only places on earth that protect the experientially righteous believer from such persecution are those countries that are governed under the principles of establishment or Biblical principles. All other protection, such as to missionaries serving in antagonistic cultures, comes to the mature believer through His overriding grace.

This beatitude continues with:

> *... for theirs is the kingdom of heaven.*
> *... ὅτι αὐτῶν ἐστιν ἡ βασιλεία τῶν οὐρανῶν.*

This beatitude continues with the conjunction OTI (ὅτι) which is often translated "for," along with the emphatic plural personal pronoun AUTOS (αὐτός) for "them." Together, they read "because of them." Therefore, the translation of this final phrase of this beatitude should be "because of them is the Kingdom of Heaven." This aspect of the Kingdom of Heaven gives us a peek into the rewards and blessings for the mature believer. If you have the capacity to bear up under such suffering as persecution brings, then God has waiting for you blessings far beyond the ordinary. A better translation of these beatitudes reads this way:

Inner happiness to those receiving persecution because of righteousness, because of them is the Kingdom of Heaven.
Matthew 5:10

Inner happiness to you when people insult you and persecute you, falsely say all kinds of evil against you, because of Me.
Matthew 5:11

This second beatitude expands upon the first. Logically or interpretively, we can place it between the first and second phrases of verse ten:

Inner happiness to you receiving persecution because of righteousness, when people insult you and persecute you and falsely saying all kinds of

evil against you because of Me. The Kingdom of Heaven is for you. Matthew 5:10-11

J. A Review of the Beatitudes

In this section, we will look at each beatitude's interpretive translation, and then address their continuity. This will serve as their summary.

Inner happiness to the spiritually destitute, for the Kingdom of Heaven is for them. Matthew 5:3

This beatitude begins with the unbeliever who has no ability to establish a relationship with God. Yet merciful God has prepared His Kingdom for them, as He has for each of us. God established this Kingdom for every member of the human race before any of us existed. As an over-all principle, there is no one on earth from whom we should withhold the Gospel.

Inner happiness to those under soul wrenching agony, for they will receive comfort from God. Matthew 5:4

This beatitude finds the unbeliever understanding who he is before God. A human being who has not benefitted from a saving relationship with God through Jesus Christ is weak, helpless and living a meaningless life of vanity. This objective truth, when understood, should drive one to the Gospel wherein lies God's ultimate comfort: salvation from eternal death through faith in Jesus Christ.

Inner happiness to the humble for they will inherit the unconditional covenants. Matthew 5:5

This beatitude applied to those who responded to our Lord's presence and the disciples' message—believing in our Lord. Only believers during the dispensation of Israel—true Jews and proselytes—inherit the provisions of the unconditional covenants. Interpretively, for Jesus' disciples, they presented to Israel the only way to benefit from the unconditional covenants, which is salvation. How does this land inheritance relate to their inner happiness? This covenant will not be fulfilled until the Millennium, at which time all Israel will inherit the Promised Land. As an application after salvation, true inner happiness always comes from fulfilling God's plan for your life, no matter what dispensation you live in. For those under the Mosaic Law, His plan was to fulfill the dictates of the Law, including all four codices. This, of course, was impossible, apart from faith in Christ. The Mosaic Law pointed to Christ who fulfilled the Law. For those in this Church Age, true happiness requires three factors: knowledge of the Word, the empowerment of the Spirit and choosing to apply principles of the Word.

Inner happiness to those who strongly desire experiential righteousness, for they shall be satisfied. Matthew 5:6

This beatitude presents the continuation of the believer's spiritual growth. If a believer in any dispensation remains "unsullied" spiritually for any length of time and immediately begins his spiritual growth, then the desire of continued spiritual growth characterizes him. God will provide the necessary resources for that believer's continued spiritual growth. Those resources include a local church with a pastor teaching the Bible accurately. Often, though, a new believer, though regenerate, returns to his prior lifestyle of sin and arrogance without spiritual growth. God is not obligated to provide that believer with the necessary accouterments of spiritual growth until his volition steers him toward spirituality. The Father often provides effective motivation in the form of discipline to persuade the believer to move toward spirituality and spiritual growth.

Blessed are the merciful, for they shall receive mercy. Matthew 5:7

This beatitude continues the progress of spiritual growth. True mercy develops in the soul and mental attitude of the believer growing in grace, taking on our Lord's thinking as his own.

Blessed are the pure in heart, for they shall see God. Matthew 5:8

In both dispensations, the Age of Israel and the Church Age, purity of heart involves learning and applying the Word. It involves keeping a short account of sin and applying doctrinal rationales through which believers come to know God. He gives the Church Age believer the Holy Spirit's empowerment to aid and assist in this endeavor. Actually, without the Spirit's power, the believer cannot grow in grace to the degree that he can "see God." We as Church Age believers "see God" by experiencing Him through His Word.

Blessed are the peacemakers, for they shall be called sons of God. Matthew 5:9

The peacemakers are those believers who carry the message of reconciliation, the Gospel, to unbelievers. This requires a thorough knowledge and understanding of the Gospel without which a believer cannot realize a certain level of spiritual growth. As a believer, you become a "son of God" by taking on His character—another picture of spiritual growth.

Inner happiness to you receiving persecution because of righteousness, when people insult you and persecute you and falsely say all kinds of evil against you because of Me. The Kingdom of Heaven is for you. Matthew 5:10-11

These last beatitudes speak of an inevitability of spiritual growth as it reaches a high level: suffering for blessing, which can take the form of persecution. When the believer has grown spiritually to the degree that he has the capacity for suffering, he has truly reached a landmark of spiritual growth.

K. Matthew 5:12—Inner Happiness Produces Outer Happiness

Rejoice and be glad, for your reward in heaven is great; for in the same way, they persecuted the prophets who were before you. Matthew 5:12

Be glad in that day and leap for joy, for behold, your reward is great in heaven. For in the same way their fathers used to treat the prophets. Luke 6:23

These beatitudes begin with God's provision for salvation, continue with spiritual growth, and finally end with the spiritual maturation of the believer. Each step the believer takes toward spiritual maturity adds another facet of inner happiness to his soul. The believer who continually grows can do only one thing: Rejoice!

Rejoice and be glad ...
χαίρετε καὶ ἀγαλλιᾶσθε,

The Greek source word for rejoice is the present active indicative of CHAIRETE (χαίρετε)! Rejoice! Whereas MAKARIOS describes inner happiness, a state of soul, this word describes an outer manifestation of it. Inward joy must find an expression! That expression is wrapped up in this word—rejoice! This outer expression of happiness finds its root in the Old Testament Scripture. The understanding of many aspects of God's grace and benefits bring this manifestation of inner happiness:

But let all who take refuge in You be glad, let them ever sing for joy; and may You shelter them, that those who love Your name may exult in You. Psalm 5:11
I will be glad and exult in You; I will sing praise to Your name, O Most High. Psalm 9:2
Therefore my heart is glad and my glory rejoices; My flesh also will dwell securely. Psalm 16:9

Be glad in the Lord and rejoice, you righteous ones; and shout for joy, all you who are upright in heart. Psalm 32:11

This is the visible manifestation of inner happiness. No matter who or what is persecuting you, if you possess inner happiness you will face pressures from adversity—and even prosperity—with relaxation and maybe even a smile![xiii] Even if you fail initially, remember that Job also failed at one time. If you do fail, recover and move on!

The present tense of this Greek verb indicates that this is to be a continual way of thinking. Keep on rejoicing! The active voice indicates that the believer produces the action of the verb. Do your thinking, feeling, and activities continually outwardly express inner happiness? You must keep on making the right decisions. Keep short accounts of your sins and continue growing spiritually. Every decision you make is paramount to maintaining your happiness. You decide what you are going to do with your life. Even though you have followed all of the steps to spiritual maturity, you cannot stop and rest on those laurels! These decisions directly affect the degree of your spiritual growth and therefore the degree of your happiness. The indicative mood indicates the reality that God means it to be.

This brings up a question. If you grow spiritually to this degree, that you outwardly rejoice, can you ever lose that happiness because of subsequent spiritual failure? According to Paul, you can. He teaches us not to lose our happiness. We can infer from Paul's words to the Hebrews that we can lose our spirituality and degree of spiritual growth, even after considerable growth:

> *Do not, therefore, throw away that confidence of yours;*
> *it brings a great reward. Hebrews 10:35*

Paul could just as easily have said, "...do not throw away your happiness," because just as your confidence results from your spiritual growth, so does your happiness. This writer had evidence that led him to assume that the Jews to whom he addressed this letter had been making great spiritual progress and maturing rapidly during their period of suffering. Now that they were prospering, they were forgetting their spiritual foundation. They were throwing their spirituality out the door; therefore, they were about to lose their confidence, their spiritual maturity and happiness.

The next word, translated, "be glad" comes from the present passive imperative of the verb AGALLIAO (ἀγαλλιάω). This word represents an intensification of the outward manifestation of inner happiness. As with the previous word, CHAIRETE, AGALLIAO indicates an ongoing expression, "keep on being glad ..." These words, "rejoice" and "be glad," having two different source words, and though they express much the same concept, differ in two areas. On one hand, rejoice, CHAIRETE (χαίρετε) is in the active voice and indicative mood. The active voice indicates that the believer produces the action of the verb, as we noted above. Second, the indicative mood presents this fact from the viewpoint of reality. "Be glad," AGALLIAO (ἀγαλλιάω), on the other hand, is in the passive voice denoting that the believer receives this expression. God gives this happiness to the believer because he has reached that certain stage of spiritual maturity when He shares His happiness with him. This verb is also in the imperative mood! Our Lord actually commands this extreme expression of inner happiness in each of one us! This is tantamount to a command to grow up spiritually so that you have the capacity to enjoy that God-given happiness. From both of these verbs we learn that we are supposed to be happy, both internally and visibly! If the Lord imparts this to us, then He has also provided everything we need to experience this happiness.

> *Cry aloud and shout for joy, O inhabitant of Zion,*
> *for great in your midst is the Holy One of Israel. Isaiah 12:6*

... for your reward in heaven is great.
... ὅτι ὁ μισθὸς ὑμῶν πολὺς ἐν τοῖς οὐρανοῖς.

The reward, MISTHOS (μισθός), delineated in the next phrase of this verse does not come to you because you are happy or persecuted but because of your spiritual growth. God rewards you, if you have matured spiritually to the degree that you possess unshakable happiness. God rewards you if you have grown spiritually to the degree that you can receive persecution without reacting and losing your spirituality. Remember that those special communicators of doctrine in past dispensations received persecution for their role in the angelic war. You have a much greater, much more crucial role, so if you fulfill it, you will receive great rewards, even as they!

Paul echoed our Lord's commands for happiness when he wrote the Philippian believers:

Finally, my brethren, rejoice in the Lord. To write the same things again is no trouble to me, and it is a safeguard for you. Philippians 3:1

Rejoice in the Lord always; again I will say, rejoice!
Philippians 4:4

... for in the same way they persecuted the prophets who were before you.
... ὅτι ὁ μισθὸς ὑμῶν πολὺς ἐν τοῖς οὐρανοῖς.

The Scripture clearly documents both the persecutions and rewards of the great prophets of old. 1 Kings 19:1-3 narrates Jezebel's persecution of Elijah. Jeremiah 26:7ff describes a plot to kill Jeremiah. Hebrews 11:36 begins a narrative of persecution of the prophets.

PART III

IMPACT OF THE MATURE BELIEVER
MATTHEW 5:13-16

A. Matthew 5:13—Salt of the Earth

You are the salt of the earth; but if the salt has become tasteless, how can it be made salty again? It is no longer good for anything, except to be thrown out and trampled underfoot by men.
Matthew 5:13

Salt is good; but if the salt becomes unsalty, with what will you make it salty again?
Have salt in yourselves, and be at peace with one another.
Mark 9:50

Therefore, salt is good; but if even salt has become tasteless, with what will it be seasoned? Luke 14:34

Jesus addressed those who had advanced through the various stages of spiritual growth, those maturing believers, calling them salt.

You are the salt of the earth ...
Ὑμεῖς ἐστε τὸ ἅλας τῆς γῆς ...

He first said, "You are..." Though this may seem straightforward, the Greek source words and their etymology offer us a greater implication. It begins with the plural second person personal pronoun of SU (σύ), translated more accurately, as "ya'll," to include everyone listening to our Lord. We English speakers use the personal pronoun, "you," to include both singular and plural. Of course, if you are from the South, you probably use the plural form, "ya'll" as both singular and plural! Perhaps Northerners say, "youse guys!" We will use "you all" in our translation.

The following word is the verb of being, EIMI (εἰμί), in the plural second person present active indicative, linear aktionsart. The present tense presents the action in progress without the completion of that action in view. This action is progressive or ongoing. Therefore, the implication of the linear aktionsart is continuity; "you all keep on being…" The active voice indicates that His disciples, who were listening and maturing, produced the action of the verb. The indicative mood means that the writer presents this action as being real. A better translation would indicate the progression of the action; "you all keep on being." In the English, this begins to sound like a command, as if He was telling His disciples to keep being like salt. However, it is a statement of a fact, not a command.

The next phrase, "the salt of the earth," is the nominative singular neuter of HALAS (ἅλας), with the genitive singular feminine of GE (γῆ), "the salt of the earth." In ancient times, salt symbolized deity because of its purifying, preserving and seasoning qualities. The Old Testament dictated its use in sacrifices by mixing it with or sprinkled on top of the sacrifice.

Every grain offering of yours, moreover, you shall season with salt, so that the salt of the covenant of your God shall not be lacking from your grain offering; with all your offerings you shall offer salt. Leviticus 2:13

Putting salt in the offerings was a picture of the believer's ratification of the treaty God presented at the instant of Gospel hearing and understanding. If you believed, you "salted" or ratified the treaty with your faith. God preserved you eternally, as salt does your food, to live in God's Kingdom forever. Salt, then, in the context of the Levitical offerings, represented God's gift of salvation and eternal preservation. Furthermore, midwives rubbed newborns with it and covenants were ratified with it.

Do you not know that the Lord God of Israel gave the rule over Israel forever to David and his sons by a covenant of salt? 2 Chronicles 13:5

The salt of the covenant follows the ancient custom that a promise or an agreement made with salt was considered perpetual and permanent, legal and binding. Jesus' hearers understood from the phrase that having inner happiness to its maximum degree meant that they would save and preserve the earth.

Today, we use salt as a food enhancer and preservative. These two concepts certainly apply to the interpretation of this verse, both to those who heard Jesus teach this and to us today. These principles cross all dispensational boundaries, applying to every advancing believer from the beginning of human history to today's modern Church Age believer. Wherever mature believers exist, either geographically or in time, God blesses and preserves not only that believer, but blesses also those in his purview even spreading throughout his nation. If enough advanced believers exist in a national entity during the Church Age, that nation becomes a blessing to the entire world by missionary activity, custodianship of the Word and providing a haven for Jews. As God prospers the client nation, so the entire world prospers. If a country faces divine judgment, a number of mature believers can cause God to refrain from destroying that nation. Those few mature believers can salt a nation, allowing God to preserve it.

Not only does salt preserve, but it also enhances the flavor of food. Believers, who have advanced spiritually, those having achieved inner happiness by spiritual growth, enhance the lives of those around them. Again, this principle applies to every dispensation. God's power works though advanced believers through three principles: the verbal witness, the lifestyle witness, and the principle of blessing by association. Nothing enhances the life of the unbeliever more than to receive and believe the Gospel of our Lord! On the other hand, because an advanced believer has capacity for blessings, those within his or her purview, by either relationship or geography, God will bless as well. Sometimes, those He blesses by association appear to prosper to a greater degree than that mature believer with whom the blessed associate! God can only bless unbelievers in time, whereas, the advanced believers' temporal blessings are only a small taste of his eternal blessings. These believers will more likely be invisible to those around them receiving divine blessings by association with them.

A good interpretive translation of this phrase includes the principle of progression and continuity of blessings:

> ***You all, with inner happiness, keep on being the salt of the Earth ...***

Our Lord continued with the salt analogy to include the principle of salt losing its saltiness.

> ***... but if the salt has become tasteless,***
> ***... ἐὰν δὲ τὸ ἅλας μωρανθῇ,***

The word, "if" is EAN (ἐάν), the third class conditional particle recognizing this possibility, if not its probability, of action. The phrase, "has become tasteless," the aorist passive subjunctive of MORAINO (μωραίνω) appears to be a play on words. Contextually, it refers to becoming tasteless, but it also refers to dullness, sluggishness, or intellectual deficiency![xiv] The implication is clear! What kind of expression did our Lord have on His face when He uttered these words? Was He implying a bit of sarcasm here?

We, in this modern age of pure chemical compounds, probably will not understand this. Our Lord understood this but He was addressing people whose salt did lose its effectiveness, its saltiness. The salt used in ancient times was not pure but contained other substances. If humidity attacked the salt, the actual sodium chloride would leach out leaving the other compounds with not a bit of saltiness. Salt harvested from the Dead Sea would lose its saltiness, acquiring an alkalinity. Furthermore, Dr. Thompson (*"The Land and the Book"*) cites the following case: "A merchant of Sidon, having farmed of the government the revenue from the importation of salt, brought over a great quantity from the marshes of Cyprus—enough, in fact, to supply the whole province for many years. This he had transferred to the mountains, to cheat the government out of some small percentage of duty. Sixty-five houses were rented and filled with salt. Such houses have merely earthen floors, and the salt next the ground was in a few years entirely spoiled. I saw large quantities of it literally thrown into the road to be trodden under foot of men and beasts. It was 'good for nothing.'"[xv] This worthless salt was not even good enough to be used to speed up the decomposition of dung! It was hardly worth throwing out!

How can believers, salted with inner happiness, become tasteless or spiritual morons? The believer who stops learning and applying God's Word loses his spiritual effectiveness. He stops appropriating God's power in his life, backsliding into reversionism! This insipid believer becomes a casualty in the angelic war! Too many believers fall into this category because they put details of life ahead of appropriating divine power by which God has designed them to live.

... how can it be made salty again?
... ἐν τίνι ἀλισθήσεται;

However, to answer our Lord's question, which I take as being rhetorical, the insipid Church Age believer can only regain his saltiness by getting back into fellowship with Him then regaining his spiritual life. Often believers will willingly walk into a state of sin for one reason or another with the misplaced confidence that they can simply regain their spirituality and level of spiritual growth. This may be true to a degree, but it is possible to become caught in a web of sin and evil from which even the most mature believer will be unable to be extricated! You can reach a point of no return!

Once you have reached this point of no return, you will never fulfill God's plan for your life. You will not have lost your salvation, but your effectiveness in the angelic war will be gone. God might as well as take you home to Heaven because there will be no reason to keep you on the Earth! The Scripture refers to the process of God taking you home early, before He had initially planned as the sin unto death or sin face-to-face with death!

It is no longer good for anything except to be thrown out and trampled underfoot by men.
εἰς οὐδὲν ἰσχύει ἔτι εἰ μὴ βληθὲν ἔξω καταπατεῖσθαι ὑπὸ τῶν ἀνθρώπων.

The final sentence in this verse reveals the destiny of the insipid believer. Understand that this no-longer-salted believer has lost his role in the angelic war. In terms of God's plan, this believer is useless. The only way he can glorify God is to die, partaking in our Lord's victory over death. He will not have lost his salvation, but he will have lost rewards and blessings the Lord had slated for him to receive at the Judgement Seat.

B. Matthew 5:14-16—Light of the World

In the previous series of verses, our Lord delineated the means of inner happiness. In this following series of verses, He explains the overflow of these blessings to others.

1. Matthew 5:14

You are the light of the world. A city set on a hill cannot be hidden; nor does anyone light a lamp and put it under a basket, but on the lampstand, and it gives light to all who are in the house.

Our Lord continued characterizing the advancing believer, the one who has progressed through the concepts presented in the beatitudes to a high level of spiritual growth. Not only does He refer to them as salt, but also as the light of the world.

You are the light of the world.
Ὑμεῖς ἐστε τὸ φῶς τοῦ κόσμου.

The syntax of the first two words in this verse echo those in the previous verse with the translation of, "You all keep on being..." The verb of being indicates an absolute, continuing status quo. In the English, too, this almost sounds like a command. It is not. It is a statement of fact. Though He had not yet sent His disciples out into Israel to offer the Kingdom, the continuity concept applied to their entire lives, not just to their assigned sojourn. We apply this in the same manner. The application of this verse applies to us, as Church Age believers, as well, applying the following principles to our entire lives.

The word translated "light" is the predicate nominative noun, PHOS (φῶς). While it most often refers to the literal light emanating from the sun, other heavenly bodies and fire, to understand its use in this context we need to look at three different subjects. First, we will look at light as energy, then to Old Testament uses, both literal and metaphoric, and finally we will look at what our Lord meant when He called Himself, "the Light of the World."

a. Light as Energy

We need to understand light's characteristics and dynamics to understand why our Lord called both Himself and His disciples, "light." Light is energy that permeates the state without energy we know as darkness. Do you notice that when you open a dark closet, light permeates the darkness? Darkness does not overflow into the light. Our Lord's power, in the form of His thinking, is the only light that permeates the darkness of satanic thought. Light is energy that overcomes and overpowers darkness. So it is with your spiritual life. The power of God, in the form of thought dynamics circulating in your soul, permeates the darkness of Satanic thought.

This physical world in which we live serves as a veil, shielding us from God's glory, which is characterized as light. We, as frail humans, cannot exist face-to-face with His glory. For all practical purposes, this world is just an illusion, yet it is the only reality our natural senses can perceive. Moses, when he came down from Mt. Sinai had absorbed so much of God's light that he needed a veil covering so that people could look at him. The prophet Daniel passed out when he saw a vision of our glorified Lord. The actual reality of the universe far supersedes what we can understand by our senses. Once having believed in Jesus Christ, God allows us to see Him and understand this greater reality through faith. Once we leave this world, then we will see Him, as the Scripture says, "As He is."

> *Beloved, now we are children of God, and it has not appeared as yet what we will be. We know that when He appears, we will be like Him, because we will see Him just as He is. 1 John 3:2*

b. Old Testament Uses

The Old Testament uses light repeatedly both literally and metaphorically. Literally, it refers to light from the sun upon which we depend in so many different ways.

> *The light is pleasant, and it is good for the eyes to see the sun. Ecclesiastes 11:7*

In this verse, Solomon reflects on enjoyment of life for the believer.

Light also symbolizes one's life. You cannot see the sun and enjoy its vitality without being alive!

> *Thus says the Lord, who gives the sun for light by day and the fixed order of the moon and the stars for light by night... Jeremiah 31:35*

The greater context of this verse describes a covenant between God and both Kingdoms of Israel. It identifies God who provides complete logistics for His people. He provides these things by means of His omnipotence; thus He faithfully provides them. Only omnipotent God can provide for them; only an omnipotent God can require such a covenant. The covenant this passage describes will be fulfilled during the millennial reign of our Lord.

Metaphorically, light illustrates God's essence and power.

> *The Lord is my light and my salvation; whom shall I fear? The Lord is the defense of my life; whom shall I dread? Psalm 27:1*

When David spoke of our Lord being light, he was referring to the understanding our Lord's thinking provides, giving capacity for life, providing guidance and power. One important result of capacity for life is freedom from fear.

> *I will lead the blind by a way they do not know; in paths they do not know I will guide them. I will make darkness into light before them and rugged places into plains. These are the things I will do, and I will not leave them undone. Isaiah 42:16*

> *No longer will you have the sun for light by day, nor for brightness will the moon give you light; but you will have the Lord for an everlasting light, and your God for your glory.*
> *Isaiah 60:19*

In this passage, Isaiah prophesied that a great light would shine in Galilee, dispelling darkness. The use of light here is metaphoric, yet all who heard this would understand that the light referred to divine power that dispels Satanic thought.

> *The people who walk in darkness will see a great light; those who live in a dark land, the light will shine on them. Isaiah 9:2*

The light in this verse refers to our Lord, Himself.

c. Jesus' Use of the Phrase

Jesus called Himself the Light of the World.

> *Then Jesus again spoke to them, saying, "I am the Light of the world; he who follows Me will not walk in the darkness, but will have the Light of life." John 8:12*

Though He spoke these words after the Sermon on the Mount, it reflects His use of the phrase we are studying. He spoke this during the Feast of the Tabernacles, popularly known as the Feast of Lights. It was called this because during this festival four massive candelabras were erected in the Court of the Women in the Temple. These lights were visible from and softly illuminated the entire city. Due to the altitude of the Temple, the lights were probably visible beyond the city. The people would celebrate by rejoicing and dancing around them. The disciples He taught were raised within this context, so they understood the quality of and importance of the light to which our Lord referred. This festival was rooted in the fact of the column of fire, which led the Israelites through the Sinai desert after they were delivered from Egypt. The column of light itself was the Shekinah Glory of our Pre-incarnate Lord.

The writer of the Psalms referred to our Lord prophetically as "His Light." John the Baptist called Him, "the True Light." Isaiah called Him, "Everlasting Light." Israelites generally referred to the Messiah as the Light. Therefore, when our Lord said that He was the Light, He was making a Messianic claim! The lampstand in the Holy Place, the only source of light in there, represented our Lord.

> *While I am in the world, I am the Light of the world. John 9:5*

Jim Oliver
I have come as Light into the world, so that everyone who believes in Me will not remain in darkness. John 12:46

No prophet, not even the greatest, was ever given this title, but He appointed His disciples as luminaries, having given to them the responsibility of witnessing for Him. As He initially addressed this to His disciples, He was indicating to them that they were representing Him to Israel. They were to continue doing that.

The question we need to answer is this: what does it mean in relationship to the inner happiness that God gives to us as we mature spiritually? When we spiritually advance, we become conduits of divine blessings to others in our purview. We transmit His light to others by verbally giving the Gospel, living a lifestyle of integrity and being a conduit of divine blessings.

This verse continues with a characteristic of light.

A city set on a hill cannot be hidden;
οὐ δύναται πόλις κρυβῆναι ἐπάνω ὄρους κειμένη·

Every city has lights. When a city is on a hill, the light permeates darkness and is visible for miles around. The Greek source word for "cannot," DUNAMAI (δύναμαι), speaks of power and ability. When used in this context, it carries much impact. This city absolutely cannot be hidden. The same principles apply to believers in every generation. Believers living the spiritual life specific to that dispensation will have a lifestyle recognized as one with integrity. Their integrity, having come from God, will not ever be hidden. In this Church Age, spiritual believers applying the Word to their lives will be like a bright city, because their lives reflect God's grace and integrity. The word "hidden" comes from the Greek KRUPTO (κρύπτω) as an aorist passive infinitive. Such light can never, ever be hidden—nor can it even conceal itself.[xvi]

2. **Matthew 5:15**

Nor does anyone light a lamp and put it under a basket, but on the lampstand, and it gives light to all who are in the house.

οὐδὲ καίουσιν λύχνον καὶ τιθέασιν αὐτὸν ὑπὸ τὸν μόδιον ἀλλ' ἐπὶ τὴν λυχνίαν, καὶ λάμπει πᾶσιν τοῖς ἐν τῇ οἰκίᾳ.

Believers in this age, when our Lord is personally absent, become lights of the world when they proclaim God's integrity by their life, actions, and speech. Believers, then, become the illuminating ones, carrying the torchlight of God's Word, the very thinking of our Lord, to unbelievers. Just as a city with its lights brightly lit, a believer thinking and living doctrine cannot be hidden from view. The light of doctrine can never be hidden or repressed. Once you experience the light of God's love and absolute integrity in your life because of your spiritual advance, then you will be as that light which is not hidden but shining on everyone in your purview. If you live in the spiritual darkness, not maturing, then you will be hiding your light under that basket. This basket, according to the

Greek source word, MODIOS (μόδιος) refers not to a basket that may leak light, but to a clay pot used to measure grain. It is light tight. No light will leak from the believer who lives his life in spiritual darkness, rejecting God's provision for spiritual growth.

3. Matthew 5:16

Let your light shine before men in such a way that they may see your good works, and glorify your Father who is in heaven.

Let your light shine ...
οὕτως λαμψάτω τὸ φῶς ὑμῶν ...

Jesus continued this dissertation with a concluding command: "In this way, let your light shine..." In the Greek, this phrase consists of the adverb of manner, HOUTOS (οὕτως), translated, "in this manner." In what manner? If each disciple followed the path set out in the Beatitudes, going from the need of salvation, to faith in Christ, and then advancing through spiritual growth, then they would have light to show others through the life they lead.

The phrase continues with the aorist active imperative of LAMPO (λάμπω) with the nominative noun PHOS (φῶς) and the second person personal pronoun SU (σύ). A translation that more accurately represents these words is, "...shine your light!" This is an imperative, a command! To the disciples this required obeying the Son, living the life as prescribed by proper interpretation of the Law. For our application as Church Age believers, it means that each of us has the responsibility to maintain the empowerment of the Spirit, continuing our spiritual growth, living the life God has designed for us. This also requires continual spiritual growth. The verse, so far, then reads this way: "In this manner, shine your light..."

... before men in such a way that they may see your good works,
... ἔμπροσθεν τῶν ἀνθρώπων, ὅπως ἴδωσιν ὑμῶν τὰ καλὰ ἔργα,

The next Greek words indicate where we are to shine our light: the preposition EMPROSTHEN (ἔμπροσθεν), the near demonstrative article HO (ὁ) with the genitive plural noun of ANTHROPOS (ἄνθρωπος). We can translate these words as, "in front of people." Your spiritual life should overflow to all aspects of your life with its attendant reflection of God's integrity. We are to shine our light in such a way that those in the human race see it! Do not hide your light under an opaque container. People need to see your light. Your light is the outward manifestation of your God-empowered spiritual life. Therefore, you need to maintain your spirituality and keep applying doctrine in your life. In this way, your life will reflect God's perfect integrity and loving kindness.

The verse continues with the words, the adverb of purpose, HOPOS (ὅπως) translated, "in order that," with aorist active subjunctive of the verb of seeing,

HORAO (ὁράω), translated, "they may see…" This durative aorist indicates that they should continually see. The active voice indicates that these people do the seeing. The "may" comes from the Greek subjunctive mood. If you live a life of integrity, they will be able to see God through you.

If you live your life reflecting God's integrity, being empowered by His Spirit, then you will produce "good works." These good works—the adjective KALOS (καλός)—"good," ascribes a quality to ERGON (ἔργον), "works." Though the Greeks used a multiplicity of words to express good in different contexts, two words stand out as being used most frequently: KALOS (καλός) and AGATHOS (ἀγαθός). We need to distinguish between these two words to understand all of the implications presented in this verse. The Holy Spirit did not inspire Matthew to write AGATHOS but KALOS instead. What does one word imply—or state—that the other one does not? AGATHOS indicates the quality of good, absolute excellence. In the New Testament, it always refers to the Divine. KALOS, on the other hand, refers to that which results from divine good. It is the visible demonstration of good.

So, the ancient Jews understood that the "good" referred to anything corresponding to God's perfect will. It did not denote an esthetic or moral value. Therefore, for the disciples, again, this refers to their adherence to obedience to our Lord and to the Mosaic Law. The Law never taught legalism, so this teaching stands in contrast to the Pharisees' interpretation of the Law. For we Church Age believers this is tantamount to the function of our spiritual life. It involves everything we, as Spirit-empowered believers, do such as the function of spiritual gifts, witnessing, prayer, giving, only to mention a few! You will be a witness if your life reflects God's integrity! Only one category of believer can fulfill this quality of good to their works: those having matured spiritually.

… and glorify your Father who is in heaven.
… καὶ δοξάσωσιν τὸν πατέρα ὑμῶν τὸν ἐν τοῖς οὐρανοῖς.

Why does our Lord command us to do this? We are to do this ultimately to glorify the Father. This is why we believe, why we live our spiritual lives. Glorification of the Father relates closely to the resolution of the angelic war. We have been given the greatest honor: that of glorifying the Father while we are alive and breathing on this earth. We can serve as witness to the Father's righteousness not only to people but also to angels, bringing glory to Him.

Glory comes from the aorist active subjunctive of the Greek word, DOXAZO (δοξάζω). The aorist tense indicates that this occurs, possibly continually as a durative aorist would indicate or more likely every so often, as the iterative aorist would indicate. You glorify God when the Holy Spirit fills you and you apply His Word. The subjunctive mood refers to the potentiality of this glorification. This is only a potential because a believer's ability to glorify the Father is directly dependent upon his level of spiritual maturity. No believer can glorify God without applying doctrines referred to in the beatitudes we have just studied! Will every believer glorify God through his lifestyle? Not unless he is living the advanced spiritual life!

PART IV

THE LORD'S RELATIONSHIP TO THE LAW
MATTHEW 5:17-20

A. Matthew 5:17—Fulfilling the Law

Do not think that I came to abolish the Law or the Prophets; I did not come to abolish but to fulfill.

To understand this verse, you need to understand the popular messianic expectation circulating around Israel at that time. They were under the despised Roman rule, so they were looking forward to a Messiah who would rise up militarily, throw off Roman rule and then establish the Israel God promised to Abraham. The Messiah would actually rule them. After God fulfilled this promise, Israel was to include much of the Mideast. After our Lord told them that they were the salt of the earth and light of the world, did they, too, think that our Lord would follow that Messianic pattern?

A second precursor to understanding this passage deals with an accusation the Pharisees leveled upon Jesus. They claimed that He was abrogating the Law by His activities. Furthermore, they accused Him of doing exactly what they were doing—teaching the Law erroneously.

Do not think ...
Μὴ νομίσητε ...

"Do not think" is the negative particle ME (μή) with the aorist active subjunctive of NOMIZO (νομίζω) which means, "do not presume" or "do not assume." The subjunctive mood when combined with the negated aorist forms an imperative. When a person presumes or assumes something, they often jump the gun, believing what they have been told without ever confirming it. Religious people, for instance, often arrogantly assume certain things true without ever consulting the Scripture. A local pastor, one Sunday, taught the proper protocol for prayer. Though his teaching was Scriptural, many of his hearers chose to reject it, relying instead on erroneous preconceived notions. Presumptions often relate to emotionalism and arrogance because those who presume the accuracy of their knowledge dogmatically defend it. How often are our presumptions false or a distortion of a truth? Believers must confirm their beliefs by accurate scriptural interpretation. Paul spoke glowingly of the Bereans who searched the Scripture to confirm his teaching.

Jesus then warned His disciples against an assumption they might make in light of a popular misconception and in light of what He had just told them.

> *... that I came ...*
> *... ὅτι ἦλθον ...*

These words, the coordinating conjunction, HOTI (ὅτι) "that" with the verb ERCHOMAI (ἔρχομαι) "I come" in the aorist active indicative, though literally "I come," form a Hebrew idiom meaning, "It is my purpose to..." This is obvious, but it is interesting to note how many Hebrew idioms pop up in what theologians generally consider to have been written from the spoken Aramaic.

Were the disciples' heads spinning at His words: "You are the salt of the earth...You are the light of the world..." Remember the men He was addressing were not in the political hierarchy or men of any influence at all. Now He had just told them that they were to have great influence. Certainly, now they are beginning to understand the responsibilities our Lord was delegating to them. They may have been wondering these things: "Is the kingdom here?" "Is the King going to stay? "Is this the beginning of the promised reign of the Messiah, the Millennium?" Many believed that now that the Messiah had arrived, He would establish an army, defeat the Romans, and usher in His millennial reign. His millennial kingdom certainly included the end of Roman rule, but that was a "side-effect," of bringing in the Millennium. His main purpose was not to start a revolution but to provide salvation through His substitutionary work. By this statement, then, He shut down that line of thinking in the disciples' minds as well as answering the Pharisaic accusation. Was Judas absent from Bible class that day?

> *... to abolish the Law or the Prophets.*
> *... καταλῦσαι τὸν νόμον ἢ τοὺς προφήτας·*

The word, "abolish," the aorist active infinitive of KATALUO (καταλύω) refers to the abrogation or to the setting aside of something, in this case of the Mosaic Law and Old Testament prophecies. Setting aside or abrogating the Mosaic Law and prophets implied ushering in the Millennium, because this ushering in would change the entire societal structure as it then existed. He is telling them that He is not going in that direction. His first advent has another purpose: to fulfill the Mosaic Law and to fulfill the prophecies of the Old Testament prophets completely. His fulfillment of the Law did not imply an instant Millennium! Also, note that the Pharisees thought that He was destroying the Law by His Sabbath activities. Nothing could have been further from the truth!

I did not come to abolish but to fulfill.
οὐκ ἦλθον καταλῦσαι ἀλλὰ πληρῶσαι.

The word "fulfill" is the aorist active infinitive of PLEROO (πληρόω), the aorist tense indicating fulfillment or completion of something in a point of time with results perpetuated forever. Our Lord's fulfillment of the Law was a permanent, one-time accomplishment with results that last eternally. No other human being could fulfill the Law. Since our Lord fulfilled it, no one else must. Our Lord fulfilled or completed the Law in two ways: by His life and by His deaths. Since our Lord gave Moses the Law, no one had been able to live up to it or fulfill it until His first advent. Actually, it is impossible for any spiritually dead human being to keep the Law, ever. That was one of its points of truth. No one can ever attain ultimate righteousness, righteousness needed for eternal life, presented by the Law. A person who was truly oriented to the Law understood his inability to attain salvation on his own and looked for Him who the Law pictured in that ritual sacrifice, namely our Lord. Ultimate righteousness comes only by grace through faith in our Lord Jesus Christ. When anyone believes in Jesus Christ, the Father bestows upon that one His own righteousness. This fact spans the dispensations.

A popular movement awash among believers today involves attempts to keep the Mosaic Law. These people try to keep certain outward tenets and requirements of the Law but do not understand its overall purpose. Its purpose was to demonstrate the inability of the human race to attain to God's righteousness, then to present Him who would: our Lord Jesus Christ. A person who truly adheres to the Law today understands that our Lord fulfilled it and then believes in Him. Once a person places his faith in our Lord, he should understand that the Age of Israel has been temporarily set aside to establish our Lord's bride, the Church. Our Lord introduced the Church Age when He saw Israel reject Him. Therefore, a person must progress beyond the Law and understand the importance of the Church Age.

What does it mean to fulfill the Law and Prophets? Generally, theologians fall into two different schools of thought on this. The first category says that by fulfilling the Law and the Prophets He did everything the prophets prophesied. The second school of thought says that He fulfilled the Law by bringing it to completion by accurately explaining it. In reality, understand that He did both.

How was He, as the Perfect God-Man, humanly able to fulfill the Law and Prophets whereas no other human being ever could? He was able to do this because He was born perfect, without an old sin nature, empowered by the Holy Spirit, and applied doctrine perfectly. How did He fulfill the Law? During His 33 years on this earth, He kept the commandments, Codex #1, perfectly. By His substitutionary saving work on the Cross, He fulfilled Codex #2. It describes perfectly the Lamb who would take away the sins of the world. He fulfilled the establishment code by His patriotism and applying the principles of establishment perfectly. Therefore, by His life, He fulfilled the first Codex, and by His work on the Cross, He fulfilled the second Codex. He fulfilled the prophets by fulfilling every prophecy taught about Him. By His fulfillment of the Law and the Prophets He gave life to them, embodying them. The Law was to reach its fullest fruition in His perfect life and substitutionary death. Note that even though I have broken apart the Law and Prophets as two concepts, they are really one concept referring to the entire Old Testament Scripture.

The terms, "to destroy" or "to abrogate" the Law compared to "fulfilling" the Law were also Hebraisms, which lends credence to the above commentary. When one Rabbi accused another of misinterpreting the Mosaic Law, he did so by saying, "You are destroying the Law!" The other, disagreeing, would say, "No! I'm fulfilling the Law!" Therefore, our Lord completely disagreed with the then-current teachers of the Law who alleged that He was misinterpreting the Law. In actuality, He was teaching correctly; furthermore, He was the embodiment of the Law.

Whenever someone teaches the Scripture erroneously, he is changing the Law, usually beyond the above seemingly innocuous points. The religious establishment in Jesus' day was teaching inaccurately by leading the people to adhere to the many legalistic requirements they had established as a means to fulfilling the Law. As an aside, over the years, they had built layers of regulations meant to protect the people from even coming close to violating the Law! However, in so doing, they had built in layers of legalism. They missed the point that no human being can fulfill the Law; its entire purpose was to point to our Lord, the Unique One who did fulfill the Law. Today, just the multiplicity of denominations—of "brands" of Christianity—indicates how many pastors from their pulpits promulgate error!

B. Matthew 5:18—Continuing the 'Fulfillment' Concept

For truly I say to you, until heaven and earth pass away, not the smallest letter or stroke shall pass from the Law until all is accomplished.

For truly I say to you ...
ἀμὴν γὰρ λέγω ὑμῖν ...

Our Lord continued talking about His fulfilling the Law and Prophets in this statement. Remember that "the Law and Prophets" refers to the entire Old Testament Scripture.

This verse begins with a very important, emphatic phrase. We see this phrase repeatedly in the Gospels. In the Greek, it looks like this: AMEN GAR LEGO HUMIN (ἀμὴν γὰρ λέγω ὑμῖν). The first word in the phrase should sound very familiar. AMEN is an Aramaic word brought into the Greek. When Jesus placed

Amen before his own sayings, He indicated emphatically that what He was about to say was both true and valid. Furthermore, this truth was no ordinary truth but that bound up in His own divinity. These words abide forever and ever both in the Scripture and in His thinking.

AMEN, translated as "truly" has great implications because history packs it in terms of its usage. The ancient Hebrews used the word to acknowledge and confirm the glory of God. Though the sayings vary in content, they always relate to God's Kingdom. "In the Amen we have all Christology in a nutshell."[xvii] Therefore, AMEN designates the ultimate category of truth.

The next word, GAR is the postpositive conjunction, translated into English as "for." GAR always goes before the preceding word in English. The translation of AMEN GAR then is, "For truth."

The next word, translated, "I say," is the present active indicative of LEGO. The linear aktionsart echoes the concept of AMEN: These words go on record permanently as the Word of God, though they have existed forever in the thinking of our Lord. The last word, HUMIN, translated "to you," is a dative of advantage from the second person personal pronoun. That dative of advantage indicates that the words our Lord was about to utter are to our advantage to hear, believe and ultimately, to apply to our lives. So, whenever our Lord introduces a statement with those words, "For truly, I say to you ...," sit up and listen very closely. Just as His disciples did then, so you need to do now. Note carefully!

... until heaven and earth pass away ...
... ἕως ἂν παρέλθῃ ὁ οὐρανὸς καὶ ἡ γῆ ...

Though the meaning seems obvious, the next phrase, "until heaven and earth pass away" needs attention for three reasons. First, the particle translated as "until" in the English implies something the Greek particle does not. Second, "heaven and earth" serves as an idiom. Finally, third, "pass away" needs to be defined.

Let us begin with the first issue. The word translated "until," comes from two Greek words EOS (ἕως) and AN (ἄν). EOS is a conjunction while AN is a particle of modality. Together they are translated as "until." Usually EOS alone reads as "until." When combined with AN, the translation should indicate some conditional implications as well as serving to confirm the actuality of the following clause.[xviii] A loose interpretive translation might read this way, "Even if heaven and earth should pass away..." The meaning is this: even if the condition stated in the first clause—the passing away of Heaven and Earth—should occur, then the second clause most assuredly is true. This does not mean that Heaven and earth will pass away!

The second issue deals with the words, "Heaven and earth." They combine to form an idiom to include the entire universe, not literally the third heaven, and this planet.

Finally, the words "pass away" come from the aorist active subjunctive of the verb PARELTHE (παρέλθῃ). The aorist tense combined with the subjunctive mood does not indicate any time issues; however, this mood does add force to the conditional aspect of the particle AN. Therefore, this "passing away" does not refer to the end of that current dispensation of Israel. Some relate this "passing away" to the destruction of the universe taught by Peter in 2 Peter 3:7. That passage, however, views the judgment of the unbeliever and refers to the cleansing of the earth, not to a literal total destruction of the universe. According to other passages, the universe will not suffer destruction at any time.[xix]

> *Say among the nations, "The Lord reigns; indeed, the world is firmly established, it will not be moved; He will judge the peoples with equity."*
> *Psalm 96:10*

Actually, I see this entire phrase as being hyperbole. Our Lord is not teaching about the destruction of the earth and universe in this message but is simply adding force to the statement He is about to make about the permanence of the Scripture. The idea is this: Heaven and Earth pass away? Never! Neither will the Scripture, not even the smallest letter or stroke!

> *For truly I say to you, even if Heaven and Earth should pass away, not the smallest letter or stroke ...*

The fulfillment that Jesus spoke of in the previous verse will be coupled with the Law, referring to both the Mosaic Law and the prophecies of the Old Testament prophets. The Law will be valid and maintain its integrity as He intended it, at least up to that point. Jesus will reveal its intent in the next several paragraphs.

> *... not the smallest letter or stroke shall pass from the Law ...*
> *... ἰῶτα ἓν ἢ μία κεραία οὐ μὴ παρέλθῃ ἀπὸ τοῦ νόμου ...*

The Law, in itself, is perfect down to its smallest detail, needing no changes at all. Our Lord communicated this thought in this next phrase: "not the smallest letter or stroke shall pass from the Law ..." The two factors representing change in the Law in the Greek are IYOTA (ἰῶτα), the tenth letter of the Hebrew alphabet and the KERAIA (κεραία), a serif or accent on a Hebrew letter. These are small, seemingly insignificant parts of the Hebrew alphabet of the Scripture; yet even those will not change until "all is fulfilled."

> *... until all is accomplished.*
> *... ἕως ἂν πάντα γένηται.*

This last phrase begins with AN (ἄν) just as the second phrase did. "Accomplished" comes from the aorist middle subjunctive of GINOMAI (γίνομαι) which literally means, "to come into being." This phrase can be better understood if translated as, "until all comes into being." The fulfillment then refers to two factors: the first, to our Lord's life on this earth, to include the completion of His salvation work on the Cross, His resurrection, His ascension and session, then second, to the completion of all prophecies, to include the Tribulation, Millennium and our Lord's eternal Kingship. The focal point of the entire Old Testament and the object of most prophecies was the coming and the atoning work of our Lord. All human history revolves around Him. Yet the Law, as the spiritual life of the disciples at that moment and of Israel during the Tribulation and Millennium, will still be valid. Jesus overlooked the coming Church Age with these words because it was not yet in view. Though both the Mosaic Law and the prophets do not specifically pertain to the Church Age spiritual life and though no prophecy exists to be fulfilled during this Age, they do remain after the Church's exit resurrection.

For truly I say to you, even if heaven and earth should pass away, not the smallest letter or stroke shall pass from the Law until all is accomplished. Matthew 5:18

C. Matthew 5:19—Jesus Stresses the Importance of the Law

Whoever then annuls one of the least of these commandments, and teaches others to do the same, shall be called least in the kingdom of heaven; but whoever keeps and teaches them, he shall be called great in the kingdom of heaven.

We have noted that the religious establishment changed the Law by erroneous teaching. Jesus warns those who do this; they will suffer penalty. In this verse, He describes the penalty for doing so. In the following, He compares his disciples' righteousness with those of that current religious establishment, and then He proceeded to clarify the Law. He presented the Law, as the religious establishment should have been teaching it, in the next section of this Sermon on the Mount.

Jesus taught this sermon during the Age of the Hypostatic Union, during His First Advent. Though we separate that unique dispensation from the Age of Israel, the Mosaic Law continued to be the order of the day for their spiritual life. The Law was still the canon for those in Israel, including the disciples. They were to continue the spiritual life that was based upon the Law—not as it was being taught by the religious establishment of the day—but the Law as our Lord taught it. Therefore, the disciples were to remain under the authority of the Mosaic Law until our Lord accomplished His salvation mission. Upon that completion, He would usher in the Church Age when the New Covenant to the Church would supersede the Law. The New Covenant to Israel belongs to the Millennium when our Lord will be enthroned in Jerusalem.

Perhaps at this point you have picked up an apparent contradiction. If our Lord completely fulfilled the Law by His salvation work, resurrection and ascension, is not the Law completely abrogated or put aside, during both this

Church Age and all following dispensations? Two issues become germane here. First, as Paul wrote, though the mystery doctrines of the Church Age supersede the Mosaic Law, it presents many valuable lessons pertaining to the spiritual life of Church Age believers.

> *For whatever was written in earlier times was written for our instruction, so that through perseverance and the encouragement of the Scriptures we might have hope. Romans 15:4*

Second, though God rejects Temple worship patterned after the Law during the Tribulation as being a substitute for obedience, Jews will reinstitute it at that time.[xx] Isaiah wrote about our Lord's attitude toward those who reestablish Temple worship during the Tribulation.

> *But he who kills an ox is like one who slays a man; He who sacrifices a lamb is like the one who breaks a dog's neck; He who offers a grain offering is like one who offers swine's blood; He who burns incense is like the one who blesses an idol. Isaiah 66:3*

God desires obedience, not Temple sacrifice. Just exactly what form of worship God will desire from Tribulational saints eludes me though I suspect that learning and applying promises as well as the development of faith through doctrinal rationales will play a major role. For Gentiles, support and protection of Israel will also play a major role.

> *To him who is humble and contrite of spirit, and who trembles at My word. Isaiah 66:2*

I am not clear on the spiritual life during the Millennium except that the Scripture describes it as a time of great celebration. The Lamb will be physically present on the Earth, sitting on His throne in Jerusalem. That the King will be on His throne as well as the fact of the completed fulfillment of the Mosaic Law will be causes of great rejoicing.

> *Whoever then annuls one of the least of these commandments ...*
> *ὃς ἐὰν οὖν λύσῃ μίαν τῶν ἐντολῶν τούτων τῶν ἐλαχίστων ...*

Returning to verse 19, it describes the eternal future of two categories of believers. We know that this refers to believers because both have futures in the Kingdom of Heaven. The first word in the verse is HOS (ὅς) a relative pronoun, translated, "who." Though not translated as a conditional sentence, the second word in this verse is the conditional particle EAN (ἐάν), generally translated "if." It introduces a hypothetical situation. Therefore, these two words, together with the inferential conjunction OUN (οὖν) translate as "Therefore whoever..." The important verb in this first sentence, translated variously as "loose, abrogate, nullify," is the aorist active subjunctive of LUO (λύω). It denotes, in this context, loss of authority the Law normally has over a person.

This loss of authority can come about in various ways. The most subtle is to teach it erroneously. In this fashion, those who think they are under the authority of the Law are complacently deceived. Those who do the deceiving are the subjects in this sentence. The false teacher does not have to teach only major doctrines erroneously to fit into this category, but as Jesus taught, only the least of the doctrines or commandments. In reality, there is no least commandment. Every doctrine, once a person has received salvation, is as important to understand correctly, as any other. Often the most innocuous doctrine taught inaccurately causes an entire doctrinal rationale to collapse. Doctrines, of course, do not really collapse, but error in one "small" area can nullify doctrines in other areas.

A popular example of this pertains to the current status of the nation of Israel. Many pastors teach that because Israel is now a nation, and turning that part of the world green, the resurrection of the Church is historically very close. Of course, it may be just around the corner! Certain historical occurrences and events seemingly poised to take place lead one to this conclusion. However, the present existence of the Jewish nation has no bearing upon the termination of the Church Age. The existence of the Nation of Israel does not cause the Church's resurrection. It is all a matter of God's perfect timing. One doctrine that this teaching nullifies is the immanency of the rapture. Are we to believe that when Israel was not a nation that the Church Age could not have ended prior to the 1940s when the current nation of Israel had yet to be established? Was the resurrection of the Church not imminent then and just as it is now, just as it will be in the future even if the current nation of Israel were to be destroyed? Our Lord will form the nation of Israel that will go through the Tribulation. We do not know what tools He may use or may have used or may be using to bring this nation about; perhaps it will not have been the British applying the principles of Zionism! We simply do not know how long the Church Age will last! Certainly, to this writer's eyes, events of the Tribulation appear to be very close. Even so, the rapture or exit resurrection of the Church is as imminent when Paul wrote the Thessalonians as it is today.

Furthermore, to teach that the terminus of the Church Age is near tends to take one's eyes off doctrines that result in spiritual growth and focus them upon the doctrines of the end times. Doctrines that pertain to the Church Age must become the bedrock of the believer's life, not focusing upon the end of the Church Age. Though providing comfort, those end-time doctrines will not give believers the spiritual tools unique to this Church Age, to build them up spiritually, no matter how fun they are to study! Do end-time doctrines give the believer mechanics and strength to face everyday problems? The only doctrines that carry one through daily challenges are those that pertain to the building up of practical faith in the soul of the believer. Therefore, one seemingly innocuous, harmless teaching may cause one's congregation to stop focusing upon spiritual growth but instead create a fascination with the end times. I do not mean by this that no pastor should teach about the end-times. These doctrines do fulfill an aspect of the believer's spiritual growth. Confidence in our future does provide great comfort! Pastors, though, should balance their teaching. No pastor should teach dogmatically that because Israel is now a nation that the rapture is close … although it may be!

Another insidious example of erroneous teaching involves incompleteness. Many churches do not teach the importance of sin confession to the Father prior to teaching the Word of God. Such confession opens the door to Holy Spirit's empowerment in believers' lives. If the believer is not filled, therefore, empowered by God the Holy Spirit, the best doctrinal preaching and instruction will not benefit him at all. Believers need to be "hyper-inculcated" to fulfill the mechanic John presented in 1 John 1:9, and mentioned by King David after his Bathsheba debacle.

I acknowledged my sin to You, and my iniquity I did not hide; I said, "I will confess my transgressions to the Lord"; and You forgave the guilt of my sin. Selah. Psalm 32:5

If we confess our sins, He is faithful and righteous to forgive us our sins and to cleanse us from all unrighteousness. 1 John 1:9

This raises a question about confession of sin. If this is as important as John teaches, then why did not Paul, James, and Peter teach it as well? Why did not all the apostles spell out the relationship between confession and fellowship clearly, as they did the Gospel? After all, the Spirit's ministry in the believer's life to bring about spiritual growth is just as important as His ministries to unbelievers to bring about salvation. Complete answers to these questions would fill a book. We will briefly answer these! First, if you consider the naming of one's sins as a return to soul purity, then the Mosaic Law presented this principle clearly through the ritual of washing before entering into the Tabernacle or Temple. Second, no apostle wrote completely everything they taught to their congregations. Perhaps they inculcated this mechanic so thoroughly that they did not think written reminders necessary. Paul does present the concept using the phrase, "judging yourself."

But if we judged ourselves rightly, we would not be judged. 1 Corinthians 11:31

In addition, just because one apostle did not delineate a spiritual mechanic or doctrine completely, it does not negate it. We must compare Scripture with Scripture, studying the entire counsel of God.

Members of a congregation can nullify the authority of doctrinal teaching as well. Whenever a parishioner takes up valuable teaching time, challenging pastoral authority, he does this. Asking for clarification is one thing, but no one should challenge pastoral teaching and take up the pastor's valuable time during his teaching. It is disrespectful to others in the congregation who are gaining from that teaching. No congregation can grow apart from systematic scriptural pastoral teaching. There is a place for believers to discuss the Scripture and doctrines amongst themselves and the pastor, as it does serve to help circulate these things through one's thinking. However, these discussions should never replace doctrinal instruction or be construed as an efficient way to bring about spiritual growth.

A good interpretive translation of that phrase reads this way:

> ***Therefore, whoever nullifies the authority of even the least of these doctrines or commandments ...***

This phrase also served to focus the disciples' thinking back onto the Scripture, upon their spiritual lives, rather than upon the many speculations about the future reign of the Messiah. It underscored the importance of following the correct interpretation of the Scripture. In the following verses, our Lord steers His hearers away from current false interpretations to the true intent of the Law.

> ***... and teaches others to do the same,***
> *καὶ διδάξῃ οὕτως τοὺς ἀνθρώπους*

The sentence continues with "and teaches others to do the same ..." A religious teacher who believed erroneously then taught that error falls into this category. Today, a pastor who believes erroneous doctrine then teaches it to his congregation is liable as well. These false teachers will be "called the least in heaven." Obviously, those who do not believe orthodox doctrine will have no effective spiritual lives, so those teachers will have no rewards, blessings or rank in heaven. God will only reward the spiritually mature with blessings and rank. Furthermore, God will reward false teachers with temporal discipline for leading their congregations astray.

On the positive side, those who grow spiritually from adherence to orthodox doctrine will be "called great in the Kingdom of Heaven," for two reasons. They will be called great because they will have fulfilled the spiritual life God designed for them and fulfilled the ministry God has for them. To the great teachers, our Lord will say this:

> ***Well done, good and faithful slave. You were faithful with a few things, I will put you in charge of many things; enter into the joy of your Master.***
> ***Matthew 25:21***

D. Matthew 5:20—Superseding Religious Righteousness

> *For I say to you that unless your righteousness surpasses that of the scribes and Pharisees, you will not enter the Kingdom of Heaven.*
>
> *λέγω γὰρ ὑμῖν ὅτι ἐὰν μὴ περισσεύσῃ ὑμῶν ἡ δικαιοσύνη πλεῖον τῶν γραμματέων καὶ Φαρισαίων, οὐ μὴ εἰσέλθητε εἰς τὴν βασιλείαν τῶν οὐρανῶν.*

Perhaps at this point in His teaching, He turned His eyes to Judas Iscariot, the one unsaved disciple. The righteousness of the Scribes and Pharisees was self-righteousness, at best human good. Neither qualifies a person—in this case, Judas Iscariot—for eternal life. Codex #1 of the Law delineates that self-righteousness based upon Jewish birth or attempting to keep the Law will not do the job. Its purpose was to prove that all are spiritually bankrupt, spiritually dead, sinners, that all need a Savior.

> *For I say to you ...*
> *λέγω γὰρ ὑμῖν ...*

Jesus concluded this lesson concerning the Law with a dogmatic statement sure to shake the religious establishment to its core! He began with formulaic words of ultimate authority. Uttered by the Creator of the Universe, these words carry the greatest authority possible. Did the earth quake at these words? Could those within earshot even remain standing? Did their legs turn to water? The words that follow must have rocked whoever heard them. The verb, LEGO (λέγω) in the present active indicative translates as, "I say." As an iterative present, it carries the connotation of emphatic continual communication. This point of doctrine our Lord is about to communicate is of utmost importance. This doctrine begins with a protasis:

> *... that unless your righteousness surpasses that of the scribes and Pharisees,*
> *... ὅτι ἐὰν μὴ περισσεύσῃ ὑμῶν ἡ δικαιοσύνη πλεῖον τῶν γραμματέων καὶ Φαρισαίων,*

The second word EAV (ἐὰν), is translated "if," when preceding a verb in the subjunctive mood that expresses a probable future event. The contingency, though, is still there. This is followed by the negating particle ME (μὴ) with the aorist active subjunctive verb, PERISSEUO (περισσεύω) that means, "to greatly exceed." All three words translate as, "if it does not greatly exceed." The subject of the verb, translated "righteousness," is the nominative singular noun DIKAIOSUNE (δικαιοσύνη).

For all practical purposes, only two categories of righteousness exist: that which pertains to humans and that which pertains to God. When it comes to God, His righteousness—perfect righteousness—is His perfect standard. That which fulfills His standard of what is right survives, that which does not He must condemn. Human righteousness is imperfect. The prophet Isaiah taught that our righteousness is comparable to dirty rags.

> *For all of us have become like one who is unclean, and all our righteous deeds are like a filthy garment; and all of us wither like a leaf, and our iniquities, like the wind, take us away.*
> *Isaiah 64:6*

The words, "righteous deeds" come from the Hebrew word TSEDAQAH

(צְדָקָה) in the plural: our "righteousnesses." This refers to our standing before God. Compared to Him we have nothing that adds up to His perfect righteousness. The translators euphemistically translated Isaiah's "filthy garment." Remember he was married and probably had occasionally to go to the supermarket to pick up feminine supplies for His wife! The garments he referred to went directly to the trash after use. That is an accurate picture of our highest standard. In no way do we qualify to live with God because we do not begin to measure up. For any human to live with God, he or she must measure up to His perfect standard.

Whose righteousness must the disciples exceed? They must exceed the righteousness of the religious hierarchy! For all of these disciples' lives—as well as the rest of the listening crowd—the role model for righteousness had been the scribes and Pharisees. Now our Lord said that their own righteousness must exceed the Pharisaic righteousness. That surpassing righteousness, that which fulfills God's perfect standard, comes only as a gift from Him upon faith in Christ.

The apodosis continues the verse:

> *... you will not enter the Kingdom of Heaven.*
> *... οὐ μὴ εἰσέλθητε εἰς τὴν βασιλείαν τῶν οὐρανῶν.*

The first three words OU ME EISERCHOMAI (οὐ μὴ εἰσέρχομαι) in the Greek express great emphasis, "where the emphatic sense may be 'under no circumstances will you enter into the kingdom.'"[xxi] Both OU and ME are strong negatives. Therefore, our Lord dogmatically states that not even the most evident, so-called human righteousness qualifies for salvation. This must have shocked our Lord's listeners!

Righteousness based upon self and human good must be surpassed to qualify for eternal life. Entering into the Kingdom of Heaven is synonymous to possessing eternal life. Only by faith in Christ can a person exceed self-righteousness. That ultimate righteousness, both the Father and Son bestow at a moment of time, when one believes in Christ and receives God's righteousness. Our Lord directed this to Judas who only had human, relative or self-righteousness, the same righteousness the Pharisees and scribes possessed. The Mosaic Law, even if a person could follow it perfectly, still could not save. The only way Judas could have God's righteousness was to believe in Christ. He might have tried keeping the Mosaic Law for salvation from eternal condemnation. However, it cannot save.[xxii]

How were, then, the disciples to attain that superior righteousness? First, they attained it through faith in Christ. This entered them into God's plan for spirituality. Whereas the Pharisees tried to attain it though works, the disciples were to do so by faith in Christ.

PART V

JESUS REFRAMES THE MOSAIC LAW
MATTHEW 5:21-48

A *Introduction*

In this section of the Sermon on the Mount, Jesus apparently reinterprets the Mosaic Law. However, He did not actually reinterpret it as much as He clarified the intent behind certain laws. Behind every law is its intent. Though He apparently raised the sin bar from the overt to the mental in the next several verses, He is actually revealing that in the intent behind the prohibition lay the core purpose of that prohibition. The overarching purpose of the Law demonstrates that no old sin nature corrupted human being, no matter how moral, can keep the Law and achieve God's righteousness. No human can keep the Law, thereby achieving his or her own salvation.

Jesus not only clarified the Law but corrected erroneous interpretation by the self-righteous, legalistic Pharisaic establishment. That religion constantly distorted the Law, making it a system of self-righteousness. Its purpose, again, was to demonstrate that every human is spiritually bankrupt, needing a Savior. For Jesus Christ to have an effective ministry in Israel He was going to have to reveal to the Israelites, often through shock treatment teaching, their legalism and self-righteousness. Jesus Christ was going to the Cross to solve the problem of spiritual death and the sin nature. He was to bear all of the world's sins in His own body when the Father would judge those sins, opening the door of salvation for every human being. The citizens needed to understand this.

Those steeped in self-righteousness and legalism reject this grace, and therefore, reject the Father's gracious provision of salvation. Not only does this rejection involve the only unforgivable sin but also continually produces human good and evil. While Jesus' salvation work paid for sin, that work totally rejects human good and evil. The Pharisaic religion taught human good: salvation and spirituality by works, which invariably parlays into evil. They taught that if the people kept the Law along with the myriad corollary rules they invented, they could achieve salvation and spirituality.

Jesus in the next several verses does two things. He shakes His disciples out of their religious complacency then prepares them to do the same to those to whom He is going to send them. Those who listened to the religious hierarchy assumed that because they had not killed someone or actually committed adultery and were Jews by birth, then they had achieved salvation. The people of Israel had to be shocked out of their religious assumptions, legalism, and self-righteousness if they were to believe in Jesus and inherit the promises He had promised them generations ago.

Where does this leave Church Age believers, those who have not been promised "the Land" as per verse 5 and other provisions in the promises to His chosen people? For what purpose do we study this Law, which God exclusively gave to Israel? First, the Pharisaic version of Judaism has no monopoly on self-righteous legalism. Modern churches also stew in it! These lessons apply every bit to us as it did to them, to shake us out of our legalism, faulty assumptions and self-righteousness! Second, Jesus is bringing the intent of these Mosaic provisions into our spiritual lives. The thought dynamics that Jesus taught on that day should be a product of our Spirit empowered spiritual lives. By the way, our rewards for spirituality far supersede Israel's, so do not upset yourself over not inheriting the Land!

B. *Matthew 5:21-22—Murder and Anger*

1. Matthew 5:21—Revisiting the Murder Prohibition

> *You have heard that the ancients were told, 'You shall not commit murder' and 'Whoever commits murder shall be liable to the court.'*
> Matthew 5:21

The Pharisees had considered sin as only being an overt act. They did not consider the person's mental attitude. Though the commandments our Lord gave to Moses prohibited the overt sin, some ancients did consider the mental motivation as sin as well. We will consider one such passage in a moment. However, to the minds of the disciples, our Lord, in the next several verses, apparently raised the sin bar from overt acts to include the mental attitude. Sometimes mental attitudes precede overt acts, sometimes not. Whether or not a mental attitude leads to an overt act is inconsequential; both fall short of God's perfect righteousness and therefore lead to loss of fellowship with God and divine discipline.

Our Lord taught that sin was committed at the point of thought, at the moment of an unrighteous mental attitude. Often the unrighteous mental attitude precedes the intent to commit an overt sin. This shook up anyone who thought they were keeping the Law by avoiding overt sins. "Look," Jesus might as well have said, "just because you haven't committed murder or violated a few other commandments I'm going to mention here doesn't mean that you've kept the Law! You need to get off your self-righteous high horse and look at the intent behind the prohibitions! You keep violating the intent behind the prohibitions. You do give into anger though you do not kill! You lust, so you have sinned though you have not actually committed adultery! You are unable to keep from these mental attitude sins! You are unable to keep the Law! You are not saved because you think you are keeping the Law!" This not only shook up the self-righteous legalistic religious establishment, but also gave the disciples, whom He was preparing to send out, a method of rattling the self-righteous, religious lost sheep of Israel. This would awaken their need for salvation though faith by grace: the grace of their Messiah.

Before we look at the passage at hand, let us look at two Old Testament passages that describe mental attitude sins. The writer of Proverbs revealed that God considers seven sins as abominations. He mentioned three categories of sin: mental, verbal, and overt. The two mental sins appear to be the worst of these seven sins.

There are six things which the Lord hates, yes, seven which are an abomination to Him: Haughty eyes, a lying tongue, and hands that shed innocent blood, a heart that devises wicked plans, feet that run rapidly to evil, a false witness who utters lies, and one who spreads strife among brothers. Proverbs 6:16-19

First, note that God does not hate. Hate is a sin. God cannot sin, author sin nor be exposed to it. He only condemns it. The term "hate," when ascribed to God, is an anthropopathism that reveals God's policy of condemnation towards anything that does not measure up to His perfect standard in a language we can understand.

"Haughty eyes" or more literally, "upward eyes" is a Hebrew idiom for the mental attitude sin of pride, "representing arrogance, a presumption of superiority, self-absorption, self-centeredness, and inordinate pride. Arrogance is the root sin that leads to other sins."[xxiii] The eyes often reveal one's mental attitude! In the Hebrew idiom the "eye is used to express knowledge, character, attitude, inclination, opinion, passion, and response. The eye is a good barometer of the inner thoughts of man."[xxiv] This arrogance, often reflected in one's eyes, was Satan's original sin as well as the original sin of Adam and his wife. The woman evidenced her arrogance when she believed the serpent's lie.

Pride is one of the most subtle of all sins. The average uninformed individual immediately assumes another one arrogant if standing erect and speaking with authority! Incredibly, the most arrogant display rounded shoulders, lowered eyes, and practice all sorts of peculiarities of hypocrisy and self-righteousness. Arrogance and pride also manifest themselves in legalism among the religious.

Legalism and all brands of arrogance are antagonistic to grace.

"A heart that devises wicked plans," representing the second mental attitude sin in this passage, refers to revenge motivation. Revenge always begins in one's thinking with the motivation to retaliate against those who hurt you, allegedly or actually, in some way. The mental attitude motivation is the key to the sin of taking revenge. The writer of the Proverbs further emphasized the role of mental attitude sin.

> *Do not eat the bread of a selfish man, or desire his delicacies; for as he thinks within himself, so he is. He says to you, "Eat and drink!" But his heart is not with you. You will vomit up the morsel you have eaten, and waste your compliments. Proverbs 23:6-8*

The key phrase in this verse for our purposes is "for as he thinks within himself, so he is." This is a picture of the mental attitude sin of arrogance. You are what you are thinking at any given moment. Contextually, this man is not hospitable and gracious as he appears, but is counting every morsel you are eating and adding up the cost! You do not want to be a guest in his home or eat the food he's providing.

Again, Jesus is speaking to His disciples who are going to the lost sheep of the house of Israel. In order to go to these people they must understand and be able to apply the Law properly themselves. They will be facing many self-righteous, religious people because this is what that current interpretation of the Mosaic Law had spawned. In order for them to break down this self-righteousness, they had to communicate accurately the intent of the entire content of the Law, that is, the Person and Work of our Lord.

> *You have heard that the ancients were told ...*
> *Ἠκούσατε ὅτι ἐρρέθη τοῖς ἀρχαίοις ...*

Now we return to Matthew 5:21. The first word, the aorist active indicative, 2nd person plural of the verb AKOUO (ἀκούω) translates as, "you have heard." OTI (ὅτι), "that" precedes the aorist passive indicative, third person plural of the verb of communication, LEGO (λέγω). These words translate as, "that it was communicated ..." Two words complete the phrase: the articular adjective in the dative plural, ARCHAIOS (ἀρχαῖος) translated "to the ancients." These ancients were generations of recipients of the Mosaic Law. By this first phrase, "You have heard that it was communicated to the ancients ..." Jesus tells them to remember, to recall, their past Biblical training.

> *'You shall not commit murder.'*
> *Οὐ φονεύσεις·*

He brought up the sixth commandment from Exodus 20:13, often mistranslated as, "You shall not kill." Both this passage and Exodus 20:13 prohibit murder, not all instances of taking human life. The verb, future active indicative from PHONEUO (φονεύω) clearly prohibits illegal intentional killing of a human being. This verb is preceded by the negative adverb OU (οὐ), negating the verb of killing. The Hebrew word RA'SAH (רצח) also refers to murder, not to all killing. The Bible authorizes killing in certain circumstances, but prohibits murder. The Bible sanctions both capital punishment and killing in warfare. "Capital punishment is vitally necessary for the enforcement of the Law. It is also a part of divine judgment actually to exterminate certain races when they become like a mad dog and must be removed, as in the case of the Canaanites, Sodom, and Gomorra, certain of the descendants of Ham such as the Carthaginians. Were it not for these divine judgments we would not be here today."[xxv]

While the Scripture authorizes killing in certain situations, it never authorizes murder. Why does the Law prohibit murder? It permanently infringes upon the victim's right to express his volition. The most important choice a person makes is to believe in Jesus Christ. A murdered person cannot believe in Christ. Furthermore, the dead believer has lost the opportunity to grow in grace. No one has the prerogative to destroy anyone's volition. Murder is not the only means of destroying one's volition; soul murder can occur by forms of child and spousal abuse. Soul murder is another topic in itself. Satan foisted soul murder upon Eve when he led her to the point of violating the tree prohibition, eating from the Tree of the Knowledge of Good and Evil. Another issue concerning murder: all the generations that a person would have generated are lost.

And 'whoever commits murder shall be liable to the court.'
ὃς δ' ἂν φονεύσῃ, ἔνοχος ἔσται τῇ κρίσει.

"Whoever shall murder" is the aorist active subjunctive of PHONEUO (φονεύω). The aorist tense refers to a certain point in time when someone violates this commandment by murdering someone. The active voice indicates that the subject, in this case you, actually commits the murder. The subjunctive mood indicates the potential of murder. If you commit murder, this tense says, but you do not have to! Nevertheless, if you do, you are liable for temporal judgment, judgment from the legal system of your country.

2. Matthew 5:22—Anger Prohibited

But I say to you that everyone who is angry with his brother shall be guilty before the court; and whoever says to his brother, 'You good-for-nothing,' shall be guilty before the supreme court; and whoever says, 'You fool,' shall be guilty enough to go into the fiery hell.

Every overt sin begins with a motivation, from either thought or emotion. Jesus addressed the source of the overt sin of murder: anger. Murder begins with anger and hatred, both mental attitude sins. Not only is the murder reason for punishment, but also the mental attitude that precedes it. Note the pattern our Lord used to communicate this truth. It takes on the progressive shape that anger often takes. His statement begins simply with anger and its penalty, and then it escalates to name-calling with a more severe penalty, then finally with an explosive expletive and the final penalty!

But I say to you ...
ἐγὼ δὲ λέγω ὑμῖν ...

Jesus continued with two words that emphatically express His complete authority: EGO LEGO (εγω λεγω), "I say," or "I communicate." EGO is the first person personal pronoun, translated, I. LEGO, in the first person present active indicative means, "I say." He did not have to use the personal pronoun as well, but it greatly increases the emphasis. The Lord of the Universe Himself is communicating this truth. The postpositive adversative conjunction, DE (δε), translated, "but," placed between the two words gives even greater contrast between the previous phrase and the words our Lord was about to say. To whom is He speaking? To His disciples, but these words are carried down through the centuries to us. The Greek HUMIN (υμιν) means, "to you." You can take this very personally!

... that everyone who is angry with his brother ...
... ὅτι πᾶς ὁ ὀργιζόμενος τῷ ἀδελφῷ αὐτοῦ ...

This phrase forms the complete subject of the sentence. The first two words, HOTI PAS (ὅτι πᾶς) mean "that all." Our Lord includes every one of us. No person can get around this. The subject of the sentence, the articular nominative present particle from ORGIZO (ὀργίζω) represents a category within which we all have fallen. It means to have hostility, hatred, the desire to destroy, or the desire to hurt someone. Why would you ever be angry with another? Perhaps someone in authority over you chews you out, so your self-righteousness suffers injury then expresses itself in anger. Perhaps someone has not treated you in a way you think you deserve to be treated! The reasons can be multifarious. The point is this: anger is never justified! When you lose your composure to anger, you have failed!

In this context, this is limited to the mental attitude. Your face may be a bit red, but you have not totally lost it! I remember my best friend in my college days; at times, I was late for an appointment with him, for no good reason. He would simply state, as a matter of fact, that he was feeling antagonistic toward me because of my tardiness! His attitude toward me was certainly justified. However, his ears would be tinged with red, so I knew, despite his matter-of-factness, that he was angry with me!

The object of your anger may be a believer, your brother in Christ. It can refer to anyone you are very close to as well, such as a fellow sibling!

... shall be guilty before the court;
... ἔνοχος ἔσται τῇ κρίσει·

The first two words in this phrase, the nominative adjective, ENOCHOS (ἔνοχος) and the future indicative of the verb EIMI (εἰμί) together mean "will be subject to" in this context. The object of the verb-phrase is the articular dative noun KRISIS (κρίσις). It referred, in Jesus' day, to the lowest court of judgment in Israel. In reality, no court is ever going to convict anyone of anger. It is not illegal. However, anger does violate God's standard of perfect righteousness. The judge, in this case, is our Lord, who justly continually evaluates every aspect of our thinking and feelings, our heart. Your mental anger or antagonism may not be visible to anyone but God, who disciplines for any thought, motive, or action, which falls short of His perfect standard: His righteousness. A good working translation of this phrase reads thusly, "... will be subject to discipline."

> *... and whoever says to his brother, 'You good-for-nothing,' shall be guilty before the supreme court;*
> *ὃς δ' ἂν εἴπῃ τῷ ἀδελφῷ αὐτοῦ, Ῥακά, ἔνοχος ἔσται τῷ συνεδρίῳ·*

In this next phrase, anger takes on verbal characteristics. Jesus then describes this verbal sin: "and whoever says to his brother, "You good-for-nothing..." That phrase "good-for-nothing" comes from the Hellenized Aramaic term, RACA (ῥακά), a derogatory word approximating profanity of the day. It expressed more outward anger, the sin that can precede murder. This kind of verbal sin can destroy a person's reputation as well. This one is liable for punishment from the next higher court, called SUNEDRION (συνέδριον). The Sanhedrin in Jesus' day was the highest council and decision-making body over the Jews. It did not have the power over life and death, however. That was reserved for the Roman government. In any case, this represents a higher level of discipline. No court is going to convict you of name-calling, even cursing someone. Nevertheless, God in Heaven knows that your anger is escalating, progressing to the next level. Your old sin nature has taken hold of you. You have not responded to our Lord's initial outlay of discipline, so He increases the discipline to the next level. This is an inference because anger is neither a crime nor a violation of civil law. It is sin, but not one punishable by a criminal or civil court.

It is important to remember a factor about the old sin nature. When anyone makes the decision to get angry or to follow any pattern of thinking or action related to one's sin nature, it is tantamount to choosing to run a "sin nature program" in your thinking computer. You may be powerless to stop it without divine intervention in the form of discipline. God does not discipline out of vindictiveness but for our protection, to prevent our old sin nature predilections and trends from getting out of control. A maturing believer can catch himself by comparing his thinking with his knowledge of Scripture, applying divine power to the situation, bringing his sin nature trend to a halt. This believer, using the words of James, stops the sin process before the lust gives birth to sin!

Note also, that Jesus is not necessarily pointing His finger at those listening to Him, saying that they are the angry ones. All are guilty of anger from time to time, of course, but Jesus is teaching this as a general principle. In the following verse, Jesus gets more personal, moving from general principles of anger, to a direct personal application of sin against another.

Everyone who is angry, whether or not that one carries that anger to the extreme of murder, is still liable for punishment. Jesus set the record straight: if you are guilty of anger, the emotion, or mental attitude that can precede murder, you are culpable. You have committed an inner sin, a mental attitude sin. This word also implies a settled, seething anger, a nursed malice liable to explode into rage. Anger may extend itself to murder, but even if it does not, culpability still exists. Before what to court are you liable for punishment? You are liable before the Supreme Court of Heaven, of which our Lord is judge. A human court may never see your anger!

> *... and whoever says, 'You fool,' shall be guilty enough to go into the fiery hell.*
> *... ὃς δ' ἂν εἴπῃ, Μωρέ, ἔνοχος ἔσται εἰς τὴν γέενναν τοῦ πυρός*

With this last phrase, Jesus does two things. First, He takes the escalated sin of anger to its maximum penalty then second, through that, taught that no one can fulfill the Law. No imperfect person can attain to God's standard of righteousness. The Law demonstrates this fact. No matter how hard a person tries, no one can perfectly keep the Law. Therefore, no one can achieve salvation by trying to keep the Law.

This anger has escalated from a mental attitude, to a curse and now to a real insult. In the Greek, that insult is calling someone MOROS (μωρός), translated, "You fool." So commonplace is cursing and name calling in our modern culture that we probably do not recognize this as an escalation to a peak of anger. Yet that context demands that we see it as such. In our culture, we have become insensitive to acts of verbal violence. The penalty, as the English translation reads, is to be subject to fiery hell. These words in the Greek are TEN GEENAN TOU PUROS (την γεενναν του πυρος). GEENAN refers to the Valley of Gehenna that began its bad reputation by being the location of child sacrifice. By Jesus' day, it was a perpetually burning refuse pile. It was an apt picture of the Lake of Fire.

To our ears, being subject to the Lake of Fire seems like an extreme punishment for calling someone a fool! Remember, though that these three phrases illustrate an escalation of anger. A person does not become a bit perturbed, and then think about raising the intensity of his anger. A person loses control of his ability to think, giving his distorted emotions control of his body. This is what happens when you give your old sin nature control of your soul. Once, as a believer, you lose the Holy Spirit's empowerment, your give your old sin nature control of your soul. You cannot even think at this point. You may commit murder in a fit of rage, not even "knowing" what you are doing! However, you do because you choose to give into your anger. However, should you still be subject to the Lake of Fire—eternal condemnation—because you give into your anger?

Our Lord began this dissertation on anger with culpability from murder, what the "ancients" said and then raised the bar to culpability from the mental attitude and emotion preceding murder. He raised the culpability bar to a simple derogatory statement, calling someone a fool. This may seem innocuous, yet even calling someone a fool violates the Mosaic Law. Anyone who violates the Law without faith in Christ is bound for the Lake of Fire. Violation of the Law does not send a person to the Lake of Fire, but simply indicates one's inability to attain to the standard of God's righteousness. For the unbeliever, it indicates his spiritual death.

The same goes for sin. A person does not go to the Lake of Fire for personal sins committed. One ends up there because of two factors. First, unbelievers join Satan and his fallen angels in the Lake of Fire because of spiritual death. The spiritually dead person does not have God's righteousness, so he does not qualify to live with God forever. The second factor deals with one's continued spiritual death. If a person rejects the Gospel and the authority of the Holy Spirit when he or she hears the Gospel, that rejection is the one unforgivable sin, one that perpetuates a person's spiritual death to the Lake of Fire. As to one's continual personal sins, Jesus Christ paid for those with His substitutionary death on the Cross. Those sins are not an issue. Only a person's rejection of His gift of eternal life though faith in Him results in eternal condemnation.

Interpretively, the verse reads this way:

> *But I say to you that everyone who is angry with his brother will be subject to discipline; and whoever says to his brother, 'You good-for-nothing,' will be subject to greater discipline; and whoever says, 'You fool,' shall be guilty enough to go into the fiery hell.*
> Matthew 5:22

C. Matthew 5:23-26—Reconciliation

1. Matthew 5:23

Therefore if you are presenting your offering at the altar, and there remember that your brother has something against you ...

Therefore if you are presenting your offering at the altar,
ἐὰν οὖν προσφέρῃς τὸ δῶρόν σου ἐπὶ τὸ θυσιαστήριον

These two verses continue the thought our Lord began in the previous verse, with "therefore if," a third class condition of the conditional particle EAN (ἐάν) with conjunction OUN (οὖν). Understand that the conditional particle does not say this will happen, but it may. The potential is there. This is a personal application of anger. It deals with a person who is preparing to worship God. We always must interpret the Scripture understanding when it was written. In Israel in those days, people worshipped in the Temple. Part of that worship involved bringing a gift of an animal sacrifice, a food offering, or money, to the altar for sacrifice. There were several different offerings for different purposes and involving different doctrines. The general principle presented here is worship. Though worship details may change from dispensation to dispensation, the basic idea does not. In this Church Age, visualize preparing to sit down, being one of a congregation, readying to worship by listening to the teaching of the Word. This principle also applies whenever you bow your head to pray or act in any capacity requiring the dynamics of your spiritual life!

... and there remember that your brother has something against you ...
... κἀκεῖ μνησθῇς ὅτι ὁ ἀδελφός σου ἔχει τι κατὰ σοῦ ...

Next, remembering that your brother has something against you must be understood from the context. Something has come between you and someone else. You are at fault. If recalling this person disturbs you because he has something against you, then you have a certain responsibility to discharge. Obviously, your conscience is bothering you! Because you wronged someone then failed to take care of that wrong, you do not qualify to worship. You have sinned by wronging someone. That wrong, following the immediate context, resulted in anger between you two. You are out of fellowship, carnal, for two reasons. First, you wronged someone. Second, you failed to take responsibility for that wrong. You must reconcile with that one whom you wronged. Why must you stop your worship? Worship has no meaning or efficacy if you are out of fellowship. You have sinned and not taken care of the matter! What should you do? In this case, our Lord gives us direction, telling us exactly what we should do.

2. Matthew 5:24

... leave your offering there before the altar and go; first be reconciled to your brother, and then come and present your offering.

... leave your offering there before the altar and go;
... ἄφες ἐκεῖ τὸ δῶρόν σου ἔμπροσθεν τοῦ θυσιαστηρίου καὶ ὕπαγε

You need to stop your worship, stated for that time period as leaving your gift at the altar, not on it. Today, you also need to stop your worship. What form may your worship take in this Church Age? True worship may find you in the pew of your local church, preparing to sing, pray or listen to the teaching of the Word. On the other hand, your worship may find you meditating upon the Scripture alone, or fulfilling the spiritual gift the Holy Spirit bestowed upon you. The possibilities are endless! If you have sinned in this Church Age, you are out of fellowship with God. You cannot worship God in any form without being in fellowship with Him. So, begin with regaining your fellowship with Him by utilizing the mechanic taught by John in 1 John 1:9, and then do what this verse teaches.

ABIDING BY THE SERMON ON THE MOUNT
... first be reconciled to your brother ...
... πρῶτον διαλλάγηθι τῷ ἀδελφῷ σου ...

You then need to reconcile yourself to the one you wronged. Make sure that the other person's attitude to you is changed. Let us look at that word, translated in your English New Testament as, "be reconciled." We need to get a full understanding of it for three interrelated reasons. First, to the exegete, even though the English word "reconcile" appears many times in the New Testament, this certain use of it demands a very close look. This is the only time this certain Greek word appears in the New Testament. When our Lord used this word, He knew that it would only appear once, so it would raise the interest of any worthy exegete. Second, why did the Holy Spirit guide Matthew to translate our Lord's use of this word, instead of another similar word, which was more frequently used? Third, the verb's etymology presents a challenge.

This word "to reconcile" DIALLASSOMAI (διαλλάσσομαι) is the key to understanding this verse. Foundational to its meaning is the principle of transformation, in the sense of converting someone's hostility to peace. The word has been translated as "make your peace with" in the TEV.

The first question we need to answer then is this: Why did our Lord choose to use this word, DIALLASSOMAI (διαλλάσσομαι)? We would have expected to see KATALLASSO (καταλλάσσω), the word generally used for reconciliation. This second word implies inequality of the parties being reconciled, such as God reconciling the world to Himself, or human beings being reconciled to God. It is also used in the marital context of separated spouses becoming reconciled. An authority structure is involved when KATALLASSO (καταλλάσσω) appears. However, our Lord chose to use the word, DIALLASSO (διαλλάσσω) instead. Friedrich Büchsel, one of the contributors to TDNT, saw no discernible difference between the meanings of these two words. He understood that during one era, one word was used while in another, the other was used. However, Lightfoot, as quoted by A. T. Robertson, saw an important distinction based upon the difference in prepositions used in the compound words. Both of these are compounded using differing prepositions, the first with KATA, the second with DIA. Lightfoot wrote this about DIALASSO: "The verb denotes mutual concession after mutual hostility, an idea absent from καταλλασσω..." These writers, Joseph B. Lightfoot and A. T. Robertson, gained this idea from the use of DIALLASSO (διαλλάσσω) in a fragment of a 2nd century papyrus letter. An estranged son seeking reconciliation appealed to his mother.[xxvi] The issue is reconciliation by mutual concession. Both parties needed to put their differences aside, resolving the issue together.

The etymology of the verb also brings in some important issues. This verb, DIALASSO is in the aorist tense, the passive voice and imperative mood. Assigning this aorist as an ingressive aorist, as A. T. Robertson did, emphasizes the beginning of the verb's action as being initiated in a moment of time. The one doing the wrong—you in this context—initiates the action of reconciliation beginning at a point in time.

The passive voice indicates that the subject of the verb, you, again, receives the action of the verb. This is a bit of a twist. I would assume that this verb would appear in the active voice, indicating that you, the reconciler would produce the action of the verb. The passive voice here works though because although you initiate the reconciliation, you receive reconciliation in the sense that you receive peace from the cessation of hostilities from the one you wronged. The son, we assume, received reconciliation from his mother when she stopped being angry with him when she received his letter. The son, who initiated the reconciliation received peace from his mother.

The imperative mood our Lord used emphasizes, along with the next verse, the strength, and purpose of this command. The strong implication is this: You reconcile! You do it now, without hesitation! Stop what you are doing and reconcile. You cannot worship the Creator of the Universe without having first reconciled with those you have wronged! Go make peace now! Go heal that broken relationship! How many spouses could save their marriages if both heeded this command?

Note that our Lord gave this command during His dispensation, during His sojourn upon this earth. Let us bring in some Church Age doctrines to expand upon this command. Initially, the first person who needs to be transformed is you. When you name your sin—the wrong you committed—to the Father, you receive transformation from carnality to spirituality, from a state of sin to that of fellowship with Him. I say, "receive" transformation because we receive transformation by grace when we name our sins, as per 1 John 1:9, to the Father by virtue of the work of our Lord's substitutionary work on the Cross. We receive this state of spirituality by grace. So, first resolve your issue of broken fellowship with the Lord by naming that sin to the Father, then, go reconcile with your brother, or sister in the Lord, as indicated by the imperative mood. Jesus directed that we reconcile with those with whom we have a conflict.

... and then come and present your offering.
... καὶ τότε ἐλθὼν πρόσφερε τὸ δῶρόν σου.

Once you have been transformed from your carnality to spirituality, received a cessation from hostilities, then continue your worship. This picture of worship during the age of Israel, offering your gift, is grammatically presented as a dramatic principle. Therefore, the emphasis here is upon your fulfillment of worship in your recovered state of spirituality, your personal transformation, then your worship. Worship always carries drama because as Paul taught, not only is this watched by the world but also by the angels. Your worship, in no matter what form, always carries great dramatic impact for the Lord.

3. Matthew 5:25

Make friends quickly with your opponent at law while you are with him on the way, so that your opponent may not hand you over to the judge, and the judge to the officer, and you be thrown into prison.

Our Lord continued with the theme He began with raising the bar from overt to mental and emotional sin. We continue to make application of that principle. Remember the one you wronged, with whom you had a conflict? In the previous verse, our Lord indicated the immediacy with which you need to reconcile with that one. He continued with an illustration. The situation has escalated. You are on your way to court, because of a suit between you two. Again, you are in the wrong, liable to suffer under the court's decision!

Make friends quickly with your opponent at law ...
ἴσθι εὐνοῶν τῷ ἀντιδίκῳ σου ταχύ ...

The phrase, "make friends," consists of two words, the present active imperative of EIMI (εἰμί) and the present active participle of EUNOEW (εὐνοέω). Generally, EIMI translates as "I am" or "I exist;" however, it works as a verb of status quo or of being as well. Along with the following participle, these words form a periphrastic of the present imperative. The verb, to be, in the imperative explains that you need to be something, that you need to get into a particular status, permanently. That status is defined by the present active participle EUNOEW (εὐνοέω). This participle denotes moving into the status of civility from hostility and antagonism. We can idiomatically translate these two words, because of their immediate context as "come to quick agreement by a generous settlement!"[xxvii]

Applying this means that you will not harbor any mental attitude sins toward this one you have wronged. Moving back into Church Age doctrine concerning the ministry of the Spirit, you cannot think this way without the power of God the Holy Spirit and applying the doctrine you have learned to this kind of situation. You must be mentally relaxed, being free from arrogance, antagonism, or dread when you face those who have reason to be antagonistic to you.

When should you do this? You approach your antagonist as soon as you can. Our Lord said, in the Greek, TACHU (ταχύ), quickly! When someone hates you, they are bound to express that in maligning and hostility! You also need to maintain your spirituality to prevent you from reacting, thereby exacerbating the antagonism. In this scenario, you and your antagonist cross each other's paths on the way to court. He is suing you for damages due to your wrong. Remember that you are entirely wrong. Do your best to resolve the issue between you two before you reach the court, as soon as possible. He has the power to hurt you by throwing you upon the "mercies" of the court.

The rest of the verse delineates the consequence for failing to reconcile.

> *... so that your opponent may not hand you over to the judge, and the judge to the officer, and you be thrown into prison.*
> *ἕως ὅτου εἶ μετ' αὐτοῦ ἐν τῇ ὁδῷ, μήποτέ σε παραδῷ ὁ ἀντίδικος τῷ κριτῇ καὶ ὁ κριτὴς τῷ ὑπηρέτῃ καὶ εἰς φυλακὴν βληθήσῃ*

"According to Roman law, if a person had a quarrel that he could not settle privately, he had the right to order his adversary to accompany him to the praetor. If he refused, the prosecutor took someone present to witness by saying, 'May I take you to witness?' If the person consented, he offered the tip of his ear, which the prosecutor touched, a form that was observed toward witnesses in some other legal ceremonies among the Romans. Then the plaintiff might drag the defendant to court by force in any way, even by the neck, but worthless persons such as thieves and robbers might be dragged before the judge without the formality of calling a witness. If on the way to the judge the difficulty was settled, no further legal steps were taken."[xxviii] Ultimately, without resolving the case, the court would throw you into debtor's prison. Once in debtor's prison, you would be unable to work off your debt or resolve the case in any other way.

4. Matthew 5:26

> *Truly I say to you, you will not come out of there until you have paid up the last cent.*

Much like today, farmers borrowed money on their crops. If the harvest was poor, they risked failure to pay off their debts. If a farmer angered his creditor, he could see to it that the debtor landed in prison where he could not work to pay off his debt. If rapport had existed between the two, they could come to terms with the debt; the farmer would stay out of prison.

This entire principle was repeated in the Old Testament, in the Gospel of Mark, and then brought into the Church Age:

> *When the ways of people please the Lord, he causes even their enemies to be at peace with them. Proverbs 16:7*

> *Salt is good; but if salt has lost its saltiness, how can you season it? Have salt in yourselves, and be at peace with one another. Mark 9:50*

> *If it is possible, so far as it depends on you, live peaceably with all. Romans 12:18*

> *Let us then pursue what makes for peace and for mutual upbuilding. Romans 14:19*

We can delve deeper into the message of this section of the Sermon on the Mount. We all owe a tremendous debt due to our fallen nature. We can never repay this debt because we all live in the debtors' prison of spiritual death. The only way possible to be released from this prison is reconciliation with the one we owe. By His substitutionary death on the Cross, our Lord continually offers the human race release from this captivity by faith in Him. Therefore, the message to the unbeliever is this: Quickly, become reconciled to God through faith in Him to be released from the prison of spiritual death.

D. Matthew 5:27-28—From Overt to Mental Adultery

1. Matthew 5:27

You have heard that it was said, 'You shall not commit adultery.'

Jesus continued the message with another rising of the sin bar. Again, He contrasts the Pharisaic teaching of the Mosaic Law with His teaching. The Mosaic Law, the ancients, prohibited adultery, defined as sexual intercourse between a man and a married woman.

2. Matthew 5:28

... but I say to you that everyone who looks at a woman with lust for her has already committed adultery with her in his heart.

In this verse, our Lord, once again contrasts the Pharisaic teaching with His own with strong authoritarian overtones:

... but I say to you ...
... εγω δε λεγω ...

There is no mistaking the great authority with which our Lord communicated. He had taught all of these principles to Moses long ago.

... that everyone who looks at a woman with lust for her ...
... υμιν οτι πας ο βλεπων γυναικα πρὸς τὸ ἐπιθυμῆσαι αὐτὴν ...

The key to this dictate is looking with extreme desire. This desire, described by the present active participle of BLEPO (βλέπω), translates as "looks at" with the articular aorist active infinitive of EPITHUMEO (ἐπιθυμέω). In this context, BLEPO refers to the sense of seeing with the eyes. The connotation is concentration upon a woman. EPITHUMIA means extreme desire. The Scripture uses this word both positively and negatively. In this case, it refers to a desire that will get you into trouble! When used as an articular infinitive preceded by the preposition PROS it expresses purpose. When a man looks at a woman and notes her attractiveness or even her appeal sexually, he has not conceived sin. However, he may be heading in that direction! When that one look results in emotional titillation and desire, it is time to look elsewhere. Lust, or extreme desire, in this case, for a woman sexually is the sin that the Scripture prohibits. The key to this then is the linking up of what the eye sees to the emotions resulting in extreme desire. From that lust comes a multitude of sins.

One time, my father, one of his cronies and I were on a bus with a couple of cheerleaders from my high school. My father's friend looked at him and said, "You can only look once!" To which my father replied, "But make it a long look!" I am not accusing my father of sin here! He loved kidding his cronies! Nevertheless, it is that long kindling look that can result in lust. The issue in lust is the desire created by the emotional response to what you see. You do not even have to look to have lustful desire, but if you have the predilection for lust, even one short look will do you! As you look at a woman, ask yourself why you are looking at her! If sexual appeal becomes the issue, better look the other way!

> *... has already committed adultery with her in his heart.*
> *... ἤδη ἐμοίχευσεν αὐτὴν ἐν τῇ καρδίᾳ αὐτοῦ.*

When emotional appeal hooks up with your old sin nature predilection to lust, it locks you into that desire. You have lost your fellowship with the Holy Spirit, Son, and Father because your concentration has changed from God to what He has created. This fits the criteria for idolatry. All of a sudden what He has created has taken on greater importance than the Creator.

"Adultery" comes from the Greek word, MOICHEUO (μοιχεύω) which refers to sexual intercourse between a man and a married woman. Adultery was usually defined in terms of the woman. If she was married, it was considered adultery whereas if she was single, it was considered fornication. However, our Lord made no distinction here. Looking at any woman, married or single, with kindled desire is sin. "In his heart," EN TE KARDIA AUTO (ἐν τῇ καρδίᾳ αὐτοῦ) refers to the thought process being coupled with emotional attraction and volition. Just as the heart pumps blood throughout the circulator system, so the volition circulates thought throughout the soul. The thought, whether or not it actually precedes the overt act, falls short of God's righteousness. Therefore, it is sin.

In those days, the woman probably needed to be near-by to be seen and lusted after. However, in these days of modern electronic communications, you can easily kindle lust by movies and printed material! These images, today so readily made available by pornographers, have resulted in an entire illicit industry that addicts men and women alike. God designed marriage to be the only framework of sexual desire.

The religious leadership took the seventh commandment too literally by only prohibiting resultant overt adultery, not understanding the reason for the commandment. They did not understand that sin begins with thought. Jesus addressed this issue because not only was adultery rampant in those days—as it is now—but also because it was a core area of self-righteousness within the religious hierarchy. These leaders could prohibit overt adultery but ignore the sinful reality of the mental attitude that precedes the overt sin. These people were prohibiting overt adultery while being heavily involved in mental adultery, themselves. Jesus, then, raised the bar from the overt activity to the mental attitude that precedes it.

That mental attitude is not simply looking at a woman, recognizing that she is attractive but looking with concentration, with either the intent to commit adultery or fantasizing adultery.

These teachers prohibiting overt adultery while being involved in mental adultery became, as a result, steeped in self-righteousness. They condemned those involved in overt adultery yet were steeped in the greater sin, self-righteousness, themselves. This led to great legalism and spiritual corruption.

Jesus, then, was more concerned with the issue of spiritual corruption and legalism that interfered with spiritual growth. He was going to send His disciples into a nation that was steeped with well-intentioned but legalistic religiosity. They needed to be prepared to deal with it by making an issue of the mental attitude, getting to the core of the problem. Legalism finds its roots in self-righteousness. Legalism begets spiritual corruption. You see, unless these citizens of Israel threw off religion with its yoke of self-righteous legalism, they would never recognize their own Messiah. Furthermore, unbelievers recognize a self-righteous legalistic façade in a moment then reject the Gospel. Nothing destroys evangelism, the presentation of the Gospel, no matter how accurate, more than self-righteousness.

E. Matthew 5:29-30—Self-Judgment

1. Matthew 5:29

If your right eye makes you stumble, tear it out and throw it from you; for it is better for you to lose one of the parts of your body, than for your whole body to be thrown into hell.

Speaking of that long, lust-producing look, Jesus gave us a great piece of advice. Get rid of the offending body part.

If your right eye makes you stumble, tear it out and throw it from you;
εἰ δὲ ὁ ὀφθαλμός σου ὁ δεξιὸς σκανδαλίζει σε ἔξελε αὐτὸν καὶ βάλε ἀπὸ σοῦ·

Everyone who reads this would have to admit that this is shocking! The English translation from the Greek certainly communicates the implication clearly. Jesus specified the right eye because for the right-handed person; it is dominant. What has this eye done to you? SKANDALIZW (σκανδαλίζω) in the present active indicative indicates that your eye produces the action of making you spiritually stumble. Your right eye caused your vision to fall upon that woman, resulting in your thinking lustfully. Your eye made you do it! So, what should you do about that eye? Excise that eye and get rid of it! Would anyone in his or her right mind actually do this?

2. Matthew 5:30

If your right hand makes you stumble, cut it off and throw it from you; for it is better for you to lose one of the parts of your body, than for your whole body to go into hell.

As we noted, the eye can be the beginning of mental adultery. However, it is not your eye's fault. Look to your volition of thought for blame! Jesus did not mean for anyone to take this advice literally, but through it He used shock as a teaching method to break up the combination of self-righteousness and religion. What are you doing in taking your eye out? You are judging that part of your body as being the source of the offense, then removing it. The key point is self-judgment. Step back from removing your "lust producing eye" or "violence producing hand" to judging the real source of your sin, your volition! How do you self-judge your volition that really produces that sin?

For Church Age believers, look into 1 Corinthians 11:31 then into 1 John 1:9. You resolve mental adultery by naming that sin to the Father. You resolve any sin enacted by your hand by naming that sin to the Father.

But if we judged ourselves rightly, we would not be judged.
1 Corinthians 11:31

If we confess our sins, He is faithful and righteous to forgive us our sins and to cleanse us from all unrighteousness. 1 John 1:9

As an aside here, one does not correct his or her mental attitude by naming their sin or sins to the Father. By this confession, the Holy Spirit puts you back into fellowship with Himself—and the Father and Son—empowering you to grow up spiritually by consistent doctrinal inculcation. Naming your sin to the Father does not resolve the spiritual weakness issue that gets you into trouble, but sets you up to grow up spiritually. Spiritual growth coupled with your volition takes care of mental attitude adultery. Spiritual growth will also grow you out of sins you may commit with your hand. As you grow spiritually, you should choose not to involve yourself in those particular sins. You must choose to use the power you have gained from the Spirit and knowledge of Scripture.

This echoes another passage Paul wrote to the Colossian believers:

Therefore consider the members of your earthly body as dead to immorality, impurity, passion, evil desire, and greed, which amounts to idolatry. Colossians 3:5

The implication of this verse, beyond self-judgment, is the severity of sin. Both mental attitude and overt sins are in view here. Mental adultery often leads to other sins, resulting in soul injury. Remember David's lust for Bathsheba! Where did that lust lead? It led to David's murder of Uriah the Hittite. Remove that mental trend from your soul, if you are a believer, because it locks you into arrogance, preventing you from growing up spiritually. Mental attitude adultery locks the unbeliever into arrogance leading to rejection of the Gospel truth, resulting in living eternity in the Lake of Fire. The problems resulting from overt sins, so often criminally destructive, are obvious.

Again, remember the context of our Lord's message here. He was preparing His disciples for evangelism toward the lost sheep in Israel who were following the legalism and self-righteousness of the Pharisees. Their mission, then, was to break into their complacent thinking by shock. If the ones to whom they witnessed agreed with the disciples, that a person is better off destroying a part of himself than having his entire being be thrown into the Lake of Fire, then they would have a better chance understanding the Gospel of Christ which results in complete salvation.

F. Matthew 5:31-32—The Case of Immoral Divorce

It was said, 'Whoever sends his wife away, let him give her a certificate of divorce,' but I say to you that everyone who divorces his wife, except for the reason of unchastity, makes her commit adultery; and whoever marries a divorced woman commits adultery.
Matthew 5:31-32

Jesus continues His dissertation by addressing another issue noted in the Mosaic Law, divorce. Before we look at this passage, let us look at what the Mosaic Law said about it. Under certain conditions, the Old Testament Law sanctioned it. If the marriage broke up because of certain conditions, the Law, in some situations, authorized remarriage!

When a man takes a wife and marries her, and it happens that she finds no favor in his eyes because he has found some indecency in her, and he writes her a certificate of divorce and puts it in her hand and sends her out from his house ... Deuteronomy 24:1

When two people marry, they fall into, or walk into, the divine structure of marriage. In Jewish marriages, the parents usually arranged the marriage, while today couples marry because of love. In either case, the couple is obligated to follow divine intents and provisions for marriage. Two important provisions God provided are these: He designed it be permanent and a union between a man and a woman. Not only is it a foundational stabilizing relationship in the human race but Christian marriage is also a picture of the union of Jesus Christ and His royal family. As such, it is vitally important. Satan continually attacks it through degenerate cultural practices. The Church Age couple who weathers its many storms and challenges receives rewards, both temporally and eternally.

"And it happens," the Hebrew conjunction WA (ן) with the verb of status HAYA (היה) in the qal, indicates that some time has passed. When the woman loses "favor" in her husband's eyes, she has lost her husband's love. He, as the responsible party in the marriage, has clearly violated Biblical marital principles. The man in marriage is responsible for the marriage, being responsible for love initiation. She responds to his love in every area of the marriage. This man has violated marital principles by becoming antagonistic toward his wife, destroying her love response toward him. This constitutes the destruction of his own capacity to love, if he had capacity to begin with. He has also destroyed his wife's choice to love her husband. He has violated her volition. How else is she to respond to a husband who no longer loves her? This husband has moved from love to dislike, and finally, to hatred. His moving into hatred of her indicates his own arrogance and sin, and then he uses his own volition to initiate hatred instead of love, violating her choice to love him. He, because of his arrogance, finds an excuse to divorce her. He finds an excuse in the Hebrew term, ARVAH (עֶרְוָה.) This term, translated, "indecency" or "uncleanness" has as its root nakedness and resultant shame.

Remember that Adam and the woman in the Garden tried to hide their nakedness from the Lord. After their sin, they perceived an imbalance in their lives then blamed it upon their nakedness. That imbalance resulted from their fall from spiritual life to spiritual death. They then, hurriedly fashioned body coverings from nearby fig leaves in an attempt to regain the balance in their lives. They were ashamed of their nakedness. They were also ashamed of their love making because it was analogous to our Lord's relationship with them.

The Scripture considers nakedness shameful in many passages. In many contexts, nakedness referred to adultery. Because the Law considered adultery a criminal offense, it was punishable by death as per Deuteronomy 22:20-24. However, in this context, nakedness did not refer to adultery because the husband was not to accuse her in the Courts of Law. The Rabbinical school of Hillel interpreted this shame as being anything that displeased the husband, including ceremonial uncleanness. According to the Mosaic Law, ceremonial uncleanness even included such things as entering a home where someone had recently died. Any excuse probably filled the bill!

We do not need to know exactly what ARVAH (עֶרְוָה) meant to the Jews at that time. They clearly understood what it meant though. Their lack of integrity spawned many divorces from it. Because a woman displeased her husband in some way, he would issue her a bill of divorce and send her away. If she had been sexually unfaithful to him, he could have taken her to court. Other displeasures also sparked these permanent divorces.

According to the next verse, the Law gave her the right of remarriage.

... *and she leaves his house and goes and becomes another man's wife, and if the latter husband turns against her and writes her a certificate of divorce and puts it in her hand and sends her out of his house, or if the latter husband dies who took her to be his wife, then her former husband who sent her away is not allowed to take her again to be his wife, since she*

has been defiled; for that is an abomination before the Lord, and you shall not bring sin on the land which the Lord your God gives you as an inheritance.
Deuteronomy 24:2-4

The Law forbade her to remarry her former husband if her second husband died. It did allow reconciliation and remarriage if no second marriage ensued.

What was the valid reason for divorce presented in this verse? We do not exactly know, nor do we need to understand it because Jesus updated it for us in this Sermon.

1. Matthew 5:31

It was said, 'Whoever sends his wife away, let him give her a certificate of divorce';

Getting back, then, to our immediate passage, Jesus referred back to the Mosaic Law. With this phrase, "it has been said," Jesus began a quotation from the Old Testament passage we have just looked at, updating its meaning. The Jews had been abusing the divorce concept for generations.

2. Matthew 5:32

... but I say to you that everyone who divorces his wife, except for the reason of unchastity, makes her commit adultery; and whoever marries a divorced woman commits adultery.

Everyone who divorces his wife and marries another commits adultery, and he who marries one who is divorced from a husband commits adultery.
Luke 16:18

And He said to them, "Whoever divorces his wife and marries another woman commits adultery against her; and if she herself divorces her husband and marries another man, she is committing adultery."
Mark 10:11-12

... but I say to you,
... ἐγὼ δὲ λέγω ὑμῖν,

"But I continually say to you," our Lord said. The present linear aktionsart of "I say," LEGO (λέγω), means that what He was about to say is doctrine, certifiable truth!

... that everyone who divorces his wife, except for the reason of unchastity ...
... ὅτι πᾶς ὁ ἀπολύων τὴν γυναῖκα αὐτοῦ παρεκτὸς λόγου πορνείας ...

He said that whoever divorces his wife, except for the case of sexual unfaithfulness puts his wife in a very difficult situation. Whatever ARVAH meant in those ancient of days was no longer an issue; our Lord's words were. Simply said, whoever divorces his wife for any other reason than PORNEIA (πορνεία), sexual unfaithfulness, violates the prohibition against divorce.

... makes her commit adultery,
... ποιεῖ αὐτὴν μοιχευθῆναι,

Divorce for any reason other than sexual unfaithfulness causes her, according to the Greek, to receive adultery if she remarries. The word translated, "makes," comes from the Greek word POIEO (ποιέω) in the present active indicative. The active voice indicates that she produces the action, committing adultery. However, MOICHEUO (μοιχεύω), adultery, appears as an aorist passive infinitive; the passive voice indicating that she receives adultery. The woman has not committed adultery in this case, because that was a valid reason for divorce. She is innocent of any wrongdoing. A man who divorces his wife, justifying it by the "uncleanness" gimmick, causes her to receive the label of adulterer. The man she marries also commits adultery. She receives adultery according to the passive voice, whereas the man commits adultery according to the active voice of the verb.

What is happening here? The man who originally divorced his wife, by his sin of unjustifiable divorce brought on by arrogance, begins a chain of sinning beyond himself. He first sinned by antagonism toward his wife. Instead of resolving the issue that brought on the antagonism, he propagated that sin into hatred leading to unjustified divorce. The divorce and woman's subsequent remarriage causes her second husband to commit adultery and her to receive adultery. Not only has Jesus clarified the one justifiable reason for divorce—sexual unfaithfulness—but He also brought out the subject of chain sinning. No one who sins remains isolated in that sin. The effects of sin always spread to others. A translation that takes into account the passive voice of "adultery" reads this way.[xxix]

... but I say to you that everyone who divorces his wife, except for the reason of sexual unfaithfulness, makes her receive adultery; and whoever marries a divorced woman commits adultery.

Let us back up for a moment. What is the man or woman whose spouse no longer pleases them to do? This is a real problem today. People get divorced for any reason they can think of to release themselves from an unsatisfactory marriage. I do not know any solution other than divorce for the unbeliever. It requires great emotional fortitude and strong establishment orientation to turn a bad marriage into one that lasts for the couple's life. With establishment orientation disappearing in this country, the mental structure necessary for an unbeliever's marriage to last has vanished.

For the Church Age believer, however, God has provided the solution to marital dissatisfaction in virtue love. This category of love is the foundation of integrity that gives the divinely provided solution for any human relationship.

Jesus Christ demonstrated this love—the fruit of the Spirit—by taking it to its furthest limits at the Cross when He died for the sins of the world. He loved every human being even though no one qualified for His perfect love. He loved the human race because of His own virtue, integrity and perfection.

G. Matthew 5:33-37—The Issue of Oaths or Swearing

Again, you have heard that the ancients were told, 'You shall not make false vows, but shall fulfill your vows to the Lord.' "But I say to you, make no oath at all, either by heaven, for it is the throne of God, or by the earth, for it is the footstool of His feet, or by Jerusalem, for it is the city of the great King. Nor shall you make an oath by your head, for you cannot make one hair white or black. But let your statement be, 'Yes, yes' or 'No, no'; anything beyond these is of evil. Matthew 5:33-37

Jesus continued His dissertation on the Mosaic Law. He quoted, for this lesson, from two more Old Testament passages.

You shall not take the name of the Lord your God in vain, for the Lord will not leave him unpunished who takes His name in vain. Exodus 20:7

You shall not swear falsely by My name, so as to profane the name of your God; I am the Lord. Leviticus 19:12

What do you do when you swear about something? You are trying to lend credibility or reliability to what you are saying by bringing in something that is reliable. In essence, you are bringing in a witness to validate what you are saying. When you bring in God's name, as the ultimate witness, would He validate what you are saying! Do you see the blasphemy in all of this?

The Pharisees were evidently famous for their oath taking. Only, they sidestepped God, by swearing "by heaven," "by earth," "by Jerusalem" or by their own heads! They claimed that they could weasel out of the oath penalty because they had not brought in God as their witness! Note that the words Jesus quoted do not forbid the utterance of an oath but only the false or frivolous one. Furthermore, the quote continues, if an oath is given, it had better be discharged as unto the Lord, with all alacrity!

Jesus had this to say about all of this oath giving. First, He promptly demonstrated that for those who swore by Heaven, they were indeed bringing in God as a witness because, according to Isaiah 66:1, Heaven is God's throne! To those who swore by the Earth, they were also bringing in God as a witness, because, according to Isaiah, the Earth is the Father's footstool!

Thus says the Lord, "Heaven is My throne and the earth is My footstool." Isaiah 66:1a

The same holds true for those who swore by Jerusalem because, according to Psalm 48:2, it is the city of the great King!

Beautiful in elevation, the joy of the whole Earth, is Mount Zion in the far north, the city of the great King. Psalm 48:2

Do you, as the Pharisees did, swear by your own head? You do not even control when your hair turns to gray! How can you swear by your own head? It has no more stability or credibility than do you! Perhaps in swearing by your head you should say, "You may take my head if what I say is false!"

Remember that what a person says is no better, no more reliable, than his or her own character. Bringing in any witness to add credibility to your statements does not add to your credence! You are responsible for whatever you say. Do not try to bring in anyone else, especially God, to co-sign your statements.

Jesus, again, after quoting a passage from the Law, communicates its intent, with the formulaic, "but I say to you…" Who is making this assertion? Our Lord Jesus Christ says this, communicating as the Lord of the Universe, the very Author of the Mosaic Law! He said not to swear at all! If you are honest, your word, "Yes," or "No" should be sufficient. If you have no integrity, you can bring in anyone you wish to underwrite your oath but it will still be worthless.

Do not take this as a prohibition against taking an oath in court. Jesus answered Caiaphas on an oath. Paul appealed to God on two occasions:

I adjure you by the Lord to have this letter read to all the brethren. 1 Thessalonians 5:27

I affirm, brethren, by the boasting in you which I have in Christ Jesus our Lord, I die daily. 1 Corinthians 15:31

H. Matthew 5:38-42—*The Case for Revenge*

You have heard that it was said, 'An eye for an eye, and a tooth for a tooth.' But I say to you, do not resist an evil person; but whoever slaps you on your right cheek, turn the other to him also. If anyone wants to sue you and take your shirt, let him have your coat also. Whoever forces you to go one mile, go with him two. Give to him who asks of you, and do not turn away from him who wants to borrow from you. Matthew 5:38-42

This is a complex passage, so we will start with a basic outline of these few verses. Many people have misapplied this passage for many years. We need to look into it very carefully:

1. Matt 5:38—Quotation from the Mosaic Law.
2. Matt 5:39a—The Intent Behind the Law
3. Matt 5:39b—Application to Personal Relationships
4. Matt 5:40—Application to Legal Situations
5. Matt 5:41—Application to Public Service
6. Matt 5:42—Application to the Demonstration of Grace

1. Matthew 5:38—Quotation from the Old Testament

You have heard that it was said, 'An eye for an eye, and a tooth for a tooth.'

Ἠκούσατε ὅτι ἐρρέθη, Ὀφθαλμὸν ἀντὶ ὀφθαλμοῦ καὶ ὀδόντα ἀντὶ ὀδόντος.

To introduce this line of teaching, Our Lord quoted an Old Testament principle. It appears in at least three verses.

... eye for eye, tooth for tooth, hand for hand, foot for foot ... Exodus 21:24

Thus you shall not show pity: life for life, eye for eye, tooth for tooth, hand for hand, foot for foot. Deuteronomy 19:21

... fracture for fracture, eye for eye, tooth for tooth; just as he has injured a man, so it shall be inflicted on him. Leviticus 24:20

This instruction had been grossly misunderstood, and misapplied. This saying, "an eye for an eye and a tooth for a tooth" has been used to justify the *lex talionis*, the supposed law of retaliation. We will not discover where the ancients went wrong with their application of those verses but discover what our Lord had to say about it. That He established the context for the next five verses by this quote is very important. The subject is retaliation, not personal policy toward criminality. This "law of retaliation" corrective presented in the following four verses does not justify pacifism or allow criminality as some have supposed.

This supposed system of retaliation did not provide for revenge in personal relationships, as was occurring in Jesus' day. Indeed, many have used this passage as a rationale for such personal revenge many times over the centuries. If someone did any injury to someone else, then the one injured could, according to some interpretations, take revenge upon the perpetrator of his injury to the level he was injured. However, if one person injures or wrongs another, the Bible never authorizes the victim to take personal retaliation, taking justice into his own hands. Even the Mosaic Law required that every believer leave justice in God's hands.

'Vengeance is Mine, and retribution, in due time their foot will slip; for the day of their calamity is near, and the impending things are hastening upon them.' Deuteronomy 32:35

Our Lord, when He communicated these words to Moses, intended that they serve as a system of justice within the national entity. Therefore, the only one ever authorized to mete out this kind of punishment was the judge sitting at the bench to whom God has delegated justice within a country. The Scripture never authorized personal retaliation in any case.

2. Matthew 5:39a—The Intent Behind the Law

Jesus continued by clarifying the intent behind the Law. Those in that day needed His clarification and reminder just as we do now. People still use the above verses to justify personal retaliation. However, many even distort His words of clarification, using them to justify pacifism in the face of criminality and war. Jesus said, as translated by numerous English translations,

> *But I say to you, do not resist an evil person.*
> *ἐγὼ δὲ λέγω ὑμῖν μὴ ἀντιστῆναι τῷ πονηρῷ.*

We need to dig into the Greek here to understand what these words mean. Specifically, we need to look at that word, "resist." The phrase "do not resist" comes from the aorist active verbal infinitive of ANTHISTEMI (ἀνθίστημι) with the negative particle ME (μή). This word is a compound one, coming from the preposition ANTI (ἀντὶ) which means against, and the verb, ISTEMI (ἵστημι), which means "to stand." The root idea is "to stand against." Certainly, the translation "resist" fits the Greek words. Except in this context of retaliation, resistance does not make sense. The evil person is not out to do you harm. He has already harmed you. That is why he is evil. You are considering retaliating against him. Do not stand against the one who has injured you to retaliate against him. Do not seek revenge. Only one English version out of my entire collection translated the word "resist" correctly. That particular translation is the paraphrase, *The Good News Translation*! The best translation, considering the context, is "do not retaliate," as in personal revenge. No one, then, is to take personal revenge upon another. Prohibiting revenge and retaliation carries a very different connotation from prohibiting resistance in the face of criminality. If someone, a criminal, for instance, tries to victimize you, you should use every means at your disposal to resist victimization. However, if he has already victimized you, do not seek revenge.

Therefore, our Lord commanded that no one take personal revenge for any wrong done to him. The corrected translation of this phrase, then should read as,

> *... do not personally retaliate against an evil person ..."*

The "evil person," the masculine substantival adjective from PONEROS (πονηρός) refers in this context to anyone with criminal intent toward you—any lowlife! In this case, he has already exacted some damage toward you.

What is evil? Evil is any system of thought that does not acknowledge God. This thinking includes motivation. Satan introduced this thinking into the world when he sought to usurp God's power. Evil people become antagonistic to divine thought and motivation. It describes the criminal because, unlike sin, it becomes a lifestyle antagonistic to principles of law and order, a part of God's Laws of Establishment. A believer can recover from sin by naming it to the Father; however, recovery from evil requires changing one's thought pattern as a result of continual Bible teaching.

What happens when you exact personal revenge upon an evil person? You lower yourself to their level of operation. You come to be an evil person, taking on the revenge thought pattern, becoming liable to punishment from not only your country's judicial system, but also from the Supreme Court of Heaven. Do not ever try to resolve this kind of problem with personal retaliation. Maintain your experiential righteousness, leaving the matter in the hands of the Supreme Court of Heaven and one of His temporal agents, civil authorities. If you maintain your spirituality, you become the plaintiff in the case that the Supreme Court of Heaven hears. If you seek personal revenge, you lose your spirituality and become subject to not only divine discipline but to civil penalties as well. The bottom line here is this: do not get in the Lord's way by involving yourself in a personal vendetta.

If you become victimized, you do have the opportunity for recourse:

Never take your own revenge, beloved, but leave room for the wrath of God, for it is written, "Vengeance is Mine, I will repay," says the Lord. Romans 12:19

Again, the Lord is teaching against personal retaliation, not to willingly submit when a criminal intends to victimize you. You are authorized to protect yourself, your family, your household and, in Texas, your neighbors household, too! He also authorizes you to protect your national entity by going to war! Jesus never intended these words to serve as a rationale for allowing an aggressor nation to overrun your national entity or an evil person to overrun your household. Never use this passage as a rationale not to go to war or to let a criminal victimize you!

3. Matthew 5:39b—Application to Personal Relationships

Jesus now illustrates the lesson by making an application to personal relationships:

... but whoever slaps you on your right cheek, turn the other to him also.
... ἀλλ' ὅστις σε ῥαπίζει εἰς τὴν δεξιὰν σιαγόνα [σου], στρέψον αὐτῷ καὶ τὴν ἄλλην.

Before we can thoroughly understand to what Jesus referred, we need to understand the historical context of slapping. Many misunderstand it today because it is not as common today as it was then. Its use was not limited to the angry woman, but authorities actually used it as an institutionalized means of control and intimidation.

Slapping was evidently common in that day. People were slapping each other all over the place for one reason or another. People publicly slapped either to insult or to intimidate. It always indicated that the one slapping was antagonistic to the slapped! The slap of the glove between so-called gentlemen early in the last century as a challenge to a dual was reminiscent of this kind of slap. Note that they did not even use the barehanded slap in a dual challenge because of its violent harshness. This is ironic! The barehanded slap was too violent but the raised dueling pistol was not. They reserved the "gentlemanly" violence for the dueling field.

A slap is very different from a hit or a slug. It does something to your thinking that a rude word or even a well-placed hit will not. Some words, colloquially called "fightin' words," can carry the sting of a slap however! The slap's insulting sting stays with you. After a hit, or even a fight, antagonists may end up friends having developed respect for each other's ability to fight. However, a slap is such an insult that the unbelieving slapped person has only two options. First, the one slapped may instantly and instinctively react, getting mad, then attempt to retaliate. The retaliation attempt may only take seconds because it is instinctive, almost as instinctive as a block thrown by a martial artist. The second option involves becoming intimidated and mentally submitting, resulting in the "whipped dog" syndrome. The "whipped dog" harbors a terrible long-lasting, deep-seated resentment. A slap, then, inflames a person so that the reaction can be instantly violent or repressed into a life-long resentful submission. I still remember, vividly, when in junior high school, a girl slapped me for no reason I comprehended! I still see her in my mind's eye! Looking back, maybe she was trying to attract my attention, like Linus of Peanut's fame, slugging a girl to whom he was attracted! He did not know what else to do!

Kings used the slap to intimidate their subjects. If the king slapped you and you reacted, his bodyguards would quickly dispatch you into the next life! However, if you valued your life, you would mentally submit and fall on to your knees! You became a whipped dog! The point is that you would most likely mentally submit to your sovereign because you valued your life. A slap would communicate these options to you very effectively. A king would easily slap his subjects into submission.

Jesus used the slap as an illustration, first, because it was common place in that day and second, because many responded with mental submission. The physical slap really covers the entire intimidation concept. A verbal slap or an insult gets the job done as well. Why would a person slap you? A person slaps you because he or she is antagonistic toward you. This mental attitude is sinful, expressed with the overt slap. If you retaliate with a slap, you lower yourself to their level, also becoming sinful.

A believer in Jesus Christ, if he is spiritual, has one more option that the unbelieving person does not. The spiritual life of the Church Age believer provides the means to bear up under anything, even an insulting slap. The slap illustrates the maximum amount of pressure a believer may go through and yet bear up under because of spiritual strength. Again, this illustration relates to personal relationships, not necessarily to the reality of maximum pressure the believer may face. Therefore, the turning of your cheek to absorb another slap does not connote pacifism or allowing yourself to become victim to criminality but illustrates your need of divine power to apply toward your antagonist in personal relationships.

To apply this to our era where slapping is not the order of the day but some physical attack may be, defend yourself. Above all, maintain your spirituality. Try to reason with your assailant if the situation allows; otherwise, bring in the local constabulary, and leave retaliation in the hands of the judicial system and the Supreme Court in Heaven. As you seek to defend yourself, your thinking—because of the virtue and integrity built into Church Age spirituality—should always reflect the virtue love our Lord had for us when He went to the Cross. Again, the intent behind the Mosaic commandment that our Lord was teaching is not the overt action but the mental attitude when the believer is under maximum pressure that can lead to overt response or reaction.

How can you, as a maturing Church Age believer absorb personal insults, up to and even beyond a physical or verbal slap? What thought dynamics must you possess in your soul to "turn your cheek?" What dynamic must reside in your soul not to react or to retaliate? You must be living your spiritual life, avoiding retaliation but allowing God to take care of the situation. You must apply the promises that God has made regarding vengeance. This takes faith beyond spiritual childhood dynamics. Become occupied with Jesus Christ so that you have His attitude toward your antagonist. To identify this attitude we need, for the ultimate illustration, to go back to the Cross and examine our Lord's attitude toward those insulting and ultimately crucifying Him. We can sum that concept up in one all-encompassing divine dynamic called virtue love! This is all humanly impossible, therefore limited to believers living the advanced spiritual life. When you are insulted or the victim of personal antagonism, you must exploit the Spirit's power, applying your virtue love, restraining any antagonism toward your antagonist on your part. By doing this, you stay out of God's way, allowing Him to apply any vengeance necessary. This mental attitude dynamic has great power toward those who watch you as well as to fallen angels. Protect yourself, at all costs, from becoming a victim of any criminality. Remember, do not become involved in personal retaliation. Leave that in the hands of the Lord and His agent, your country's judicial system!

4. Matthew 5:40—Application to Legal Situations

Jesus illustrated the lesson to civil law.

If anyone wants to sue you and take your shirt, let him have your coat also.
καὶ τῷ θέλοντί σοι κριθῆναι καὶ τὸν χιτῶνά σου λαβεῖν, ἄφες αὐτῷ καὶ τὸ ἱμάτιον.

In this illustration, someone wants your personal property. Someone is even willing to sue for your clothing! I cannot imagine a wrong a person could commit that would result in someone wanting to sue for clothes! I am sure Judge Judy has seen this though! This is tantamount to legal theft. Jesus did not go into any particulars: someone wants what you have so they sue you for it. There is no question of liability involved. The first item of clothing, the shirt, called a KITON (χιτών) in the Greek, was an open neck T-shirt type of garment that went down to one's knees. Everyone had at least one of these. It was of little value. The HIMATION (ἱμάτιον), the coat, was valued because it not only served as an outer garment or coat but as a blanket at night as well. Jewish law forbad anyone to borrow it without returning it before sundown because it was so important. The two garments went together as a suit. If you were out and about, or even in bed, you probably would have both garments on your or near you.

If we bring this situation into modern English, we might say if someone sues you for the shirt on your back, give him your pants, too. After all, if someone is suing you for your clothes, even your suit, he must need or want them pretty badly! If things were bad economically, this might be the only property you own! The point Jesus is making here relates, not to the fact of your personal, even your most personal, property, but to your relationship with Him. Clothing is just a detail of life, your need of which God is perfectly aware. He will always provide everything you need to live, logistically; up to the moment He takes you home. Therefore, be assured, if someone does sue you for your last piece of personal property, even the shirt off your back, God will provide you everything you need to live.

Getting back to someone suing you: what course of action do people generally take when sued? They usually counter-sue, retaliation being the motivation. You sue me for my clothes; I will sue you for yours plus legal fees! Are we, as believers, ever to retaliate for a wrong done to us, even when the person suing you is a low-life, after the most personal of your property? Emphatically not! Your responsibility is to extend grace!

What is your life really? The property you own or the Lord who provides perfectly for you? The important thing in your life is not what you own but your relationship with God. What grace you illustrate if someone sues you for a single item of clothing but you give him or her your entire suit! What is more important, that you keep your clothes or that you illustrate God's great gracious character by your willingness to have the shirt sued off your back? We all enjoy possessions but you must focus on the Lord in your life. You need to understand that your possessions are of no consequence compared to your relationship with God.

How does this relate to personal revenge, the backdrop for this verse? The things you possess, though their removal from you, especially through legal theft may offend greatly, your relationship with the Lord must hold a much greater place in your life than your possessions. If you do not react when someone takes your possessions but maintain your spirituality, the Lord will take care of you and deal with the one who has wronged you. Furthermore, both people and angels will see your focus upon the Lord. This is a wonderful application of your ambassadorship. God will reward you for your application of doctrine, in this and every circumstance. Why not be wronged?

5. Matthew 5:41—Application to Public Service

Jesus continued this lesson with an illustration that relates to public servitude:

Whoever forces you to go one mile, go with him two.
καὶ ὅστις σε ἀγγαρεύσει μίλιον ἕν, ὕπαγε μετ' αὐτοῦ δύο.

To the average English reader, the picture is benign: if someone wants you to go some distance, then go further. After all, you are well intentioned! However, the idea behind "force" here is much more distasteful. The key to this command, then, lays in the word translated, "forces." This is future active indicative from the Greek word AGGAREUO (ἀγγαρεύω), a loan word from the Persians. It refers to a particular type of force, that of a royal messenger pressing a private citizen into service for the government or of a military official pressing a citizen into duty. Either way, being pressed into public servitude often resulted in great inconvenience and expense on the part of the citizen. So inconvenient was this kind of service that Jews taught that students of the Law were not to be pressed.[xxx] A reasonable human response to such a situation is resentment and even thoughts of passive-aggressive revenge behavior, or not fulfilling one's duty as prescribed under the law. The word was used only once more in the New Testament describing Simon the Cyrene's impressment into service to carry our Lord's Cross, as per Matthew 27:32.

For the spiritual believer, then, the lesson is one of mental attitude. To go the extra mile, especially when impressed into service, willingly, without implacability, requires the spiritual dynamic of virtue love.

6. Matthew 5:42—Application to the Demonstration of Grace

Give to him who asks of you, and do not turn away from him who wants to borrow from you.
... and lend, expecting nothing in return ... Luke 6:35b

In the final sentence of this paragraph, Jesus extends the principle of grace from responding in grace to those who are, in one form or another, antagonistic to you, to extending grace in a situation which may be distasteful to you. Jesus said, as translated in the NASB,

Give to him who asks of you,
τῷ αἰτοῦντί σε δός,

Jesus presents two categories of people in need who come to you. They are in need because they are financially short. The first category asks for a donation. The mandate regarding this category begins with the articular dative present active participle of AITEO (αἰτέω) being used as a noun. Rather than being a simple request, this verb denotes an urgent demand. This is followed by the pronoun, "you, SE (σύ). It should read as, "to the demanding ones" or "to those who demand from you." The command comes from the short aorist active imperative of DIDOMI (δίδωμι), DOS; "you give!" You demonstrate much more grace when responding to those who demand from you than toward those patiently asking! These who demand from you evidently have no confidence of being able to pull themselves out of their difficult financial situation. It appears hopeless to them so they feel justified to make financial demands of you.

> *... and do not turn away from him who wants to borrow from you.*
> *... καὶ τὸν θέλοντα ἀπὸ σοῦ δανίσασθαι μὴ ἀποστραφῇς.*

The second category needs a loan to tide them over. Our Lord described those who desire to borrow from you. Perhaps they have over extended themselves for one reason or another or perhaps they are temporarily out of a job but see that they will be able to pay you back after they are on their feet again. In both cases, you are to respond in grace. In both situations, our Lord commands that we extend grace just as we have had grace extended to us.

You may ask how God has extended grace to us. Remember that our Lord went to the Cross, bore our sins, and paved the way for us to believe in Him that we may have eternal life. Your demonstration of grace just may lead to someone's salvation!

Why is this command placed in the same paragraph as going the extra mile and turning one's cheek to a slap? Every situation the Lord presents in this paragraph requires a dynamic of thought which the unbeliever or carnal believer will not have. That attitude is virtue love. The mental attitude is the issue. Do you ever resent people you asking for money? It is easy to be resentful of one who asks of you especially if you know they have squandered their funds due to a lack of wisdom. The solution to that resentfulness is the Spirit-given attitude and doctrinal foundation of virtue love. You always have a choice in the matter; grace should control your decision and your mental attitude.

Remember, when you apply this doctrine, that Jesus was addressing an extremely legalistic culture. He was addressing Jews living in the Dispensation of Israel. We, as Church Age believers, are to take general principles from these doctrines yet look to Church Age doctrines for specific guidance when applying them. We are also to compare Scripture with Scripture to gain a greater understanding of the Biblical concepts of giving. This list of a few verses may give you greater guidance for spiritual giving.

The Psalmist taught discernment and judgment in giving:

> *It is well with the man who is gracious and lends; He will maintain his cause in judgment. Psalm 112:5*

Paul carefully delineated several principles for us to follow:

> *Each one must do just as he has purposed in his heart, not grudgingly or under compulsion, for God loves a cheerful giver.*
> *2 Corinthians 9:7*

"Purposing in your heart" does not refer to giving under emotional duress. In our culture, we normally associate any reference to our hearts as being emotional. No wonder fundamentalist preachers try to appeal to the emotions of their followers to give up their money! To the Greek, the heart referred to the totality of the person, to include the seat of thought, volition and some emotion! Paul is mandating that we all give thoughtfully, adhering to every principle of Christian giving. Give in such a way so as not to violate your norms and standards. This is the only way you will possess the inner freedom to be a willing, generous, and cheerful giver!

And God is able to make all grace abound to you, that always having all sufficiency in everything you may have an abundance for every good deed. 2 Corinthians 9:8

This verse presents the key to giving. God is the ultimate source for all we have. It is He who understands our motivation to give as well as the relationship to giving to His plan for our lives. He also knows your capacity for generosity. Considering all, He provides every resource you need to be able to give.

Now He who supplies seed to the sower and bread for food, He will supply and multiply your seed for sowing and increase the harvest of your righteousness. You will be made rich in every way so that you can be generous on every occasion, and through us your generosity will result in thanksgiving to God. 2 Corinthians 9:10-11

I. Matthew 5:43-48—Virtue Love Commanded and Illustrated

1. Matthew 5:43

You have heard that it was said, 'You shall love your neighbor and hate your enemy.'

Jesus continued the dissertation following the same pattern as in previous verses with "You have heard that it was said…" referring to the teaching they had been receiving from the religious establishment. He then then quoted a part of Leviticus 19:18.

… you shall love your neighbor as yourself; I am the Lord. Leviticus 19:18b

The Hebrew word for love, AHAB (אהב) appears to be very general, not developed nearly to the degree of the Greek. The teachers of the day just taught the phrase about loving your neighbor, and then evidently inferred from that the opposite; that they should hate their enemies as well. There is no command for enemy hating in the Scripture! They also ignored the rest of the verse.

The word for love Matthew quoted or translated from what our Lord said, out of all of the Greek words translated as "love," was AGAPAO (ἀγαπάω).

Jim Oliver
You shall love your neighbor.
Ἀγαπήσεις τὸν πλησίον σου.

The exegete can parse the verb form as either the future tense, active voice, indicative mood or as a present tense, active voice, and imperative mood. Its use is evidently ambiguous. As a future, one can consider it as a deliberative future, which infers an expectation of completion of the action in the immediate future. The context, the use of the word, always defines it. In this case, we can infer that AGAPE refers to virtue love where the subject—the one doing the loving—produces the love because of personal virtue and integrity.

Our Lord's spiritual and physical death on the Cross serves as the ultimate expression of this virtue love. He died on the Cross, paying for the sins of the entire world because of His perfect love. No one in the human race has ever deserved what He did for each of us. Following His pattern, we should demonstrate this kind of love to everyone we meet. After all, who was the Samaritan's neighbor?

2. Matthew 5:44

But I say to you, love your enemies and pray for those who persecute you...

But love your enemies, and do good ... Luke 35a

Jesus continued by teaching an application from the original commandment, saying the formulaic: "But I say to you," EGO DE LEGO HUMIN (ἐγὼ δὲ λέγω ὑμῖν). Once again, our Lord has issued a command to each one of us that we are to obey without hesitation! He is our ultimate authority, continually communicating to us through His Word and Holy Spirit. His words are in direct contrast to what the Pharisees were teaching.

... love your enemies ...
... ἀγαπᾶτε τοὺς ἐχθροὺς ὑμῶν ...

Contrary to what the Pharisees were saying, He taught love for one's enemies. The command to love comes from the present active imperative of the verb AGAPAO (ἀγαπάω). He demonstrated this mandated love—virtue love—that we are to have for our enemies by His sacrificial life and work on the Cross.

There are many stories of how Americans demonstrated virtue love toward Japanese POWs during the Second World War resulting in many becoming evangelized and remaining in the United States. How do we demonstrate this love toward all those we meet? This involves two categories of dynamics in the Spirit-filled believer's life: both the negative and positive. The negative means that the believer will be free of any antagonism, hatred, and hostility toward his enemy. These emotional sins prevent the Spirit's work in the believer. In the extreme circumstance, for the soldier who must to kill his nation's enemies, this calls for objectivity and concentration upon his or her mission. The emotional soldier is liable to die in action. After the battle, virtue love calls for care for the wounded and when possible, evangelism. On the positive or aggressive side, virtue love calls for going out of one's way to be thoughtful toward everyone. It calls for presenting the Gospel even to those whom you do not think would respond. The Good Samaritan demonstrated virtue to love toward the fallen Israelite.

> *... and pray for those who persecute you,*
> *... καὶ προσεύχεσθε ὑπὲρ τῶν διωκόντων ὑμᾶς,*

Prayer is one demonstration of virtue love for enemies. The Greek word for prayer is PROSUECHOMAI (προσεύχομαι). Here it is in the imperative mood, a command. As indicated by the present tense, it should be an ongoing activity by the believer. When combined with an accurate presentation of the Gospel, prayer is the most effective tool of reconciliation possible. These are not to be imprecatory prayers but prayers of intercession, for their understanding of the Gospel. You cannot pray for one's salvation because God does not interfere with a person's volition. You can pray, however, that they come to an accurate understanding of the Gospel so that they can make a decision based upon fact instead of misinformation. If you encounter your enemy or persecutor, be ready for the Holy Spirit to use you to present the Gospel to them.

Every Church Age believer should be skillful prayer warriors, thoroughly understanding and applying it as a weapon unique to this Church Age. First believers should be cognizant of the effectiveness of prayer. Whenever a believer prays within the will of the Father, He will answer that prayer affirmatively and often powerfully! This is one reason believers need to have a complete knowledge of the Scripture. God reveals His will to us through the Scripture. Second, believers need to understand how the Spirit uniquely empowers prayers of spiritual Church Age believers. Third, believers need to understand the four stages of prayer, to pray in an organized and effective manner. These include:
1. Confession of sin to bring about lost spirituality,
2. Thanksgiving to express praise and gratitude toward the Father,
3. Intercession being prayer for others and finally,
4. Petition that is praying for one's own needs.

3. Matthew 5:45

> *... so that you may be sons of your Father who is in heaven; for He causes His sun to rise on the evil and the good, and sends rain on the righteous and the unrighteous.*
>
> *... and your reward will be great, and you will be sons of the Most High; for He Himself is kind to ungrateful and evil men. Luke 6:35d*

> *... so that you may be sons of your Father who is in heaven;*
> *... ὅπως γένησθε υἱοὶ τοῦ πατρὸς ὑμῶν τοῦ ἐν οὐρανοῖς,*

The next verse continues this sentence with the subordinating conjunction

HOPOS (ὅπως) which means, "in order that" or "so that" which leads us into the purpose of our expressing virtue love toward those antagonistic toward us. "You may be" is the aorist middle subjunctive of GINOMAI (γίνομαι), more accurately translated, "you might become." The difference between the NASB translation and the one suggested may seem like splitting hairs. We will discuss it in a minute. "Sons of the Father" translated from HUIOS (υἱός), PATER (πατήρ) HUMON (ὑμῶν) is accurate, but we must consider further explanation. The NASB also correctly translates, TOU EN OURONOS (του εν ουρανοις) literally translated, "who in heaven." This is a reference to God the Father, the Author of the plan for the human race.

Looking again at GINOMAI, the difference between "that you may be" and "that you may become," is twofold. The first translation infers that the hearers are not believers, but will be believers upon fulfillment of the previous verse. However, our Lord directed this to His disciples, who did believe in Him. Second, it implies that becoming a son of the Father" is instantaneous. One moment you are not a son of the Father, the next you are. Salvation—gaining the entire package—*is* instantaneous, but His disciples are already believers. Therefore, this sentence does not say that anyone will be a son of the Father immediately after loving his or her neighbor. To become a son of the Father—meaning faith in Christ—is not in view here. The translation, "becoming a son of Father" infers a process, the fulfillment of which is loving one's neighbor. Only one kind of believer can truly love his neighbor, an advanced one, who has progressed through spiritual childhood to spiritual adulthood.

What characterized a son at the time our Lord spoke these words? A son was one who took on the characteristics of his father. No blood relationship was necessary. In this case, when the believer has taken on the same thought structure of his Heavenly Father, he becomes a Son of his Father. That thought structure is virtue love.

> *... for He causes His sun to rise on the evil and the good, and sends rain on the righteous and the unrighteous.*
> ὅτι τὸν ἥλιον αὐτοῦ ἀνατέλλει ἐπὶ πονηροὺς καὶ ἀγαθοὺς καὶ βρέχει ἐπὶ δικαίους καὶ ἀδίκους.

The phrase that completes this sentence illustrates an application of virtue love that is unique to the Godhead. "The good" and "the righteous" represent believers while "the evil" and "the unrighteous" represent unbelievers. Not every unbeliever is necessarily evil; that is another study. Nor does every believer escape evil! By providing the benefits of the sun and rain for all people, whether or not they believe, illustrates virtue love. He provides survival necessities for those who believe and for those who do not. He provides these things for all because of His virtue and integrity, His divine virtue love. Furthermore, He provides these things, even for the evil, who are His enemies. Evil, as we have noted, is Satan's policy for overthrowing our Lord. The fact that our Lord characterizes the sun is as the Father's own possession further personalizes His provision. He personally provides both the sun's rays and rain, which He gives to all people.

Addressing the issue of virtue love again, it belongs uniquely to all three persons of the Godhead. Any virtue love the believer possesses and expresses is God's work. His Holy Spirit directly empowers spiritual believers allowing His love to work through them as they mature spiritually. Unbelievers can produce what appears to be virtue love but it is limited in scope and temporary. It is based upon God's provision for the entire human race, found in the Laws of Divine Establishment.

4. Matthew 5:46-47

In the next two verses, our Lord illustrates how virtue love far supersedes personal love. Only the believer who has matured to spiritual adulthood can fulfill this kind of love. Unbelievers, the unrighteous, immature believers, even the evil are limited to personal love. These verses also illustrate the lesson that the spiritual life of any dispensation is something that the unbeliever cannot fulfill. All believers must live lives that far supersede what unbelievers or carnal believers can accomplish. Believers are to live divinely empowered lives, lives that the unbeliever cannot live.

For if you love those who love you, what reward do you have? Do not even the tax collectors do the same? If you greet only your brothers, what more are you doing than others? Do not even the Gentiles do the same? Matthew 5:46-47

If you love those who love you, what credit is that to you? For even sinners love those who love them. If you do good to those who do good to you, what credit is that to you? For even sinners do the same. Luke 6:32-33

Any unbeliever can love back or respond to one who loves them. The vocabulary word for "love" is very important. The Greek source word is, as above, AGAPE. I would have thought that our Lord would have used PHILOS here, indicating rapport love or personal love, which PHILOS usually designates. Our Lord used AGAPAO that generally refers to virtue love. However, we must strongly consider the context when defining words. Context, the use of the word in the sentence, ultimately defines it. As we have noted above, human virtue love is limited to those empowered by the Holy Spirit and, to a limited degree, to those unbelievers living by the Laws of Divine Establishment. For that reason, we must define AGAPAO, in this context, as the kind of love available to the entire human race; primarily, personal love or love that depends upon rapport between people.

What is the point of these verses? God will not reward someone for loving back someone who loves you. Anyone can do this. If anyone can do this, then it is not the divinely empowered spiritual life. The unbeliever cannot live the supernaturally empowered life that our Lord calls every believer to live.

The Jews in Jesus day despised the tax collector because he worked for Rome and collected a surplus to fund his desired lifestyle. A tax collector was able to love in a human way, but, again, the love a believer is to express is a love that far supersedes what any low-life can! Are you able to love a low-life or anyone who does not fit your standards of friendship? God does command us to love these people, but not in the sense of affection. We are to love those who do not stand up to our standards of friendship and affection by treating them with virtue and integrity; the same kind of love our Lord had for us when He paid for our sins upon the Cross!

5. Matthew 5:48

Therefore you are to be perfect, as your heavenly Father is perfect.
Matthew 5:48

Therefore you are to be perfect,
Ἔσεσθε οὖν ὑμεῖς τέλειοι,

The final sentence in this paragraph begins with the postpositive conjunction, OUN (οὖν), translated as "therefore." In the Greek word order, it falls second, but it makes sense in the English to make it the first word. It forces us to draw a conclusion from what our Lord taught in the preceding verses. Starting with the verse in which our Lord began issuing corrective teaching, He admonished the disciples to stop following the Pharisees' teaching. In that light, we are to apply this verse

This word becomes very important to the translation, therefore, to the interpretation of this verse. The reason behind this importance lies in the apparent ambiguity of the next word's conjugation. The first word, in the Greek, translated in the NASB as "you are" comes from the verb of being, EIMI (εἰμί). Its conjugation is ambiguous so it makes for a fascinating study for the exegete! According to the Logos Greek, it is parsed as future middle indicative, second person plural. Its translation, in that case, should be "therefore, you-all will be" or "you will become." This would be a dogmatic statement of fact from the viewpoint of the writer, Holy Spirit-filled and inspired Matthew. According to the Friberg, it is a present active imperative, second person plural, translated as, "you-all be," as in a command. A good translation of Friberg's conjugation would be "therefore, you-all become something you are not now." We should understand this as a command. Different theologians and commentators take one translation or the other, and then run with it.

Though these two appear to be in conflict, actually, because of the Greek idiom, their meaning is the same. The future indicative, according to D. B. Wallace, "… is sometimes used for a command," especially when the concept is brought in from the Old Testament Hebrew.[xxxi] We would be on safer ground to say this dogmatically if this were a direct quote from the Old Testament; however, the New Testament repeatedly presents this truth. So, this is a command to believers to take on the thought structure of the Father, namely, virtue love.

The next word is SU (συ), the nominative plural 2nd person personal pronoun, translated "you-all." The Greek source word for "perfect" is the predicate adjective TELEIOS (τέλειος), better translated as "complete" or "mature." It modifies "you." The translation of this phrase, then, should read as, "Therefore, you-all become perfect, complete or mature…"

> *… as your heavenly Father is perfect.*
> *… ὡς ὁ πατὴρ ὑμῶν ὁ οὐράνιος τέλειός ἐστιν.*

The sentence continues with a comparison, indicating to us the measure or the goal of our maturity, completeness, or perfection. The NASB translation is quite clear! Our measure is ultimately God's level of perfection! These Old Testament verses make our Lord's mandate an echo of what the ancients heard and learned. These verses also partially justify our imperatival translation of the verb of being.

> *You shall be blameless before the Lord your God.*
> *Deuteronomy 18:13*

> *You shall be holy, for I the Lord your God am holy. Leviticus 19:2*

> *… it is written, "You shall be holy, for I am holy." 1 Peter 1:16*

The other justification lies in the "therefore" that begins the sentence. To this writer, it does not make sense to issue corrective advice then to make a prediction of the future, such as "you will be perfect, complete, or mature." One theologian interpreted this to be a prophecy of the Church Age. It is true that the Father sees Church Age believers as being complete, perfect, and mature due to our position in Christ. However, our Lord did not turn His attention to the present Church Age until Matthew 13. It makes much more sense that our Lord issue these corrective admonishments then command us to mature.

The word TELIOS needs some explanation. Though often translated as "perfect," no believer is going to be perfect and sinless in this lifetime. That status will await us in Heaven. We can become spiritually mature; however, becoming conformed to our Lord's thinking, living the life He has designed for us. We of the Church Age can strive, through the Spirit's empowerment, to fulfill our Lord's teaching in this section. We can apply virtue love to our marriages, not expecting perfection from our spouses, thereby protecting the marriage from disappoints, and disagreements that often lead to divorce. We can pray for our enemies and seek to evangelize them. We can help our fellow believer's needs because we understand that God has taken complete care of us. Love, always divinely empowered, should guide us in all of our human relationships. In this manner, we can be mature.

PART VI

A WARNING AGAINST PHARISAIC HYPOCRISIES
MATTHEW 6:1-18

In this collection of verses, Jesus teaches against the Pharisaic displays of so-called spirituality. The Pharisees were at the top of the religious hierarchy at that time, so were emulated by the general populace. Jesus, in the following verses, takes some of their practices and gives correctional admonishments.

A. Matthew 6:1—The Principle of the Warning

Beware of practicing your righteousness before men to be noticed by them; otherwise you have no reward with your Father who is in heaven.
Matthew 6:1

God has built a tremendous system of rewards and blessings, both temporal and eternal, into the life He has designed for us. There is nothing wrong with anticipating these blessings as being a motivation for living the spiritual life. What parent does not seek positively to motivate children by a system of rewards? Especially in spiritual childhood, God uses immediate rewards and blessings to motivate believers to pursue their spiritual lives. As one spiritually progresses, motivation must change from anticipation of rewards to love for God. If your love for the Father motivates you as He reveals Himself, then He becomes free to test you, leading to greater spiritual maturity and greater rewards. You can track your maturity level by noting what motivates you to pursue your spiritual life.

However, our Lord's rewards and blessings did not even motivate these Pharisees; they practiced their so-called spirituality in response to their approbation lust. They had created a system of works that they had designed for observation. They assumed these pleased God. The approbation of people who saw their displays of so-called righteousness motivated them. If you have no spirituality, then approbation lust will invariably motivate you, especially if this lust is one trend of your old sin nature. The Pharisees had set up at least three "acts of righteousness" which our Lord deals with in the following verses: alms giving or charity, prayer and fasting.

Beware of practicing your righteousness ...
Προσέχετε [δὲ] τὴν δικαιοσύνην ὑμῶν μὴ ποιεῖν ...

The verse begins with the verb, in the present active imperative, PROSECHO (προσέχω), which means, "to be alert to" to or "to consider carefully." As a progressive present, this verb indicates that this must be a continual action. You always need to be alert with a view to this warning from our Lord. It is in the imperative so consider it as a personal command from our Lord. Perhaps your spiritual gift does not place you in a position for people's praise, though often it might, unexpectedly. Pastors and evangelists are continually in front of people where they receive praise for a message well taught. They will even receive approbation for a message not well taught! Even those with gifts that do not usually find themselves in front of a mass of people need to pay attention to this command. A person with the gift of helps can receive accolades when delivering a meal! While undertaking any ministry, watch out! Let us see what we need to be heeding.

The second word is DE (δέ), the post-positive conjunction, translated as, "but." So far, we have then, "But take heed" or "But watch out ..." Next is the articular accusative singular noun, DIKIAOSUNE (δικαιοσύνη), translated, "righteousness." As articular, the definite article precedes it, emphasizing the quality of this righteousness. The righteousness you possess comes from God; therefore, it is of the highest quality. This is followed by the genitive second person personal pronoun, translated, "of you" or "your." Therefore, this is "But watch out ... your righteousness..." Righteousness, being in the accusative, has to be the object of a predicate. Next, we have a helping verb, that is, the present active infinitive of POIEO (ποιέω) preceded by the negative adverb or particle ME (μή). This is the verbal use of the infinitive. POIEO can be translated in a variety of ways, generally dealing with making or doing something. The negative adverb negates the infinitive it precedes. We can translate these words as, "But watch out not to do your righteousness..." We will smooth this out by saying "acts of righteousness" to fulfill the meaning of doing something from POIEO, something done because of your righteousness. You do not have to be in a position of Christian leadership to make application of this. Anytime you begin to get a bit fatheaded about activities you undertake which relate to your spiritual life, you need to heed this warning.

... before men to be noticed by them,
... ἔμπροσθεν τῶν ἀνθρώπων πρὸς τὸ θεαθῆναι αὐτοῖς,

The next three words are the preposition EMPROSTHEN (ἔμπροσθεν), and the articular genitive plural noun ANTHROPOS (ἄνθρωπος), translated, "in front of men." The preposition PROS (πρός) continues the sentence with the aorist active infinitive of THEAOMAI (θεάομαι). These words are translated, "in order to be seen ..." The next word is the personal pronoun, AUTOS (αὐτός) in the third person dative, translated, "by them." These words, then, are a prohibition against doing any activities that specifically relate to your spiritual life, such as a pastor teaching, an evangelist exhorting, a singer singing and so on, to be noticed by people. Love for God should always motivate you to do things related to your spiritual life. The activities will probably relate to your spiritual gifting. Even those with the gift of helps could slip into this because often that spiritual gift influences people very deeply. It is easy to be caught in the trap of being motivated by applause and approbation from others. We have all experienced it from one time or another and often we can be properly motivated this way early in life. Nevertheless, it is not to be the motivation for your spiritual life.

... otherwise you have no reward ...
... εἰ δὲ μή γε, μισθὸν οὐκ ἔχετε ...

The next phrase denotes the penalty of such a motivation. The phrase begins with the subordinating conjunction EI (εἰ), translated, "if" and contrastive conjunction DE (δέ), 'but," with two particles, the negative particle ME (μή), translated, "not" and the emphatic particle, GE (γέ). The NASB translated these four words, "if + but + not + an untranslated particle as "otherwise." We have already visited ME, the negative particle. A. T. Robertson, quoting others and writing originally, waxed extensively about emphatic particles, GE in particular. It would be difficult to express the role particles play in the Koine Greek because they can be difficult, if not impossible, to translate them into the English. They, GE included, were tools of subtle yet decisive expressions of emotion. Though the NASB translates these two particles as, "otherwise," consider this much more hard-hitting. We do not have an English equivalent to emphasize the strong contrast presented in this verse.

The next word denotes the normal object of performance, MISTHOS (μισθός), reward, recompense, or pay. This is an accusative singular noun, the object of a verb found a bit later in the sentence. The negative particle OU (οὐ) follows. Next, the present active indicative verb ECHO (ἔχω) follows. The present tense is the progressive present, the most common use of the present indicative. It indicates action in progress. Believers do, every day, go through the motions of their spiritual life to please people instead of to please God. The above noun is this verb's object. Together translated, "you have no" with the noun we looked at above, MISTHOS, reward. The message of this verse is clear. If approbation from people motivates you instead of love for God, then you absolutely will have no reward from God.

... with your Father who is in Heaven.
... παρὰ τῷ πατρὶ ὑμῶν τῷ ἐν τοῖς οὐρανοῖς.

The rest of this verse bears this out. The next words are the preposition

PARA (παρά) with the dative of PATER (πατήρ), and the second person personal pronoun SU (σύ) translated "from your Father." PARA is a preposition of source, so it can be translated as "from." The next words define which Father: the definite article HA (ὁ) with the preposition EN (ἐν). The dative plural masculine definitive article HA (ὁ) with the dative of URANAS (οὐρανός), heaven continues the verse. Those words mean, "… who is in Heaven." The first definite article serves as an emphasis, while the second, in the dative, sets this Heaven apart as being the highest quality. We can interpretively translate this verse as:

Keep on being aware of the dangers of practicing your righteousness before men to be noticed by them; otherwise, you definitely will have no reward from your Father who is in the Heaven.
Matthew 6:1

A question you may have after studying this verse is this: What rewards does the Father give to believers who are both properly motivated and spiritual when they produce *bona fide* spiritual works? We will discuss these rewards later.

A second issue in this phrase, "your Father who is in the Heaven," brings up the issue of differentiation of the members of the Godhead. It deals with the introduction of God the Father. Though a number of Old Testament verses refer to God as the Father of Israel, emphasizing the father-son relationship between Israel and God, that relationship was based upon our Lord as Creator, Provider, and Protector of Israel. The following references to God as Father refer to our Pre-Incarnate Lord, not the God the Father, as we understand Him in this dispensation. First, let us look at some Old Testament verses that refer to God as Father:

He will cry to Me, 'You are my Father, My God, and the Rock of my Salvation.' Psalm 89:26

For You are our Father, though Abraham does not know us and Israel does not recognize us. You, O Lord, are our Father, our Redeemer from of old is Your name. Isaiah 63:16

But now, O Lord, You are our Father, We are the clay, and You our potter; and all of us are the work of Your hand. Isaiah 64:8

So David blessed the Lord in the sight of all the assembly; and David said, "Blessed are You, O Lord God of Israel our father, forever and ever". 1 Chronicles 29:10

Our Lord's reference to "your Father who is in Heaven" is a new revelation. No longer did Father refer to our Lord as the God of Israel, Himself, as in the Old Testament, but to God the Father as Author of the Divine plan and chief authority of the Godhead. Here, our Lord differentiates Himself from the God the Father. He also brought attention to believer's intimacy with the Father previously reserved for the Son, as the God of Israel.

B. Matthew 6:2-4 —Application: Charity

So when you give to the poor, do not sound a trumpet before you, as the hypocrites do in the synagogues and in the streets, so that they may be honored by men. Truly I say to you, they have their reward in full. But when you give to the poor, do not let your left hand know what your right hand is doing, so that your giving will be in secret; and your Father who sees what is done in secret will reward you.

Jesus demonstrated in verse one the principle with an example of Pharisaic righteous acts: giving to the poor or needy, charity in other words. This was an appropriate example to give because giving to the needy or giving alms was an important part of the Jewish legalistic religious life. However, the Mosaic Law did not teach that charitable giving was separate from the system of taxation in the theocracy. Israel, as a theocracy, took care of the poor through an every third year tithe (10%) to the Temple. The Temple or governmental authorities then distributed the funds.

Charitable giving was included as a part of taxation. That tri-yearly tithe was collected and put into the Temple treasury. This is how the theocracy of Israel handled charitable giving. Evidently, begging was virtually unknown during periods when this system was in place. During this era, the system had failed so begging was rampant. The Pharisees, then, went beyond the requirements of the Law, which no one applied anyway and gave free-will gifts. "These were made known to the congregation in the synagogues and at fasting services on the open street. Those who gave very generously were allotted special places alongside the rabbis."[xxxii] " Many later forgot to pay the sums promised."[xxxiii]

As to application for the Church Age believer, there are both right ways and wrong ways to accomplish any spiritual life activity. Because giving is a part of every believer's spiritual life, if accomplished correctly, the Father rewards it. However, if given under false pretenses, then the giving becomes human good. This is never acceptable to Him. Categorically, for the Church Age believer, both spiritual status and motivation become issues in giving. A believer should be filled with the Holy Spirit and motivated by love for the Godhead. Paul also delineates other specifics as well. As we will see, the Pharisees were not giving for the correct reason.

1. Matthew 6:2

So whenever you give alms, do not sound a trumpet before you, as the hypocrites do in the synagogues and in the streets, so that they may be praised by others. Truly I tell you, they have received their reward.

ABIDING BY THE SERMON ON THE MOUNT
So whenever you give alms,
Ὅταν οὖν ποιῇς ἐλεημοσύνην,

In the Greek, verse two begins with the adverbial conjunction HOTAN (ὅταν) translated, "when." The next word, which appears in the English as the first word, is the logical inferential conjunction OUN (οὖν), translated, "therefore," or "so." The verse begins then with "Therefore, when…" drawing a conclusion from the preceding verse. The principle we need to bring forward concerns spiritual activities: Do not do them for human approbation.

The verb, modified by the above phrase, is POIEO (ποιέω) in the present active subjunctive. The root meaning of the word includes, "to do," "to make," "to act" and "to behave." The present tense is progressive meaning that the action is timeless, ongoing, or habitual, occurring in the present time from the perspective of the reader. The active voice means that the subject produces the action of the verb and the subjunctive presents contingent; you may or may not do this, but the possibility, even probability is there.

What is being done? The next word describes the activity: the accusative noun ELE'EMOSEN (ἐλεημοσύνη), acts of charity or "alms-giving." The TDNT delineates the history of the word, giving us a clear picture of the circumstances in which people gave alms. ELEOS is an "emotion aroused by contact with an affliction which comes undeservedly on someone else."[xxxiv] The word, emotion, is the key motivation to give charity in this context. Any time anyone gives, as either charity or spiritual giving, he or she should do so from one's thinking, not emotion. Always resist those who try to get into your back pocket, wallet, or bank account by emotion. This is not to say that every organization that tries to appeal to your emotion is a bad cause to support, but you need to scrutinize organizations to which you give. Late night television is full of ads that appeal to your emotions to give. Some ads feature forlorn felines photographed in slow motion to poor children in other countries. Do not give into your emotions. Always give according to your thinking!

The emotion that is aroused by the needy is said to be mercy. Yet true mercy is not related to emotions but to thought and understanding the plight of those in need as well as awareness of what you can do for them and how they respond to your generosity. Gauging your giving by the recipient's response may seem cold, but someone asking for food money, then heads directly to the nearest package store, violates your trust!

… do not sound a trumpet before you,
… μὴ σαλπίσῃς ἔμπροσθέν σου,

The next three words tell us how not to give. These words are the negative adverb ME (μή) with the verb, the aorist active subjunctive of SALPIZO (σαλπίζω), together meaning, "do not sound a trumpet." According to James

Broyer's writing, "the aorist imperative is used to command or request an action that is specific and occasional, dealing with everyday procedural decisions, or in general admonitions simply to say, "Do it.""ˣˣˣᵛ In this case, "don't do it," because of the negative ME. Original language students may question the use of the subjunctive mood, instead of the imperative mood, since it, to our ears better expresses a command. Evidently, the imperative mood is more recent in its formation; therefore, the subjunctive mood was used to express the imperative. We have much the same thing when we say, in the third person imperative, "let him do that." This also was Boyer's observation.

Next is the genitive preposition, EMPROSTHEN (ἔμπροσθεν), meaning, as before, "in front of" or "before," with the genitive personal pronoun, SU (σύ): "in front of you." We can interpretively translate this as, "Therefore, when you go about your charitable giving, don't sound a trumpet in front of you …"

To our ears, this sounds like hyperbole, for an extreme announcement preceding what you do. Nevertheless, through history, according to both Thieme and Robertson, we find that our Lord was not using hyperbole at all. This is what the Pharisees actually did when giving! They would have musical accompaniment when they clinked their money down on the table in the synagogue. Would they clink their money in time with the music? There would always be a crowd admiring the amount of money the Pharisees gave. Would this kind of attention make one drunk with lust for further approbation?

> *… as the hypocrites do in the synagogues and in the streets,*
> *… ὥσπερ οἱ ὑποκριταὶ ποιοῦσιν ἐν ταῖς συναγωγαῖς καὶ ἐν ταῖς ῥύμαις,*

With the next few words, our Lord tells us His "opinion" of them as well as where they would do this. His opinion is absolute truth! He called them HUPOKRITES (ὑποκριτής). Preceding this word is comparative adverb, HOSPER (ὥσπερ), translated, "just as." HUPOKRITES (ὑποκριτής), here articular because of the preceding definite article, is the Greek word for an actor, one who acts, not representing himself accurately. This word seems to have taken on its negative connotation, being defined as "pretender," in the Old Testament; perhaps in the Hebrew culture, it was always negative. The ancient Greeks, who revered drama, did not use the word negatively. However, our Lord did, criticizing the Pharisees with these terms. The next word is POIEO (ποιέω), in the present active indicative, translated "do." These words are translated, "just as the hypocrites do …"

These Pharisees were acting, in their own thinking, righteously. They thought that what they were doing demonstrated righteousness as a part of their spiritual life, pleasing God. However, what they did was evil, making an issue of themselves not of the Lord. In so doing they mislead the people terribly. Therein lies the evil. This was legalism because they were forcing their false standards as the key to righteousness upon the people. This legalism needed to be exposed because no one steeped in legalism can either enter the Father's plan by responding to the Gospel, or fulfill the Father's plan by growing up spiritually. A country living under enforced legalism cannot respond to our Lord's leadership—His goal being the ushering in of His Millennial rule.

When giving in this manner, the Pharisees could even compare their so-called righteousness with someone else's! Who gave more? Who received the greater approbation? Where did they do this? As the NASB translation says, "…in the synagogue and in the narrow street." They sought to show their good works everywhere, every time they had the opportunity!

So when you give to the poor, do not sound a trumpet before you, just as the hypocrites do in the synagogue and in the narrow street.

… so that they may be praised by others.
ὅπως δοξασθῶσιν ὑπὸ τῶν ἀνθρώπων.

The verse continues with a subordinating conjunction, HAPOS (ὅπως) which means, "so that." The word, DOXAZO (δοξάζω) in the aorist passive subjunctive third person plural meaning "they might receive praise or glorify" continues this subordinating purpose clause. The preposition HUPO (ὑπό) precedes the genitive plural masculine of ANTHROPOS (ἄνθρωπος), which means, "from people." This line clearly shows that the purpose behind this Pharisaic giving was to receive approbation from people. Their giving had nothing to do with spirituality at all.

So when you give to the poor, do not sound a trumpet before you just as the hypocrites do in the synagogue and in the narrow street so that they may receive glory from people.

Truly I tell you, they have received their reward.
ἀμὴν λέγω ὑμῖν, ἀπέχουσιν τὸν μισθὸν αὐτῶν.

This verse is wrapped up with a principle any person motivated by approbation needs to hear. It begins with a word our Lord used often to introduce principles He taught. By this word, we know that what He was about to say was undeniably divine truth. That word is AMEN (ἀμήν), a particle, which is most often translated as "truly." It is not Greek but a Hebrew loan word introduced into the language. Not being Greek, it is not subject to normal Greek parsing. It is also called a sentential word because it precedes a given sentence, influencing the entire sentence. The next two words are translated, "to you." These words are translated, "Truly I say to you…" This phrase introduces the following words as divine thought, a thought of supreme importance. Note that these Pharisees produced certain deeds of so-called righteousness, in front of people, yet expected rewards from God, thinking that their deeds fulfilled the spiritual life. What our Lord was about to say would have crushed a Pharisee who thought this way. Our Lord's next words were of the highest importance whenever He spoke, but these words, in this context really punctuated a contrasting, great doctrine.

> *... they have received their reward.*
> *... ἀπέχουσιν τὸν μισθὸν αὐτῶν.*

The next three words, APECHO (ἀπέχω) translated, "they receive in full," with MISTHOS (μισθός), "reward," and AUTOS (αὐτός), "their own." These words read as, "Truly I say to you, they have their reward in full." There is one very strong reason for this, being a consequence of their motivation for giving. Simply stated, these Pharisees were not living the spiritual life that the Father rewards. To carry this into the Church Age, for Him to reward a believer for any act of righteousness, he must be living the spiritual life the Father has designed. A Church Age believer must be in fellowship with the Holy Spirit, therefore, divinely empowered to produce acts of or the fruits of righteousness. To be giving to gain approbation is not a part of the Father's plan today, nor was it then.

2. Matthew 6:3

> *But when you give alms, do not let your left hand know what your right hand is doing,*

The next verse continues with our Lord's instruction for giving, how to give in such a way that it fulfills the Father's plan. Again, He presented a general principle here that contrasts with what the Pharisees were doing at that time. It also contrasts with what people through the ages have done and continue to do. His instruction does not present certain technicalities applicable to every dispensation, but presents a contrasting principle applicable to every dispensation. A technicality He does not present, for instance, applies to the necessity of being empowered by the Holy Spirit for the Church Age believer; however, the principle He does present is very applicable to this and every other dispensation.

> *But when you give alms,*
> *σοῦ δὲ ποιοῦντος ἐλεημοσύνην,*

The verse begins with the genitive second person personal pronoun, SU (σύ), translated "you." Because this pronoun begins the sentence, it is highly emphasized. You need to understand that the Lord is personally addressing you! We begin the English translation with this second word. It is the contrasting conjunction, DE (δέ), translated, "but" or "on the contrary." The implication here is obvious; whereas the Pharisees do that, you do this. The next two words are familiar to us: the present active participle POIEO (ποιέω) with the accusative noun ELE'EMOSEN (ἐλεημοσύνη) which forms an idiom for charitable giving. Translated these words read, "You, but when *you* give charitably..."

> *... do not let your left hand know what your right hand is doing ...*
> *... μὴ γνώτω ἡ ἀριστερά σου τί ποιεῖ ἡ δεξιά σου,*

The next words are the negative particle ME (μή) with the aorist active imperative of the verb GINOSKO (γινώσκω). This is the verb of knowledge or acknowledgment. As an imperative, this is a command, which when combined with the particle of prohibition, means that we should not acknowledge something. "You, when you give charitably do not acknowledge …"

The subject of the verb is the articular adjective ARISTEROS (ἀριστερός), literally, "left," referring to your left hand. The personal pronoun SU (σύ), translated, "your" follows: "You, when you give charitably, do not let your left hand know …" The verse continues, "…what your right hand is doing." This is hyperbole, just the opposite of making a grand announcement of your giving. Be subtle about it! There is some evidence that the phrase is idiomatic for, "Don't even let your best friend know about your giving." What is the issue? Do not give in such a way that you appease your desire for approbation, if that is one trend of your sin nature. Do not give into the temptation to show off your giving or any activity related to your spirituality!

3. Matthew 6:4

… so that your giving will be in secret; and your Father who sees what is done in secret will reward you.

The last verse in this paragraph continues the previous sentence and offers no exegetical or syntactical surprises. The entire paragraph, translated, reads this way:

So when you do your charitable giving, do not sound a trumpet before you, as the hypocrites do in the synagogues and in the narrow streets, so that they may be honored by men. Truly I say to you, they have their reward in full. But when you give to the poor, do not let your left hand know what your right hand is doing, so that your giving will be in secret; and your Father who sees what is done in secret will reward you.
Matthew 6:2-4

Principles:
1. The Pharisees, in one way or another, were giving charitably in a manner that all could see.
2. They were giving apart from the system our Lord had designed and presented in the Mosaic Law.
3. The system our Lord designed did not make an issue of the individual giver but all the money collected was gathered together for distribution among the poor.
4. These Pharisees had found a way to give in such a way that people could see them, give recognition then praise them for it.
5. The Pharisees did not give according to the spiritual life God had designed for them.
6. If your motivation for any activity considered spiritual is accomplished so that others can see how great you are, then you will have no spiritual reward because you are not fulfilling your spiritual life.
7. Your spiritual life includes your motivation as well as your actual

activity.

C. Matthew 6:5-13—Application: Prayer

When you pray, you are not to be like the hypocrites; for they love to stand and pray in the synagogues and on the street corners so that they may be seen by men. Truly I say to you, they have their reward in full. Matthew 6:5

But you, when you pray, go into your inner room, close your door and pray to your Father who is in secret, and your Father who sees what is done in secret will reward you. And when you are praying, do not use meaningless repetition as the Gentiles do, for they suppose that they will be heard for their many words. So do not be like them; for your Father knows what you need before you ask Him.
Matthew 6:6-8

Pray, then, in this way: 'Our Father who is in heaven, Hallowed be Your name. Your kingdom come. Your will be done, on earth as it is in heaven. Give us this day our daily bread. And forgive us our debts, as we also have forgiven our debtors. And do not lead us into temptation, but deliver us from evil. [For Yours is the kingdom and the power and the glory forever. Amen.]'. Matthew 6:9-13

In this passage, our Lord illustrated the principle previously stated with another function of the Pharisaic spiritual life: prayer. In contrast to the last application, that of charity, prayer is most definitely a *bona fide* function of the spiritual life of every generation. Two issues are in focus here. First, the method of praying displayed by the Pharisees was false; therefore, enforcement of it as the spiritual life became legalism. Secondly, any prayer offered under the Pharisaic modus operandi was not at all effective. Nevertheless, there is a right way and a wrong way to pray. Just as in the last passage, our Lord applies the previously covered principle but does not get into specifics of prayer for each dispensation. Any specifics garnered from this passage had direct application to His disciples who were being prepared to go out into Israel to offer the Jews the Millennial Kingdom.

An outline of this passage is appropriate because it is complex and includes a misunderstood but important prayer.
1. The Wrong Way to Pray
2. The Right Way to Pray
3. A Sample Prayer

1. Matthew 6:5—The Wrong Way to Pray

When you pray, you are not to be like the hypocrites; for they love to stand and pray in the synagogues and on the street corners so that they may be seen by men. Truly I say to you, they have their reward in full.

ABIDING BY THE SERMON ON THE MOUNT
Matthew 6:5

Our Lord continued the sermon by setting people straight about another Pharisaic error, error promulgated into legalism. In the last series of verses, Jesus addressed one of the three main activities the Pharisees considered the most important to demonstrate their spirituality. They emphasized that which they could be observed fulfilling. Being observed become their sole motivation for the activities they accomplished. The previous passage dealt with charitable giving. This passage deals with prayer.

When you pray
Καὶ ὅταν προσεύχησθε,

The verse begins with three words, the conjunction KAI (καί), the adverbial subordinating conjunction OTAN (ὅταν), with the present middle or passive subjunctive second person plural verb PROSEUCHOMAI (προσεύχομαι), translated, "and when you pray..." Because of this verb's form, being considered deponent, we consider it a present tense. In this case, it is a progressive present because it refers to an action considered as being one in continual progress. In other words, every believer, the "you" here, should make prayer a habitual action. The subjunctive mood is one of contingency. Maybe you will pray, maybe you will not. There is a further contingency: will the prayers you offer be effective? To personalize this into our Church Age, the question of prayer effectiveness lies in understanding and applying the proper protocol for prayer. For the disciples, our Lord delineates prayer protocol later in this passage.

The next few words, with the previous three translate as, "And when you pray, don't be like the hypocrites ..." The hypocrites our Lord referred to are the Pharisees. They put on a religious, pseudo-sanctified front to impress others. They were misleading the populace, so our Lord's goal was to correct the misinterpretation of the proper use of prayer for both the disciples and others who heard.

... for they love to stand and pray in the synagogues and on the street corners so that they may be seen by men.
... ὅτι φιλοῦσιν ἐν ταῖς συναγωγαῖς καὶ ἐν ταῖς γωνίαις τῶν πλατειῶν ἑστῶτες προσεύχεσθαι,

The next words, "for they love..." Love is PHILEO (φιλέω). It does not refer to virtue love but love based upon attraction or appeal. Even those without virtue can love this way. The implication from this love is that the Pharisees take great pleasure in doing this. The progressive present again implies that they continually take pleasure from this activity. With the next few words: "for they love, in the synagogues and on the street corner, to stand and pray that they may be seen by men." The word, "to stand" comes from the perfect active participle from HISTEMI (ἵστημι). As a participle, it can be either verbal or adjectival. Either way, in this case, it means the same thing. Either they love "to stand," or they love "standing." The use of this participle as a perfect is unusual, but there is no significance to that. However, according to the Pharisees, "Obligatory prayer had to be offered up in the synagogue or wherever one was. The Rabbis gave detailed directions as to the proper demeanor in public prayer."[xxxvi] The Pharisees our Lord referred to in this verse would purposely "find" themselves on the street at prayer time in order to parade their piety.[xxxvii] Was this their thinking? "Oops! Is it time to pray? I did not really mean to be in the street. All of these people, they'll be looking at me!"

Truly I say to you, they have their reward in full.
ἀμὴν λέγω ὑμῖν, ἀπέχουσιν τὸν μισθὸν αὐτῶν.

Our Lord continued with "Truly I say to you, they have their reward in full." We have already discussed the importance of "truly" as introducing divine thought, dogmatic doctrine. The word translated, "they have in full..." is the Greek word, APECHO (ἀπέχω). It is a business term, referring to receiving receipts. It is not a reward per se but due payment for services rendered or products sold. Our Lord used this business term because what the Pharisees produced was works for which they received their due payment. There is no grace in this. Their payment was approbation received, not grace rewards for fulfilling the Father's plan. The Father's bases His relationship to us upon grace, not upon our work.

When you pray, you are not to be like the hypocrites; for they love to stand and pray in the synagogues and on the street corners so that they may be seen by men. Truly I say to you, they have their payment in full.
Matthew 6:5

2. Matthew 6:6-8—The Right Way to Pray

But you, when you pray, go into your inner room, close your door and pray to your Father who is in secret, and your Father who sees what is done in secret will reward you. And when you are praying, do not use meaningless repetition as the Gentiles do, for they suppose that they will be heard for their many words. So do not be like them; for your Father knows what you need before you ask Him.
Matthew 6:6-8

a. Matthew 6:6

But you, when you pray, go into your inner room, close your door and pray to your Father who is in secret, and your Father who sees what is done in secret will reward you.

But you, when you pray,
σὺ δὲ ὅταν προσεύχῃ,

With the first two words in this passage, our Lord first emphasizes the strong contrast between Pharisaic prayer practices and His correct instruction. Secondly, He strongly emphasizes believers' prayer practices. Visualize Him looking askance at a Pharisee praying loudly, in a showy manner, but then turns His attention to them with a direct concentrated look. Those words, SU (σύ), the second personal pronoun in the nominative case with DE (δέ), the postpositive, contrastive conjunction, translate as, "but you."

The next two words, "when you pray," consist of HOTAN (ὅταν), "a temporal conjunction used to show indefinite time for repeated or contingent action"[xxxviii] and the verb, PROSEUCHOMAI (προσεύχομαι), in the present middle subjunctive second person, translate as, "when you pray." The present tense presents the action of prayer as occurring in the present time but without a definite end. Your praying should be on going then. The subjunctive mood presents prayer as being a probable action. As a growing believer, in contrast to the Pharisees, you most likely will pray.

... go into your inner room close your door ...
... εἴσελθε εἰς τὸ ταμεῖόν σου καὶ κλείσας τὴν θύραν σου ...

So, what are we to do when we pray, which is different from what the Pharisees do? The next word the aorist active imperative of EISERCHOMAI (εἰσέρχομαι), means "to go." When combined with the preposition EIS (εἰς) the two words are translated, "go into." As an imperative, it is an order, a command from our Lord. You are to go into your TAMEION (ταμεῖον), your private room, then close your door behind you. This is a picture of praying in private in contrast to the public prayers offered by the Pharisees. What a contrast to what these Pharisees were teaching and doing by example.

... and pray to your Father who is in secret ...
... καὶ πρόσευξαι τῷ πατρί σου τῷ ἐν τῷ κρυπτῷ ...

This phrase begins with the conjunction KAI (καὶ) followed by the verb in the aorist middle imperative PROSEUCHOMAI (προσεύχομαι), translated "and pray." As an imperative, this is a command from the Lord of the Universe! We are to pray to God the Father, PATER SU (πατήρ σύ). All prayers, from this time, were to be offered to the Father.

This was a big change on so many levels. First, to whom did the Old Testament saints pray? They prayed to the Lord, the God of Israel, who was Christ before the Incarnation, not to the Father. At that time, because our Lord was walking the Earth, they were not to pray to Him. In this Church Age, our Lord has been resurrected, ascended, and seated next to the Father, He intercedes for us, and so we pray to the Father through Him. This in itself was a big change to those Jews. Second, addressing the God of the universe as Father denotes a new relationship. God was now addressed as Father, as the Head of the divine family. Never before was God the Father so close to every believer! The phrase continues with a description of the Father's visibility. Because of the Father's invisibility, believer's prayers can stay private.

> *... and your Father who sees what is done in secret ...*
> *... καὶ ὁ πατήρ σου ὁ βλέπων ἐν τῷ κρυπτῷ ...*

He hears believer's prayers even though they pray privately; no need for flowery public prayers! What counts in prayer is praying correctly and faith. Our Heavenly Father hears the prayers we pray privately. We know He hears them because of our faith in His care and provision for us. Though He often answers our prayers dramatically, often only the believer-recipient and the Father need know about the prayer and His answer.

> *... will reward you.*
> *... ἀποδώσει σοι.*

Our Lord addressed the issue of reward as well. The word "reward" is from the Greek word APODIDOMI (ἀποδίδωμι). That is what the Pharisees thought it was all about. As we have studied earlier, certainly, anticipation of rewards is a *bona fide* motivation, but it must change as the believer grows. Motivation should develop from an emphasis on reward to love for God. The Pharisees were stuck on the reward factor because they were not even beginning to grow. Also, by praying aloud being seen by all also inferred that God needs prayers to be visible, aloud and verbal in order to be recognized then answered. Jesus put the kibosh on that thought as well.

The key word here is "secret," KRUPTOS (κρυπτός), the dative singular adjective. You pray in secret; the prayer should be a private matter between you and God the Father, apart from any distraction or any false motivation such as approbation lust. That prayer will be effective, according to our Lord, when He said, "your Father who sees what is done in secret will reward you." When you pray according to procedure, God will reward you. Further, omniscient God, does not need prayer to be announced to be effective. We need to pray procedurally correctly in order to be effective.

b. Matthew 6:7

> **When you are praying, do not heap up empty phrases as the Gentiles do; for they think that they will be heard because of their many words.**

In the next verse, our Lord distinguishes between a common Gentile prayer practice, which the Pharisees emulated and proper prayer procedure: "do not use meaningless repetition as the Gentiles do." History records countless examples of prayers offered in a flowery and verbose manner, as if God responds to these things, obligating Him to answer. The issue is always prayer protocol. You must pray in the right manner, following the correct procedure, being properly motivated for God to hear prayers. The closer your prayers are to His will, the more likely He will answer your prayer positively. As a child in Japan, I remember hearing prayers offered in Japanese temples that sounded like repeated chants. Obviously, in that situation, God does not ever hear or answer. However, the sound illustrates this concept. God does not hear prayer because of flowery and verbose repetition.

c. Matthew 6:8

Do not be like them, for your Father knows what you need before you ask him.

This next verse relates God's omniscience to answering your prayers and petitions: "for your Father knows what you need before you ask Him." God the Father has always known about your concerns and needs because He is outside of time and space. He knows simultaneously the past, present and future. He is not on a timeline the way we are. Not only is He omniscient, knowing everything about you, but also omnipotent, having the ability to answer every prayer you offer to Him. Three important doctrines to master about prayer include the Doctrine of the Divine Decree, Doctrine of Prayer, and Doctrine of Logistical Grace.

3. Matthew 6:9-13—The Disciples' Prayer

This next series of verse, popularly known as "The Lord's Prayer," is probably the best-known series of verses in the Bible. However, just because it is well known does not mean that everyone correctly understands it. In order to understand this prayer, we need to remember that its context gives us a foundation for understanding it. Our Lord gave this prayer to the disciples during His walk on Earth, a unique era in history. The question we need generally to answer is this: were these words our Lord spoke designed to cover all dispensations or were they specific to one?

a. Matthew 6:9

Pray, then, in this way: 'Our Father who is in heaven, hallowed be Your name.

Pray, then, in this way,
Οὕτως οὖν προσεύχεσθε ὑμεῖς,

Following the Greek word order, HOUTOS (οὕτως), an adverb, translated, "in this manner" is the first word. The second, the conjunction OUN (οὖν), translated, "therefore" draws a conclusion from the previous instruction. The previous adverb modifies the next word, the second person verb in the present middle imperative, PROSEUCHOMAI (προσεύχομαι), translated, "you pray." It is a compound word made up of PROS (πρός), with a core meaning of "to," and EUCHOMAI (εὔχομαι) meaning "to desire something, with the implication of a pious wish."[xxxix] As an imperative, it is a command to pray, modified by the previous adverb, so, the translation is this: "Therefore you pray in this manner..."

Note that it is not an order to pray using the exact words as presented, but is a pattern for prayer. So, why do many churches quote it verbatim? This is meant to be a rhetorical question, but I imagine it stems from the desire to bring ritual of the previous dispensation over into this Church Age. We in the Church Age need to be careful not to bring unauthorized ritual into our worship. Ours is a dispensation of applying divine power through thought, not ritual. To the degree that ritual was *bona fide* during the Age of Israel, to that degree, it is not authorized today. The only authorized ritual for this dispensation, the Church Age, is the Eucharist or Lord's Table.

There are two reasons that the rituals of the previous dispensation have been archived and not brought into this Age. The first relates to the completion of our Lord's work. The rituals pointed to our Lord's work. Having been completed, we no longer go through the rituals that looked forward to His first incarnation. The second reason deals with the filling of God the Holy Spirit. He fulfills a function of spiritual teaching which was unavailable to those in earlier dispensations. Because He personally teaches and causes recall of those things for the spiritual believer, we no longer require the rituals prescribed by the Mosaic Law.

The next word, the last in this phrase, is the nominative second person personal pronoun, SU (σύ), translated, "you." As the nominative, it serves as the subject of the sentence. In the Greek, exegetes understand it as a part of the verb tense as well, so it serves to be emphatic: "You pray, then, in this manner…"

This pattern for prayer includes principles of prayer for all dispensations but also includes some petitions specific to our Lord's dispensation. We will discover them as we move through our word-by-word study.

Our Father who is in Heaven …
Πάτερ ἡμῶν ὁ ἐν τοῖς οὐρανοῖς …

These next words define the first rule of prayer for every dispensation since the incarnation of our Lord: the vocative noun PATER (πατήρ), "father," with the first person plural personal pronoun EGO (ἐγώ), "our," with the HO (ὁ) EN (ἐν) HO (ὁ) with the locative of OURANOS (οὐρανός), translated, "who in Heaven." We had noted earlier that the Jews had been praying to our pre-incarnate Lord, directly, which was appropriate. Now that He was in hypostatic union, this was no longer appropriate. All prayers were to be addressed to the Father, as of that time. Therefore, this is a principle that applies to all dispensations from that time: all prayers are to be directed to the Father. If you pray to the Son, or to the Holy Spirit, or even to Mary, as some do, you will not be following *bona fide* prayer protocol; your prayer will not be heard. We pray to the Father because we are in Christ and He intercedes for us as our High Priest. The disciples, though not in Christ until the Day of Pentecost, still prayed to the Father because the God of Israel to whom they did pray was now God Incarnate.

The word, "our" carries much importance. It denotes not only believers' individual closeness but also an intimate familial relationship with the Father. The recognition that He is the Father of all believers makes us all related to each other as well as intimate with Him.

At this point in our study, it would be appropriate to do an extended study on Heaven. The history of this term, as the abode of God, is extensive. Suffice it to say now, that it is a locale that is outside of space and time, outside of our ability to comprehend. Where in Heaven believers live now we do not know, though we know that physical death brings us to a place "face to face" with our Lord. This also distinguishes our Heavenly Father from our earthly fathers, yet implies His direct authority over us, demanding our greatest respect to Him and greatest awe toward Him.

> *... hallowed be Your name.*
> *... ἁγιασθήτω τὸ ὄνομά σου*

The phrase directs us to another issue in prayer protocol: "hallowed be Your name..." Hallowed is the aorist passive imperative third person singular form of HAGIAZO (ἁγιάζω). This verb should very familiar to you if you have studied the Doctrine of Sanctification. The basic concept is separation, being set apart from all others as holy. It directs us to the concept of reverence toward the Father. It carries with it the first aspect of worship: utmost awe and respect. There is a mechanic related to these concepts. To hallow the Father's name is not an emotional operation but one of thought and soul preparation. Looking closely at this verb, we see that it is an imperative—meaning that we are all commanded to fulfill it or to embrace the concept. This part of prayer crosses all dispensations. God's ONOMA (ὄνομα), name, or person must be, according to this directive, sanctified or set apart. Not only is HAGIAZO in the imperative, mandating that we must set God's person apart, but also in the passive voice, meaning that He must receive the action. The aorist tense means that this must occur at the time you pray. According to Thieme, this is an idiom, which we, as Church Age believers, fulfill every time we name our sins to the Father, resuming fellowship with Him after we sin. This mechanic, according to 1 John 1:9, allows the Father to forgive us "our sin and cleanse us from all unrighteousness." The Old Testament also required that the believer be cleansed from sin.

> *If I regard wickedness in my heart, the Lord will not hear; Psalm 66:18*

Luke repeated this instruction:

> *And He said to them, "When you pray, say: 'Father, hallowed be Your name." Luke 11:2a*

The instruction is the same in both verses except, "pray in this manner" in the Luke verse, he very clearly states, "when you pray, say..." which implies using the exact words. We cannot misunderstand the word for "say," the present active imperative of the verb LEGO (λέγω)! However, as noted by Jamieson, Robert, and Fausset, there is no record in any subsequent part of the New Testament where this prayer is quoted verbatim, as a ritual. We, as Church Age believers, need to understand it in order to apply the truths within it, but we do not make quoting its words in any translation a worship ritual.

b. Matthew 6:10

> '*Your kingdom come. Your will be done, on earth as it is in heaven.*
> *Matthew 6:10*
>
> *Your kingdom come. Luke 11:2b*

Your kingdom come.
ἐλθέτω ἡ βασιλεία σου·

The first word in Matthew 6:10 is the aorist active imperative from the verb ERCHOMAI (ἔρχομαι), translated, "come." As an aorist tense, it is timeless, therefore, the expression of a principle not limited by time. As an imperative, it is a command that this activity should occur. The next word is "kingdom," from the articular nominative singular noun, BASILEA (βασιλεία). The preceding definite article qualitatively particularizes this kingdom as being of the highest quality. This is followed by the personal pronoun SU (σύ), in the second personal plural. These words translate as, "Your Kingdom come." An imperative in this situation is hard to translate accurately. The kingdom is commanded to come!

The first question we need to answer is "What Kingdom?" We know from the context that the kingdom belongs to God the Father. We also know that the immediate context of this prayer was early in Jesus' ministry when His focus was on Israel to offer her the earthly kingdom which had been promised Abraham. One interpretation states that this kingdom is the Millennial Kingdom when our Lord will personally rule the world from Jerusalem. The earth will be characterized by perfect environment and perfect justice from our Lord's rule. This possibly is the Kingdom that is commanded to come. This also fits in with the fact that the Father has delegated all authority to the Son.

> *And Jesus came up and spoke to them, saying, "All authority has been given to Me in heaven and on earth." Matthew 28:18*

This introduces an advanced confidence we are allowed or expected to have because of our spiritual growth. As you develop confidence in God and His plan, you can correctly expect, with confidence, His provision. For instance, you know that God will bless you within the context of His plan for your life, so that you can pray with confidence for those blessings. As you mature, you can gain confidence in the principle of blessing by association, so that you can pray for those in your purview knowing that God will bring blessing to those within it.

The question arises, then, can we pray for God to usher in the Millennium, His Kingdom, now? The disciples could because our Lord wanted to usher in His Millennial Rule at that time. Israel only had to accept Him as her Messiah. Therefore, it was a valid prayer for them. However, we cannot pray for that. The next item on the historical agenda for the Church Age is her exit resurrection, the Rapture. Sometime after that, the completion of the Age of Israel will come about during the seven years of Tribulation. Those going through the Tribulation will certainly be encouraged to pray this! Finally, our Lord will usher in His 1000-year rule. Therefore, the prayer for the arrival of the Millennium was valid for the disciples as well as for the saints of the Tribulation, but not necessarily for us.

Having said that, one problem plagues the above analysis. Even though, if taken literally, that we should not pray for the Father's Kingdom to arrive now, we need to look at prayer in terms of general principle. Otherwise, we fall into the trap of quoting these words as a ritual, without much thought for the principle behind the arrival of the Father's Kingdom. So, we ask again, what characteristics does the Father's Kingdom entail? If such a kingdom exists that can be ushered in now, what characterizes it? If it were to exist now, what would it be like?

First, the Father is the author and ultimate authority of that plan, the fulfillment being His kingdom. What, then, characterizes the Father's kingdom is adherence to His plan and authority. When you pray for the Father's kingdom to arrive, you are praying for, in this dispensation, pastors to be teaching their congregations accurate and applicable doctrines for their parishioner's spiritual growth. In only this way can the general populace adhere to the Father's plan. When people grow in grace and in knowledge of our Lord and Savior Jesus Christ, a vacuum is established which must be filled with divine blessing. Wherever capacity for divine blessing exists, God the Father, because He is just, blesses. So, you are praying for the establishment of local churches to serve local communities that they may fulfill their role in enriching the community. The list goes on. What does it take a given community to fulfill the Father's plan? That is for what you are praying. You always start with a community. You add up enough communities and you have a nation, one that fulfills the Father's plan, adhering to His authority.

As an aside here, some churches encourage us to pray for our Lord to resurrect the Church. Is there a believer alive who does not want to be raptured up into our Lord's arms, receive a resurrection body, and live with Him forever? We know that the Church can be resurrected at any moment, though He may tarry, adding many more souls to His bride! As an opinion, I do not think praying for Him to resurrect us will change the Father's perfect timing for that occasion.

The next sentence gives us a condition that also characterizes the Father's kingdom.

Your will be done,
γενηθήτω τὸ θέλημά σου,

This verse continues with the third imperative, which indicates another petition or in this case, an extension of the previous one, the aorist passive imperative, third person singular of GINOMAI (γίνομαι), translated "to become." As an imperative, it is a command for a status to be realized. As a passive, the next word designates whom or what receives the action, but does not tell us who or what produces the action. Therefore, this status needs to be realized.

The phrase continues with the noun THELEMA (θέλημα), translated "will" or "desire," with the genitive second person personal pronoun SU (σύ), "your." This sentence is correctly translated as, "Your will be done." We can be confident that God's will or His decree will be fulfilled in every aspect. It is being played out now as evidenced in the outpouring of greater grace in this Dispensation of Grace. Had Israel responded to our Lord's invitation, perhaps He would have already ushered in His Millennial rule. But she did not, so God extended greater grace to the world and ushered in the Church Age. Ultimately, the Divine Decree describes and designates the Father's will. The status that must be realized is that will or desire, characterized as the Father's will. Therefore, your prayer here is for the fulfillment of the Divine Decree.

> *... on earth as it is in heaven.*
> *... ὡς ἐν οὐρανῷ καὶ ἐπὶ γῆς.*

The verse continues with the phrase, "on earth as it is in Heaven." At this present time, in the envelope of time and space, the Father is carrying out His decree. The angelic war is being played out, to be concluded with the defeat of Satan and his fallen angels. Do we long for the completion of this conflict? Do we yearn to be released from this time of evil on the earth? Absolutely! Do we echo David's sentiments? Absolutely!

> *O let the evil of the wicked come to an end, but establish the righteous; for the righteous God tries the hearts and minds. Psalm 7:9*

> *And blessed be His glorious name forever; and may the whole earth be filled with His glory. Amen, and Amen. Psalm 72:19*

In summation, then, in order to understand this prayer the Church Age believer needs to understand the aspects of God's Kingdom. The one aspect, applicable to Church Age believers, deals with acceptance of His authority. For the Church Age believer to pray this, he must understand that he is praying that unbelievers accept the authority of the Holy Spirit and believe that Jesus Christ is the Son of God. He is also praying that pastors will teach the Bible accurately so that their congregations can grow up spiritually. He is also praying that believers will understand accurate Bible teaching so that they can believe it, apply it and grow up spiritually. If believers apply the Word in this Church Age, the Father will bring prosperity through blessing.

Can the Church Age believer pray that God resurrect the Church sooner instead of later? Can we pray for our Lord meet us in the air, sooner instead of later? This writer does not think that the Father will answer that prayer positively. If He does, it will set the Rapture and Tribulation into motion, not bring in the Son's perfect rule for several more years. We do not know how many generations of believers the Father desires to offer the glories of the Church Age to! Why would we pray for Him to shorten the Church Age just to deliver us from our current sufferings? He has provided every spiritual asset for us to prosper, no matter how bad things look!

c. Matthew 6:11

Give us this day our daily bread.

Give us each day our daily bread. Luke 11:3

Give us this day our daily bread.
Τὸν ἄρτον ἡμῶν τὸν ἐπιούσιον δὸς ἡμῖν σήμερον.

This next petition is for our temporal needs. It begins with the articular singular accusative noun, ARTOS (ἄρτος), translated, "bread." It can refer literally to a loaf or also, more symbolically, to those things we need to survive on a daily basis. What we eat is just one category of those things. The first person plural personal pronoun, EGO (ἐγώ) in the genitive, meaning "our," follows. So far then, our translation is "our bread." The articular noun EPIOUSIOS (ἐπιούσιος) follows, which refers to those things necessary on a daily basis for our survival. We could call it a daily ration of whatever we need. One connotation possibly refers to what we need tomorrow. We pray today for tomorrow's sustenance, with the confidence that God will provide what we need on a day-by-day basis. The grammatical argument for that implication is not strong, but the next word includes the concept of repeated action, which includes today, tomorrow and the next day.

The next word is the aorist active imperative verb DIDOMI (δίδωμι) with the dative plural personal pronoun, EGO (ἐγώ). Because this is an aorist, it does not implicitly refer to any set time. This imperative mood with the personal pronoun translates as a command, "give us." Luke uses this same verb, but uses the present imperative instead of the aorist. The iterative present presents the action as being repetitive and ongoing. It is interesting that the mood of this verb, the imperative, usually referring to giving a gift, is in the imperative. However, by the prayer, we are not demanding the gift of daily sustenance, but acknowledging, as an expression of faith, that He will so provide for us. This fact is the subject of the Doctrine of Logistical Grace that appears many times in both the Old and New Testaments.

The eternal God is thy refuge, and underneath are the everlasting arms. Deuteronomy 33:27

I have been young but now I am old; yet I have never seen the righteous forsaken nor His seed begging bread. Psalm 37:25

My God shall supply all your needs according to His riches in glory in Christ Jesus. Philippians 4:19

And we know that God causes all things to work together for good to

those who love God, to those who are called according to His purpose.
Romans 8:28

Another possible reason for Luke's use of the present imperative is that it serves as a lead-in for our Lord's illustration about requesting something persistently (Luke 11:5-8), which is applicable to prayer. Even though God has promised us sustenance through logistical grace, many commentators note that He allows us to pray for these things, even persistently.

And he said to them, "Suppose one of you has a friend, and you go to him at midnight and say to him, 'Friend, lend me three loaves of bread; for a friend of mine has arrived, and I have nothing to set before him.' And he answers from within, 'Do not bother me; the door has already been locked, and my children are with me in bed; I cannot get up and give you anything.' I tell you, even though he will not get up and give him anything because he is his friend, at least because of his persistence he will get up and give him whatever he needs. Luke 11:5-8

d. Matthew 6:12

And forgive us our debts, as we also have forgiven our debtors.

And forgive us our sins, for we ourselves also forgive everyone who is indebted to us ... Luke 11:4

And forgive us our debts ...
καὶ ἄφες ἡμῖν τὰ ὀφειλήματα ἡμῶν,

Three key words in this verse are "forgive," the Greek root word being APHIEMI (ἀφίημι), used twice; "debts," the Greek being OPHEILEMA (ὀφείλημα), also used twice and "as," the Greek word, HOS (ὡς). Each of these is significant to the interpretation of this verse. We will look at the lesson as it appears in Matthew, then compare it to Luke's quote as it helps us to determine a meaning for some of these words.

"Forgive" is the aorist active imperative of the verb APHIEMI (ἀφίημι), meaning "send away," or "to cancel a debt." As an aorist imperative, because it is not in the indicative mood, the action of the verb does not relate to time at all. Because of the prayer context, we can expand its meaning to be "continually be forgiving." As the in the last verb, this is an imperative, expressing a command toward the Father to whom we offer this prayer. This is a grace word. It does not include any connotation of working off a debt. To the ancient Greeks it meant to release from a legal obligation. In contrast to this Greek use is that of the Hebrews. To the Hebrews, God is the one who releases one from the debt. In the Septuagint, it carried the concept of remission or and release from sin guilt.

The word "debt," in the Greek, OPHEILEMA (ὀφείλημα) is important as well. It does not refer only to owing money but also in some circumstances, to one specific debt, sin. This refers to the debt we owe God; we can never repay or atone. This theme is sin then, because the debt concept contained in both words, forgive and debt, is sin. Considered a parallel passage, Luke wrote, "And forgive us our sins…" instead of "forgive us our debt" which makes us consider from the context that Matthew is referring to our sin debt to God. This brings us back to the original context, not doing what the Pharisees did. The Pharisees believed in working off their debt to God, as if it were possible, in the form of good works instead of accepting God's grace.

So, having narrowed down the meaning of debts in this verse as sin, the question comes up: do believers ever have to pray to the Father for the forgiveness of sins? Many commentators note that the solution for our post-salvation sins is to name the sin or sins to the Father. This is true for both the Old and New Testaments. What is the point of asking the Father to forgive our sins when our Lord died, paying the price for them on the Cross, then adding to that the mechanic of naming our sins to Him for forgiveness? However, one writer, Clifford Rapp, Jr., in Chafer Theological Seminary Journal, Volume 5, noted some passages that teach us to pray for things for which He has have already provided. In John 14:27, our Lord is quoted as leaving peace with us. However, Paul in Philippians 4:6-7, tells us to pray for this peace.[xl]

… as we also have forgiven our debtors.
… ὡς καὶ ἡμεῖς ἀφήκαμεν τοῖς ὀφειλέταις ἡμῶν

The next phrase introduces a condition under which the first phrase is to be fulfilled. It begins with HOS (ὡς) KAI (καί) meaning "also as" or "just as" making a comparison with the previous phrase. The phrase continues with the same verb as above, APHEIMI (ἀφίημι) only here, it is an aorist active indicative. This aorist indicates that this verb is fulfilled previous to the fulfillment of its previous use. Its previous use, in the last phrase, as an aorist imperative, is the main verb. The action of the second use occurs at the same time as the action of the main verb. In other words, we continually forgive those who are indebted to us, having wronged us in whatever form, as the Father forgives us for our sin-debt. This is not strictly a condition of the Father's forgiveness, but should be a continual action that accompanies or precedes the Father's forgiveness.

Forgiveness and the virtue love that accompanies it is one manifestation of the Spirit's ministry to the believer both maturing and mature. Both should be patterns in the believer's life: the Father's forgiveness of sins coterminous with virtue love and resultant forgiveness to others. If you are oriented to God's grace, then you will consistently keep short account of your sins, continually naming them to the Father. If you are grace oriented, then you will also keep a short memory of wrongs done to you, consistently disregarding them, maintaining gracious relationships with others. We are talking about keeping a spiritual equilibrium! In addition, if you maintain a personal grudge, then you are carnal. God the Father will not forgive your sin-grudge until you name it to Him. The point is this. We should keep a spiritual equilibrium.

Interpretively, then, this verse reads this way:

And keep forgiving us our sin-debts to You, as we also keep on forgiving those who wrong us. Matthew 6:12

e. Matthew 6:13

And do not lead us into temptation, but deliver us from evil. [For Yours is the kingdom and the power and the glory forever. Amen.]

And lead us not into temptation Luke 11:4c

Let us begin our study of this verse by eliminating much of it. The original manuscripts do not include what the NASB puts in brackets. It is certainly true but not found here. What remains, the actual verse, seems straight forward, but despite its simplicity, it is a difficult sentence to understand. We will note this in our discussion.

And do not lead us into temptation,
καὶ μὴ εἰσενέγκῃς ἡμᾶς εἰς πειρασμόν,

Looking at the Greek text, "do not lead" is the negating particle ME (μή) with the second person singular, aorist active imperative verb EISPHERO (εἰσφέρω). This verb has several possibilities of meaning, ranging from "cause to," "bring into an event or state," "speak about," "carry in to a state," and "lead into." We will have to look at the context to get a specific meaning. As the second person singular, the subject of the verb "you," refers contextually to God the Father. The aorist tense in the imperative carries with it no designation of time. This pure ingressive views the action of the imperative as an action that is not momentary. The active voice indicates that the subject produces the action of the verb. For the time being, our translation reads, "You (God the Father) do not lead, carry or bring us in to a state of ..."

The next word, "temptation," the accusative noun PEIRASMOS (πειρασμός) carries with it concepts of both testing and temptation. It is interesting that one word should mean both testing and temptation, both being different though related concepts. We must differentiate these.

God allows us to be tested. When we are in fellowship with Him, He allows us to come face to face with situations that induce us to use, or to give us the option, to apply the doctrines that should be resident in our souls. Applying these doctrines allows us to maintain our state of spirituality and fellowship with Him. For the Father to allow us to be tested, certain criteria must be present. First, we need to be, as just mentioned, in fellowship with Him. We need to be constantly aware of sin in our lives, keeping short account of it. Once you name a sin or series of sins, though, forget them, putting them behind you. Secondly, we must be growing up spiritually. We must be in a state of learning doctrine, constantly building our inventory of applicable doctrine. The primary source of gaining this inventory should be systematic teaching from your pastor.

For the Father to allow you to be tested fairly or justly for your mastery of a certain category of doctrine, you must have had the opportunity to learn and to believe the doctrines that relate to that test. If you are keeping current with your doctrinal education, when you face testing, you simply, under the ministry of the Holy Spirit, recall and apply the pertinent doctrine. If you do this successfully, then, you have passed that test. You constantly gain spiritual strength as you keep passing tests. Therefore, the purpose of testing us, as one possible interpretation of this word implies, is to develop spiritual strength. This is a positive thing, for our benefit. As the following verse states, God never unfairly allows you to face testing for which you are not ready. This implies that you have had the opportunity to both learn and to believe the doctrines pertinent to the test.

No testing has overtaken you but such as is common to man; and God is faithful, who will not allow you to be tested beyond what you are able, but with the testing will provide the way of escape also, so that you will be able to endure it. 1 Corinthians 10:13

Note that in keeping with differentiation between testing and temptation, I have replaced temptation in this verse with testing.

Temptation is a horse of a different color! We place ourselves in a state of vulnerability to temptation when we have squelched or quenched the Holy Spirit's empowerment. We face temptation when we are out of fellowship, under the control of our sinful nature. We cannot recall, much less apply doctrines pertinent to our lives in the state of carnality. The only doctrine you can recall and apply is the reminder to name your sin to the Father in order to resume your spirituality. The Father is not going to you lead you anywhere but to discipline when you are in a state of carnality!

Getting back to testing, if you fail to apply the pertinent doctrine to a given test, failing it and becoming carnal; that same test has become a temptation to further sin. If you maintain your carnality, you will certainly succumb to that temptation. As a Church Age believer, without the power of the Holy Spirit and doctrine, you have not the chance of a snowball in hell of resisting temptation then getting into a sin spiral! As James noted, we lead ourselves into temptation by carnality.

However, each one is tempted when he is carried away and enticed by his own lust. James 1:14

In this verse James relates temptation to being enticed by lust, the power our sin nature has over us when we allow it. You become carnal when facing a test either because you did not learn the necessary doctrine though you heard it, or you did not believe it.

Why does God not tempt us? The only thing He does when we are out of fellowship is to lead us back into the fold of fellowship with Him. He usually uses one of three categories of divine discipline, depending upon our level of our recalcitrance to get us back in to fellowship with Him. It is contrary to His character, contrary to His integrity, to lead us into a state of sin. He does only one thing with regard to sin: He condemns it. James also addressed this subject:

> **Let no one say when he is tempted, "I am being tempted by God"; for God cannot be tempted by evil, and He Himself does not tempt anyone. James 1:13**

If, then, we look at this verse as we have so far defined the words, "You (God the Father) do not lead, carry or bring us in to a state of testing..." we have to ask a question. Why would we petition the Father to keep us from being tested, especially, if it be by testing that we confirm and strengthen our faith? Admittedly, there are those of us who would rather maintain our immature status quo, exploiting the Father's grace to no good cause, expressing our total laziness! That we should avoid testing, and thereby greater grace, is not the Father's intention. We have already established that the Father will not lead us into temptation; it is against His integrity to do so. However, He does lead us into testing. To answer that question, we need go no further than our Lord's words to His disciples just prior to His arrest by the religious authorities:

> **Keep watching and praying that you may not enter into temptation; the spirit is willing, but the flesh is weak. Matthew 26:41**

The same principles delineated above applied to the disciples who our Lord was teaching, though He taught them to pray for protection from temptation. He also mentioned watchfulness. This is key because we need to be continuously aware of testing, which we can convert to temptation by our refusal to apply the doctrines we have been taught. We are also, as the Lord mentioned, weak and frail of memory, especially when being tempted by a sin that appeals to our areas of weakness. Therefore, we are not out of line to petition God to make us aware of the mechanics of our failure when we do fail. Remember that James taught that sinning is a four-step process involving our volition, though we seem to commit some sins instantaneously. Pray that the Father will grant you wisdom to be aware of the testing you are facing. You can pray for greater wisdom in the area of doctrinal application to pass the tests you are facing. So many tests appeal directly to our areas of weakness, so we tend not to be aware of the subtle demands upon our volition when we are called upon to use it! So, again, you can pray for protection from things for which you possess a weakness or affinity because you do not think you have the spiritual strength to handle them. God, of course, knows better!

The verse continues.

> **... but deliver us from evil.**
> **ἀλλὰ ῥῦσαι ἡμᾶς ἀπὸ τοῦ πονηροῦ.**

This final phrase begins with the contrasting conjunction, ALLA (ἀλλά), "but," with the aorist imperative verb RUOMAI (ῥύομαι), "save" or "preserve."

RUOMAI closely relates to another word translated as "save," SOZO (σῴζω). We can better understand what the phrase means if we know, specifically how these words are used and distinguished. RUOMAI appears in the New Testament only 15 times, whereas SOZO's use numbers at more than a hundred. SOZO's meanings then are very general, defined specifically only from context. Because of RUOMAI's limited use, we would assume that it has a specific meaning and use. However, looking at even its limited uses, we can determine that its use refers both to an immediate deliverance from danger and evil situations as well as to eternal deliverance from evil through salvation by faith in Christ. We can note that "men" are always the object, and God is always the author of salvation."[xli] In this context, because the first phrase speaks about the possibility of entering into personal sin by failure to pass tests, then this use must refer to the evil that we ourselves enter into because of our own carnality from failure to pass tests.

Evil, PONEROS (πονηρός) in this context, refers to Satan's policy for his operational plan. It is in direct contrast to the Father's plan of grace. This would be an appropriate time to study the Doctrine of Evil. In this document, we will simply summarize the concept. Because Satan's plan is to supplant God, totally replacing His plan with his own deception and counterfeit, it includes every deception that he uses to distract the human race, especially believers, from God's plan. A believer is not necessarily involved in evil if he keeps short account of his sins, consistently naming them to the Father. A believer becomes evil when he stays out of fellowship, outside of God's plan and provision, becoming involved in Satan's deception and counterfeit. On one hand, evil includes every so-called good that replaces God's good. For instance, altruism, though considered good, is evil because, ignoring God's plan, it simply humanly "improves" the world. On the other hand, evil includes violent and subtle acts that fly in the face of God's perfect provision. For the believer, then, evil becomes the consequence of continual or a lifestyle of sin and resultant human good and rejection of God.

The Scripture also used the word evil, in other contexts to refer to the occurrence of unfortunate events, worthlessness, maliciousness, and degeneracy.

This prayer then becomes a prayer for the delivery from the consequences of sins and becoming involved in the evil of satanic rejection of God.

D. Commentary on Forgiveness – Matthew 6:14-15

For if you forgive others for their transgressions, your heavenly Father will also forgive you. But if you do not forgive others, then your Father will not forgive your transgressions. Matthew 6:14-15

1. Matthew 6:14

For if you forgive others their transgressions, your heavenly Father will also forgive you;

In the next two verses, our Lords gives detail to the above petition for the forgiveness of sin.

Jim Oliver
For if you forgive others for their transgressions ...
Ἐὰν γὰρ ἀφῆτε τοῖς ἀνθρώποις τὰ παραπτώματα αὐτῶν,

One key word in this verse is "forgive," APHIEMI (ἀφίημι), used before, but this time as an aorist subjunctive instead of an aorist imperative. The conditional conjunction EAN (ἐάν), translated, "if" begins this verse by introducing a contingency. This is followed by the positive conjunction GAR (γάρ), translated "for." The aorist subjunctive verb of APHIEMI (ἀφίημι), follows, as we mentioned above. When you precede this subjunctive with EAN (ἐάν), you have a third class condition. Maybe this will occur, maybe it will not. As an aorist subjunctive, it is a timeless principle, repeatedly occurring at certain points in time. It is a second person plural, so translated, "if you all continuously or timelessly, forgive, making it a principle in your life whenever the need to arises ..."

The next word is ANTHROPOS (ἄνθρωπος) translated literally, "men," though here it works as "others," as in "other people." If you continually forgive others ..."

The next key word is "transgressions," the accusative plural neuter noun, PARAPTOMA (παράπτωμα) which is correctly translated. A transgression is different from the debt indicated above because it refers to a specific sin against you. The question arises: do you forgive those who wrong you, or do you hang onto a grudge? If you continually forgive those for wronging you, even forgetting that they did, this reflects the dynamics of the spiritual life, the fruit of the Spirit.

... your heavenly Father will also forgive you.
... ἀφήσει καὶ ὑμῖν ὁ πατὴρ ὑμῶν ὁ οὐράνιος.

The verse continues from the apodosis of that conditional sentence, "the Father will forgive you." The Greek rubricates this gracious forgiveness by placing it at the beginning of the phrase. The clause begins with the future active indicative, third person singular of APHEIMI (ἀφίημι), meaning, "He will forgive." The conjunction KAI (καὶ) follows, translated as "also." The next word is the dative second person personal pronoun, translated you. Therefore, these words translate, "He will also forgive you." The next five words form the attributive principle where HO URONOS (ὁ οὐρανός), "in Heaven" modifies HO PATER UMON (ὁ πατήρ ὑμῶν), "your Father." Those five words form the subject of the clause. The translation then, stands as, "Your Heavenly Father will also forgive you." The Greek word order places great emphasis on the fact of His forgiveness.

The law of retribution under which the disciples had lived demanded satisfaction from the victim, not grace forgiveness from the one wronged. Our Lord was orienting the disciples, teaching them to live by grace not legalism. Therefore, the point here is not that this verse presents the mechanic of the forgiveness of sin but that it presents a contrast between grace and legalism. This, then, is hyperbole to teach that point. The Father expected grace from the disciples whom He sent out instead of legalism that was rampant in Israel at that time.

2. Matthew 6:15

... but if you do not forgive others, neither will your Father forgive your transgressions.
... ἐὰν δὲ μὴ ἀφῆτε τοῖς ἀνθρώποις, οὐδὲ ὁ πατὴρ ὑμῶν ἀφήσει τὰ παραπτώματα ὑμῶν.

These words sound harsh, however, no harsher than any kind of legalism. This line very accurately portrays the attitude the Pharisees had to those who wronged them. This is not cause and effect. In this context, the legalist, the one who does not forgive a wrong done to him, has not received grace from the Father because he has not received the Father's gift of salvation. If he were not legalistic, he would be open to grace, forgiving others, having received the Father's grace.

We cannot leave this section of this Sermon without a deeper look into the concept of transgressions. The Greek word it represents, PARAPTOMA (παράπτωμα) describes one of the many facets of sin. The Greek language has many words that describe these different facets. Trench wrote a short paragraph naming these words with a succinct summation of its type of sin. I have placed capitalized phonetic spellings of Trench's Greek words.

"It may be regarded as the missing of a mark or aim; it is then HAMARTIA (ἁμαρτία) or HAMARTEMA (ἁμάρτημα): the overpassing or transgressing of a line; it is then PARABASIS (παράβασις): the disobedience to a voice; in which case it is PARKOE (παρκοή): the falling where one should have stood upright; this will be PARAPTOMA (παράπτωμα): ignorance of what one ought to have known; this will be AGNOEMA (ἀγνόημα): diminishing of that which should have been rendered in full measure, which is HETEMA (ἥττημα): non-observance of a law, which is ANOMIA (ἀνομία) or PARANOMIA (παρανομία): a discord in the harmonies of God's universe, when it is PLEMELEIA (πλημμέλεια): and in other ways almost out of number."[xlii]

E. *Matthew 6:16-18—Application: Fasting*

And whenever you fast, do not look dismal, like the hypocrites, for they disfigure their faces so as to show others that they are fasting. Truly I tell you, they have received their reward. But you, when you fast, anoint your head and wash your face so that your fasting will not be noticed by men, but by your Father who is in secret; and your Father who sees what is done in secret will reward you.

These next three verses continue and conclude our Lord's warning against the Pharisee's religious priorities and practices. This section warns against the third Pharisaic pet religious tradition, fasting. Our first item of business with this first phrase is to define fasting.

Fasting, NESTEUO (νηστεύω) is the act of avoiding food and nourishment resulting in hunger. In antiquity, it described a hungry person, but more commonly described a religious rite. The original and most powerful motive for fasting in antiquity was to due to fear of demons who supposedly gained power over men through eating.[xliii] An application that indicated this was the fasting of the one watching over a corpse. The thought was that one risked infection from demons by eating and drinking around the soul of a recently departed one. On the opposite side, it was used in preparation for intimacy with the heathen deity; for preparing one's self to share in the magic and power brought on from demon possession. The ancient Greeks and Romans understood that hunger made one more receptive to ecstatic revelations. In Christianity, we understand correctly that such ecstatic behaviors play a role in demonic activity. Fasting, to those in antiquity, did not relate to asceticism but to relationships with demons.

The Old Testament saints fasted. Related to the death of a loved one, fasting was a part of expressing grief, not of the fear of demons. However, fasting also related to communication with God. Moses fasted for forty days and nights when he received the Ten Commandments:

So he was there with the Lord forty days and forty nights; he did not eat bread or drink water. And he wrote on the tablets the words of the covenant, the Ten Commandments. Exodus 34:28

Daniel also fasted when preparing for prophetic visions:

So I gave my attention to the Lord God to seek Him by prayer and supplications, with fasting, sackcloth and ashes. Daniel 9:3

Apparently, it seems that there was a parallel between the heathen practice and the Jewish practice, though demonic substitutions for *bona fide* spiritual practices appear though out history. Despite appearances, the Jews related the practice to humility and submission to God, not to making one ready for demon possession.

The Old Testament records many instances of fasting, among both Jews and Gentiles. The Book of Leviticus records the Divine command to fast as a part of the Day of Atonement, translated as "…you shall deny yourselves…" in Lev. 16:29-31 and Lev. 23:26-32.

In many of these instances, entire groups of people fasted apparently to get God's attention, but perhaps it was more an emotional expression of their remorse or fear of God's discipline. They thought God would be impressed, to the degree that He would answer or at least listen to their petitions, with their fasting. However, prayer often accompanied such fasting. In many instances, those fasting only restrained themselves from eating during the day; they ate and drank at night. There are recorded instances of a total fast, but the Psalmist warned against persistent fasting:

> *My knees are weak from fasting, and my flesh has grown lean, without fatness. Psalm 109:24*

One big problem with fasting, as with any observable rite, was its visibility. It was, as we will see later in this passage, only an external rite, often undertaken for approbation.

> *Say to all the people of the land and to the priests, 'When you fasted and mourned in the fifth and seventh months these seventy years, was it actually for Me that you fasted?' Zechariah 7:5*

> *When they fast, I am not going to listen to their cry; and when they offer burnt offering and grain offering, I am not going to accept them. Rather I am going to make an end of them by the sword, famine and pestilence. Jeremiah 14:12*

Jesus, when attacked by the Pharisees because His disciples were eating instead of fasting, answered using a wedding analogy. He said that wedding guests do not fast while the groom is present. That was a time for celebration, not mourning. In other words, there may be a time for fasting, but that was not it! Matthew, Mark, and Luke all record our Lord's answer to the Pharisees.

As for today in our American culture, fasting from eating, apart from health benefits for some, does not make much sense. Understand that God never has been impressed with people not eating. That is not the point. The point is to spend the time that you normally eat to study, pray, and meditate. God is always interested in your prayers and studies, not in your hunger! In our American culture where we spend 15 minutes eating, what is taking an additional 15 minutes to pray and study? In cultures where mealtimes last an hour or more, this makes a great deal of sense. How should we Americans fast today? Take an hour away from television watching, from football games, from video games to study and pray! Fast from your entertainment!

1. Matthew 6:16

> *Whenever you fast, do not put on a gloomy face as the hypocrites do, for they neglect their appearance so that they will be noticed by men when they are fasting. Truly I say to you, they have their reward in full.*

Whenever you fast
Ὅταν δὲ νηστεύητε,

This verse begins with the HOTAN (ὅταν), an adverbial conjunction that deals with time. It indicates an activity engaged in periodically. In the Greek word order, the next word is the postpositive connective conjunction, DE (δὲ) translated, "and" or "furthermore" continuing the previous subject: separation from Pharisaic religious traditions. Then follows the present active subjunctive of NESTEUO (νηστεύω) translated, "fast." We have already discussed this word.

Fasting was the third favorite Pharisaic religious rite which had been very misapplied even though established as a *bona fide* limited spiritual life function. The Mosaic Law required fasting for use only in certain festivals, including the Day of Atonement, though the Pharisees used it to "prove" their spirituality much more often. The present tense indicates action in progress. Those whom our Lord was addressing fasted. It was a part of the Jewish spiritual life. They could fast correctly, during certain festivals, or erroneously, frequently for approbation, as the Pharisees had. The subjunctive mood introduces contingency; perhaps you fast this way, perhaps you do not. The possibility, if not the probability, exists especially if you are following the Pharisees as the guide to your spirituality.

The words are translated, "Furthermore, whenever you fast..." Because fasting was *bona fide* in that dispensation, the disciples did fast. Everyone did. Fasting was a part of spiritual discipline, used in private, in conjunction with prayer and sometimes publically during certain festivals.

... do not put on a gloomy face as the hypocrites do,
... μὴ γίνεσθε ὡς οἱ ὑποκριταὶ σκυθρωποί,

The next word, a negative adverb, introduces a negative command, ME (μή), our Lord giving His disciples a spiritual corrective. The verb of being, GINOMAI (γίνομαι), in the present middle imperative operates as a helper with another word which appears later in the Greek word order. The middle voice of this verb implies the participation of the subject in the action. Following the Greek word order, the next word HOS (ὡς), is a comparative adverb, translated, "as." The next word, the articular noun HUPOCRITES (ὑποκριτής), defined as "pretender" or transliterated, "hypocrite" indicates that you are not to become an actor, a pretender, like the Pharisees. This next word only appears in one other verse, SKUTHROPOS (σκυθρωπός), which refers to a gloomy or sad face. These Pharisees made sure everyone knew they were fasting by looking sad and gloomy then wearing torn and tragic looking clothing. "Beyond the fast prescribed in the Law for the Day of Atonement and other officially ordained fasts, fasts were often undertaken for personal reasons or for the sake of merit. Several accompanying ceremonies were prescribed, e.g., putting on sackcloth, sitting in ashes, the sprinkling of ashes on the head (Mt. 11:21), refraining from washing and anointing the body (Mt. 6:17), the putting off of sandals etc."[xliv] "There was a great temptation to attract the attention of others by making a particularly sorry spectacle of oneself. This widespread attitude, which could even vaunt itself before God, finds living embodiment in the Pharisee ..."[xlv]

Furthermore, whenever you fast, do not become as the pretenders ...

The next few words address their clothing.

... for they neglect their appearance ...
... ἀφανίζουσιν γὰρ τὰ πρόσωπα αὐτῶν ...

It begins with the verb, APHANIZO (ἀφανίζω) in the present active indicative, meaning, "they neglect," or "they make ugly." This is followed by the accusative noun, PROSOPON (πρόσωπον), meaning "face" or "appearance," with the reflexive pronoun, AUTOS (αὐτός).

Furthermore, whenever you fast, do not become, as the pretenders; for they make their appearance ugly ...

The verse continues with same pattern as above:

... so that they will be noticed by men when they are fasting. Truly I say to you, they have their payment in full. Matthew 6:16

The point is this: Do nothing in your spiritual life for others to observe. Your spiritual life should remain a matter between you and your Heavenly Father. In the next verse, our Lord tells us how to accomplish this:

2. Matthew 6:17

But you, when you fast, anoint your head and wash your face ...

Appear and behave as you always do: fix your hair and keep your face clean! Do not make a spectacle of yourself when you fast!

3. Matthew 6:18

... so that your fasting will not be noticed by men, but by your Father who is in secret; and your Father who sees what is done in secret will reward you.

PART VII

PRIORITIES FOR SPIRITUAL LIVING
MATTHEW 6:19-24

A. *Matthew 6:19-21—A Scale of Values*
1. Matthew 6:19

Do not store up for yourselves treasures on earth, where moth and rust destroy, and where thieves break in and steal.

We need to remember the context of this sermon in order to interpret these three verses correctly. Jesus was training His disciples, preparing to send them out into Israel for the purpose of evangelization. They were to announce to Israel that her Messiah had come. In order to fulfill that ministry, these disciples needed to have the right scale of values. No one can selflessly serve our Lord without the correct scale of values. The self-centered or wrongly motivated person cannot effectively serve in a manner pleasing to the Lord.

Do not store up for yourselves treasures on earth ...
Μὴ θησαυρίζετε ὑμῖν θησαυροὺς ἐπὶ τῆς γῆς,

Verse 19 begins with verb, THESAURIZO (θησαυρίζω) in the present active imperative preceded by the strong negative particle ME (μή). The translation "do not store up" implies a system of values. You only store up and save what you value. Being a present tense, this refers to a state of being, one that you continually do. The active voice means that the subject, you, produces the action of this imperative. Being an imperative, this is a command from the Lord Himself. We will see the lexical cognate or the root of this verb used as a noun just a word away, only we will see it translated as "treasure." The implication here is value. This, then, is a command not to value something or not to place something on your scale of values.

The next word is the reflexive use of the dative second person plural personal pronoun, SU (σύ) serving as the indirect object of the verb, translated "for yourselves."

The next word is the plural noun form of the verb we just noted, THESAUROS (θησαυρός), translated, "treasure." A good translation reads thusly: "Do not store up treasures for yourselves…" The implication is, again, not to place value on something, described or characterized by the next words. These begin with EPI (ἐπί) GE (γῆ) translated, "on the earth." Our Lord, then, addressed the disciples' scale of values. He did not want them to place too much value upon on earthly things.

> *… where moth and rust destroy, and where thieves break in and steal.*
> *ὅπου σὴς καὶ βρῶσις ἀφανίζει καὶ ὅπου κλέπται διορύσσουσιν καὶ κλέπτουσιν·*

With the next phrase, He gave three reasons not to place untoward value on those earthly things; it deals with perishability of the material. Though this list emphasizes material things, we can extend this concept to anything earthly, even beyond the material. The words, correctly translated are, "where the moth and rust destroy, and thieves break in and steal." Though moths do not bother us now as much as they used to, they ate up clothing in ancient days. They still get into and ruin bulk food supplies. The word translated as "rust," the noun BROSIS (βρῶσις), has quite the range of meanings, referring to meat, as in offered to idols; referring to a meal or food, as in the Last Supper; referring to something consumed. Anything consumed is destroyed from its former form! Metal appears to be consumed by rust, though it is becoming oxidized, becoming worthless as metal. Today, rust is especially destructive when salt meets certain metals. Ocean going vessels need to be constantly painted to protect them from corrosion. Automobiles also suffer from corrosion from salted winter roads. The next problem with material goods is their appeal to the criminal who seeks to appropriate things you own. Anyone who lives in a big city has fallen victim to thieves burgling beloved belongings.

The point is that nothing material or related to the material on this earth, in this life, is permanent. So why place so much value on it when our Lord gives us a fantastic option? The issue, as we will see, is choosing spiritual values, that which is permanent, over earthly, visible, material things.

2. Matthew 6:20

> *But store up for yourselves treasures in heaven, where neither moth nor rust destroys, and where thieves do not break in or steal;*

> *But store up for yourselves treasures in heaven,*
> *θησαυρίζετε δὲ ὑμῖν θησαυροὺς ἐν οὐρανῷ,*

The next verse stands in contrast to the previous, beginning, as far as the English word order is concerned, with the adversative conjunction DE (δέ), translated, "but." This is followed by many of the same words of the previous verse, translated correctly, "but store up for yourselves treasures in Heaven..." This is clearly a command to set your scale of values upon the heavenly. Only then will your life be unencumbered by distractions of this earthly life. This all sounds very good! We should all be motivated to place our priorities upon heavenly things, actually storing up treasures in Heaven. However, unless you understand that God has provided us mechanics for actually doing so, we may default into interpreting these two verses allegorically, not literally. You may be tempted to assume that to apply it means to do "good things" of altruism and leave it at that.

However, our Lord meant for us to take this very literally. We can build up treasures in Heaven by applying the mechanics of our spiritual life. This brings to mind two questions. What are these treasures in Heaven that we can build up? Secondly, what are the mechanics for building up these treasures? We are well aware of various methods of wealth building in this life. For many, these methods remain academic because most of us are not wealthy!

To answer the first question, many passages teach the existence of rewards and blessings, both temporal and eternal, imputed to believers who fulfill the spiritual life God has provided. The Scripture characterizes these blessings but does not specifically describe them. A partial Biblical vocabulary that describes the existence of our heavenly treasure includes three words: reward, crown, and inheritance.

Reward

... each man's work will become evident; for the day will show it because it is to be revealed with fire, and the fire itself will test the quality of each man's work. If any man's work which he has built on it remains, he will receive a reward. 1 Corinthians 3:13-14

Behold, I am coming quickly, and My reward is with Me, to render to every man according to what he has done. Revelation 22:12

But you, when you pray, go into your inner room, close your door and pray to your Father who is in secret, and your Father who sees what is done in secret will reward you. Matthew 6:6

He who receives a prophet in the name of a prophet shall receive a prophet's reward; and he who receives a righteous man in the name of a righteous man shall receive a righteous man's reward.
Matthew 10:41

And without faith it is impossible to please Him, for he who comes to God must believe that He is and that He is a rewarder of those who seek

Him. Hebrews 11:6

Watch yourselves, that you do not lose what we have accomplished, but that you may receive a full reward. 2 John 8

For if I do this voluntarily, I have a reward; 1 Corinthians 9:17a

Crowns

I have fought a good fight. I have finished the course. I have kept the doctrine. In the future there is laid up for me the crown of righteousness which the Lord, the righteous judge, will award to me on that day, and not to me only, but to all who love His appearing.
2 Timothy 4:7-8

Do not fear what you are about to suffer. Behold, the devil is about to cast some of you into prison, so that you will be tested, and you will have tribulation for ten days. Be faithful until death, and I will give you the crown of life. Revelation 2:10

Blessed is a man who perseveres under trial; for once he has been approved, he will receive the crown of life which the Lord has promised to those who love Him. James 1:12

Shepherd the flock of God with you, exercising oversight not under compulsion, but voluntarily on the basis of the will of God; and not for sordid gain, but with a ready mentality; nor yet as lording it over those allotted to your charge, but proving to be examples to the flock. And when the Chief Shepherd appears, you will receive the unfading crown of glory.
1 Peter 5:2-4

Inheritance

And now I commend you to God and to the Word of His grace, which is able to build you up and to give you the inheritance among all those who are sanctified. Acts 20:32

Then the King will say to those on His right, 'Come, you who are blessed of My Father, inherit the Kingdom prepared for you from the foundation of the world.' Matthew 25:34

... knowing that from the Lord you will receive the reward of the inheritance. It is the Lord Christ whom you serve. Colossians 3:24

... also we have obtained an inheritance, having been predestined according to His purpose who works all things after the counsel of His will ... Ephesians 1:11

Kingdom of God

... envying, drunkenness, carousing, and things like these, of which I forewarn you, just as I have forewarned you, that those who practice such things will not inherit the kingdom of God.
Galatians 5:21

In this compilation of verses, I have not distinguished between the inheritance every believer receives by virtue of his position in Christ and rewards for spiritual accomplishment. We receive rewards or "greater grace" for our fulfillment of our spiritual life that involves constant fellowship with God, through the filling of God the Holy Spirit and learning and applying doctrines, the very thinking of our Lord, in the Word of God.

We each need to keep our thinking sharp enough to discern our spiritual status on a minute-by-minute basis. Are we spiritual, being filled with God the Holy Spirit, therefore in fellowship with the Son and Father, or are we under the control of our old sin nature, in sin and evil? Everything we think and do while spiritual is subject to reward by the Father temporally and in the eternal state. If you continually concentrate upon your spirituality, attempting to apply the principles of the Word of God as brought to your thinking by the Spirit, then you are expressing your scale of values. If you are continually mindful of this principle, striving to maintain your spirituality and use of doctrinal principles, then the things of Heaven are at the top of your scale of values. Also, remember that our Lord is not telling His disciples to ignore totally their temporal responsibilities, but to keep the things of Heaven at the top of their system of values.

We can find the mechanics of spirituality in 1 John 1:9; simply name your sin or sins to the Father. To maintain your sinless state, you need to apply the doctrines of the Word to counter temptations to sin and becoming involved in human good and evil. One key word found in 1 John 1:9, HOMOLOGEO, the verb usually translated "name" goes beyond flippant naming of one's sin or sins but implies being totally on-board with applying the necessary doctrines to avoid areas of sin that so consume us. Flippant thinking will put you right out of fellowship and back into sin and evil. Because we still have intact old sin natures, we default to sin, human good and evil, rejecting the Father's plan and provision for us. It takes concentration upon spiritual values to maintain our spirituality. For the disciples to successfully evangelize, they needed to live by God's power, not their own. The only way to live in the sphere of God's power is to maintain spirituality. The same applies to each of us as we seek to fulfill the Father's plan for us.

Paul taught this to the Colossian believers:

Set your mind on the things above, not on the things that are on earth.
Colossians 3:2

3. Matthew 6:21

... for where your treasure is, there your heart will be also.
... ὅπου γάρ ἐστιν ὁ θησαυρός σου, ἐκεῖ ἔσται καὶ ἡ καρδία σου.

This brings us to the last phrase in this passage. The only word possibly misunderstood in this phrase is "heart." This is from the Greek noun, KARDIA (καρδία). It does mean heart. However, the Greeks, for the most part, understood the heart to be the seat of thinking, not the muscle that pumps one's blood. Granted they understood the physiological process of blood circulation but used that blood-pumping organ to express the concept of thought that circulated throughout one's soul. The principle our Lord communicated here, deals with priorities. Interpretively, the idea is this: "Therefore if the things of Heaven are what you set at the top of your scale of values, that is where your concentration will be."

This is an important lesson in today's entertainment focused world. Most everyone fixates upon the myriad forms of entertainment, from immediately available movies, television programs, and video games to sports and other public events. These things distract us from the very source of our happiness. What is entertainment but a means to distract though sense stimulation from harsh and often miserable realities of life? I could add every distraction from God's provision to this list, but you get the idea!

God gave us life to glorify Him! Does that mean that we are to live strained, dry, and difficult lives? Absolutely not! Would that glorify Him? His plan for us includes great happiness and satisfaction, beyond what we can humanly imagine, but it is only available to us though His supernatural power.

B. Matthew 6:22-23—*Understanding the Possibility of Failure*

The eye is the lamp of the body; so then if your eye is clear, your whole body will be full of light. But if your eye is bad, your whole body will be full of darkness. If then the light that is in you is darkness, how great is the darkness! Matthew 6:22-23

The eye is the lamp of your body; when your eye is clear; your whole body also is full of light; but when it is bad, your body also is full of darkness. Then watch out that the light in you is not darkness. If therefore your whole body is full of light, with no dark part in it, it will be wholly illumined, as when the lamp illumines you with its rays. Luke 11:34-36

In our quest to learn the lesson our Lord taught with these words, we first look at the Greek sources for the major words to understand their meaning. Secondly, we will look at the sentence syntax, how the words relate to each other, to discover an accurate or interpretive translation. Remember that a working translation can be more interpretive than literal, that is, word for word.

This passage, just as all previous verses, fits the overall context of this sermon, that is, to prepare His disciples to go out and evangelize legalistic Israel. This category of evangelism was the announcement that the long-awaited Messiah had come. They also needed to be spiritually prepared themselves, lest they fall into the same error that consumed Israel. Once we understand how this lesson applied to them, then we can derive important lessons for us in this Church Age as well. We will concentrate upon Matthew's presentation, and then go to Luke's presentation, for clarification.

1. Matthew 6:22

The eye is the lamp of the body; so then if your eye is clear, your whole body will be full of light.

The first phrase reads this way:

The lamp of the body is the eye;
Ὁ λύχνος τοῦ σώματός ἐστιν ὁ ὀφθαλμός.

The first word, correctly translated as "lamp," is the articular nominative masculine singular noun LUCHNOS (λύχνος). It is an old word used since the days of Homer. It refers to a vessel that contained a flame that gives off light. It is not the light itself; it only carries and reveals the light within it. In secular literature, ancient Greek writers used it to describe a literal lamp. However, in the Old Testament, it metaphorically denoted, "length of days, vitality, the possibility of action…the source of strength, helping power and the grace of preservation…"[xlvi]

But Abishai the son of Zeruiah helped him, and struck the Philistine and killed him. Then the men of David swore to him, saying, "You shall not go out again with us to battle, so that you do not extinguish the lamp of Israel." 2 Samuel 21:17

In this context, David's men characterized him as the "lamp of Israel," signifying his delegated leadership over Israel. He was not the Light, but the lamp containing and revealing the Divine Light of leadership.

For You are my lamp, O Lord; And the Lord illumines my darkness. 2 Samuel 22:29

In this hymn of praise, David characterizes the Lord as a lamp, lighting his way, signifying divine leadership. This is a blending of light into the concept of lamp. This is often the case as in some of the following verses.

When His lamp shone over my head, by His light I walked through darkness; Job 29:3

How often is the lamp of the wicked put out, or does their calamity fall on them? Does God apportion destruction in His anger? Job 21:17

For the commandment is a lamp and the teaching is light; and reproofs for discipline are the way of life. Proverbs 6:23

Your word is a lamp to my feet and a light to my path. Psalm 119:105

And the city has no need of the sun or of the moon to shine on it, for the glory of God has illumined it, and its lamp is the Lamb. Revelation 21:23

These verses demonstrate the wide range of meanings this word carries. In this case, we can return to the basic meaning of the word, that which contains and gives off light.

The next phrase, correctly translated "of the body," is the genitive masculine article with the genitive singular noun, SOMA (σῶμα). In this context, it refers to the entire person, body, soul, and spirit. The phrase "...is the eye" is translated from ESTIN HO OPHTHALMOS (ἐστιν ὁ ὀφθαλμός). The translation reflects the Greek words accurately, without any surprises. The translation of these words together is, "The lamp of the body is the eye." This sentence means that the eye reveals the life, energy force, or vitality in the person. In this context, the life transmitted through the eye is the animation from the spiritual life. While the lamp is not the light, nor the eye the actual vitality or animation of the body, it reveals it. Where there is life in the body, the eye reveals that life. The eye reveals the sparkle of life within the spiritually mature person. Thieme called this the animation of the body. Without life in the body, there is no animation. Often the eye reveals the condition of that animation. We speak about a person with a sparkle in his eye or conversely, one who is sick or depressed, as having dull eyes.

So then if your eye is clear,
ἐὰν οὖν ᾖ ὁ ὀφθαλμός σου ἁπλοῦς,

This phrase begins with the adverbial conjunction EAN (ἐάν), translated "if," which introduces a conditional clause in the third class condition. The idea is this: if and it is possible, even likely to be true, but it is uncertain. The expanded translation of this phrase from the NASB would read as, "so then, if your eye is clear, perhaps it is ..." The conditional clause continues with the inferential conjunction, OUN (οὖν), translated, "therefore," or "then." It is a possibly true condition related to the fact of the eye being the light of the body. Perhaps there is light in that body, perhaps not! This phrase reveals the condition of the eye in revealing an internal light or animation. In the Greek word order, the verb of being EIMI (εἰμί) in the present active indicative follows. The subject of that verb is the same word for eye as above.

The word translated, "clear," is nominative adjective HAPLOUS (ἁπλοῦς). The root meaning deals with simplicity, though in the ancient Hebrew texts, it took on the connotation of purity. In the sense of preparedness for sacrifice, the one sacrificing had to be "clear," meaning without guile or ulterior motive. Also translated "without folds," it applied specifically to the time in which this verse was written. In those days, one purchased cloth in quantity, as in bolts. The vender could fold it over in such a way as to hide flaws. If he sold it without folds, then it was without flaws. The seller was honest and without guile or ulterior motives. The NASB translates it as, "clear," in the sense of "transparent motives." These two phrases, then, can be interpretively translated this way:

> *The life or animation of the body is the eye; therefore, if your eye does not reveal flaws, ulterior motives or impurity, maybe it does, but then maybe it does not...*

How is the Church Age believer's eye to reveal a life without guile or flaw when spiritual death flaws every person in the human race from the moment of birth? Even a believer's eye can reveal guile and imperfections. The only experiential purity, for the Church Age believer, comes from the filling and resultant empowerment of the Holy Spirit coupled with continual learning and applying the Mind of Christ, leading to spiritual maturity. The spiritually mature believer's eye will reveal the animation from the fruit of the Spirit.

> *But the fruit of the Spirit is love, joy, peace, patience, kindness, goodness, faithfulness, gentleness, self-control; against such things there is no law. Galatians 5:22-23*

> *... your whole body will be full of light.*
> *... ὅλον τὸ σῶμά σου φωτεινὸν ἔσται.*

The word, "whole" comes from the nominative Greek adjective, HOLOS (ὅλος), which includes the concept of complete and undivided, inferring integrity. The implication is that what the eye reveals about the person will be true about the entire person. Often believers will compartmentalize their lives, living spiritually on Sunday in church, but on Monday through Friday, conducting business greedily and dishonestly. What about Saturdays? Live for yourself on Saturday! The spiritual life, however, should overflow to every aspect of your life, active every day! If your eye is "clear," revealing no guile and flaws, meaning spiritual, then your whole person will fulfill the next few words, "be full of light." The word describing light is different from the word previously used, lamp, which inferred light as coming through a conduit. In this case, light is PHOTEINOS (φωτεινός), the source of light. The source of light that illuminates the eye and the whole person is God.

> *O send out Your light and Your truth, let them lead me; Let them bring me to Your holy hill and to Your dwelling places. Psalm 43:3*

> *Arise, shine; for your light has come, and the glory of the Lord has risen upon you. Isaiah 60:1*

> *... for you are all sons of Light and sons of day. We are not of night nor of darkness; 1 Thessalonians 5:5*

While you have the Light, believe in the Light, so that you may become sons of Light. John 12:36a

2. Matthew 6:23

But if your eye is bad, your whole body will be full of darkness. If then the light that is in you is darkness, how great is the darkness!

The eye is the lamp of your body; when your eye is clear, your whole body also is full of light; but when it is bad, your body also is full of darkness. Then watch out that the light in you is not darkness. If therefore your whole body is full of light, with no dark part in it, it will be wholly illumined, as when the lamp illumines you with its rays. Luke 11:34-36

But if your eye is bad, your whole body will be full of darkness.
ἐὰν δὲ ὁ ὀφθαλμός σου πονηρὸς ᾖ, ὅλον τὸ σῶμά σου σκοτεινὸν ἔσται.

This passage continues with a presentation of the antithetical. The sentence begins with the third class conditional adverbial conjunction EAN (ἐάν), translated "if." The third class condition may or may not be fulfilled, but it is likely that it will be fulfilled. The important words here are "bad" and "darkness." "Bad" the nominative masculine singular adjective of PONEROS (πονηρός), translated as evil, wicked, or worthless, refers to the failure to adhere to God's precepts and commands. "Full of darkness" comes from the adjective SKOTEINOS (σκοτεινός), referring to that which is antithetical to light. The term "light" embodies God's power in the form of His word circulating within the believer's soul. If the believer, however much he has matured, in turn, rejects it, then he possesses no light at all. His body's animation, seen through the eye, reveals no divine energy.

The next phrase speaks of the whole body being full of darkness. You cannot have 90% light in your body, meaning that you reject 10% of the truth you have been taught. You cannot successfully apply the Word to 90% of your life situations but reject the remaining 10% to other certain situations. You cannot apply God's Word to 90% of your life, then allow your old sin nature to flourish in the remaining 10%. In this example then, there is a 10% compartment in your soul where you do not apply the doctrine in your soul. If you willingly do this, choosing to ignore God's directives for a given situation, you are entirely in darkness! Chances are that if you are struggling with the one 10% area, constantly rationalizing, justifying yourself, then your lust or avarice in that area will preoccupy you, coloring your entire being. Furthermore, that 10% will grieve the Holy Spirit, quenching His power in your entire life.

As examples, consider these: Many German officers during World War II, "loving Christian men," taking care of their families, attended Church and fulfilled other Christian duties, yet fulfilled Hitler's extermination dictates on the other. How many businessmen apply Christian principles 90% of the time, yet let their greed set policy in their business practices? One bad compartment in your soul ruins the rest of you!

> ***If then the light that is in you is darkness, how great is the darkness!***
> *εἰ οὖν τὸ φῶς τὸ ἐν σοὶ σκότος ἐστίν, τὸ σκότος πόσον.*

When is the light within you darkness? The light within you is darkness if you have shut out the light! It is darkness when you choose to let one area of your life resist God's power to bring it into line. That darkness will permeate and influence the rest of you, taking your entire being into slavery to your sin nature, drawing you down into the well of reversionism. Because you do this willingly, despite continual teaching of God's Word, you might as well be standing precipitously on the edge of a cliff on a mountain of spiritual success that has taken you years to gain! We all have pet areas of carnality, areas of our lives that we do not want to "give over to God." These pet areas can ruin your life, unless you bring every thought, motive, and action into subordination to God's Word! We can interpretively translate the last phrase as, "how great is the influence of the darkness!"

So far, an interpretive translation sounds like this. However, without the accompanying explanation, it really does not tell the whole story behind the verse!

> ***The life or animation of the body is the eye; therefore, if your eye does not reveal flaws, ulterior motives, or impurity, maybe it does, but then maybe it does not, your whole body will be full of light. However, if your eye is bad, revealing no light, your whole body will be full of darkness. If then the light that is in you is darkness, how great is the darkness!***

C. Matthew 6:24—The Exclusivity of Divine Power

> *No one can serve two masters; for either he will hate the one and love the other, or he will be devoted to one and despise the other. You cannot serve God and wealth.*

> *No servant can serve two masters; for either he will hate the one and love the other, or else he will be devoted to one and despise the other. You cannot serve God and wealth. Luke 16:13*

The passage continues with a further development of the divided soul. We used as an example in the last verse, a person who just has 10% errant thinking in his soul. In actuality, we all probably have much more than that. As you resolve one area of weakness in your depraved soul, another area reveals itself. Then you go to work developing rationales as a defense against it or to resolve it by continual doctrinal inculcation. When you hang on to an area of soul weakness, never even wanting to overcome it, you in essence serve a second master. You serve Satan by maintaining a pet area of weakness. Our Lord used money lust, greed, as an example of the divided soul because this was such an issue among the Pharisees.

No one can serve two masters;
Οὐδεὶς δύναται δυσὶ κυρίοις δουλεύειν;

The verlse begins with the nominative singular adjective, OUDEIS (οὐδεὶς), translated, "no one." This means that what our Lord is communicating applies to every one of us. Not one of us can weasel out of this. We all have to take responsibility for the second master we continue to serve. The next word translated "can" comes from DUNAMAI (δύναμαι) in the present active indicative. This is a power word! The closest English derived word is dynamite! The present tense denotes continual action. No one is ever able; no one has the power necessary to fulfill this.

The next words are DUO (δύο) KURIOS (κύριος), "two masters." The main verb, to serve, is the present active infinitive of DOULEUO (δουλεύω), implying slavery servitude. The present tense indicates an ongoing action, without a beginning or end in sight. The active voice indicates that the subject produces the action. You, in this case, are the subject. From the English translation, one can visualize a servant trying to serve two different masters, in an honorable way. However, the Greek words impart a sense of self-induced slavery to an area of carnality, in this case, money-lust, from which there is no release without the believer applying God's power. The idea of addiction comes through very strongly. Yes, you choose to remain in servitude to your area of weakness because you do not apply the words of our Lord coupled with the power of the Spirit to overcome it. In so doing you do not serve our Lord but remain locked-in to servitude toward your second master, Satan, who has deceived you through your old sin nature.

...for either he will hate the one and love the other,
... ἢ γὰρ τὸν ἕνα μισήσει καὶ τὸν ἕτερον ἀγαπήσει,

This phrase delineates the mutual exclusivity of the divine and the cosmic. It begins, following the Greek word order, with AY (ἤ), a particle usually used in pairs, indicating a distinction. We will come across its other half later in this phrase. Together, they translate as "either...or" here.

The postpositive conjunction GAR (γάρ) follows, translated "for" or "because." The next words are the accusative masculine articular adjective with the attributive article, HO HEIS (ὁ εἷς), translated with the article, "the one." Next is the future active indicative verb in the third person singular, MISEO (μισέω), translated, "he will hate." MISEO carries an entire range of meanings, from indifference to sinful extreme abhorrence. In this context, indifference, aversion and resentment or hate work well as translations. As we will see, these two masters conflict with each other. You cannot sit on both sides of a fence at the same time. Because loyalty and concentration are at issue when serving someone superior to you in rank, you simply cannot support both. You cannot be loyal to two antithetical forces. If you are serving your old sin nature trend, greed in this case, you are going to have an extreme aversion to righteousness.

The verse continues with the connective conjunction, KAI (καί), translated "and" giving equal weight to each phrase. "The other" comes from the articular adjective HETEROS (ἕτερος), referring to another of a different kind. These two masters are on two different sides, being distinct from each other. Perhaps a person could serve two bosses if they are on the same team, with the same goals, but even then trying to fulfill the wishes of two different personalities with different responsibilities is difficult. The military doctrine of chain of command addresses this issue. You should only respond to the commands of the one person designated as your leader. Even those with higher authority than your boss should still go through your immediate supervisor to command you.

The next word is the future active indicative verb AGAPAO (ἀγαπάω), generally translated, "to love." In this context, this love refers to the thought, motivation, and humility it takes to be subordinate to another person. Though you do not have to love your boss to serve him, you still need to focus your thought upon that person, reading that person's nuances so that you can anticipate what he or she needs from your service. It takes singularity of concentration to serve someone. In this context, service to Satan who has tempted you through your old sin nature's greed trend requires much thought and motivation. Making money in the right way takes enough concentration, but when you add the complication of greed, your motivation leans toward ill-gotten gain, adding complication upon complication. In this context, hatred serves to contrast with love. An interpretive translation of this phrase is:

... for either he will hate the one and concentrate with the intensity of love on the other.

This next phrase expands the concept of trying to serve two masters.

... or he will be devoted to the one and despise the other.
... ἢ ἑνὸς ἀνθέξεται καὶ τοῦ ἑτέρου καταφρονήσει.

This phrase begins with AY (ἤ), which completes the "either–or" combination of particles we mentioned above. "Being devoted to," ANTECHO (ἀντέχω) stands in contrast to KATAPHRONEO (καταφρονέω) despising. ANTECHO is a compound word, composed of the preposition, ANTI, "against" with ECHO, "to have and to hold." The connotation, then, is holding close to yourself what you value. KATOPHRONEO carries the connotation of disparaging or as translated, despising. Can you imagine being a loyal democrat and flaming republican at the same time? Alternatively, is it flaming democrat and loyal republican? Again, you cannot be loyal to two contrasting or opposing concepts. In this case, the contrast is extreme: divine power against satanic power, the righteousness resulting from the filling of the Spirit against satanic evil transmitted through your old sin nature, integrity opposing dishonesty and righteousness standing in contrast to unrighteousness and evil.

The next phrase concludes this lesson:

> *You cannot serve God and wealth.*
> *οὐ δύνασθε θεῷ δουλεύειν καὶ μαμωνᾷ.*

As we mentioned above, greed, the wrong way to acquire wealth, is one trend of the old sin nature our Lord is using to illustrate the antagonism between God's righteousness and satanic human good, sin and evil. There are many other trends. In addition, wealth, which you acquire because of God's plan for you, is not sinful or contrary to righteousness. However, wealth in this context, the acquisition of which was a major source of evil among the Pharisees, also severely taints our current system of free enterprise. All businesses must run on principles of integrity from righteousness, which always over-rule the wanton desire for the creation of wealth at any cost.

You cannot serve God and pursue your old sin nature generated lusts simultaneously. Choose whom you will serve. If you choose to follow our Lord, growing in grace and in knowledge of Him, you will live a happy and fulfilled life, no matter what circumstances surround you. If, on the other hand, you follow the lusts of your flesh, chasing every fleshly desire you have, be prepared to live a miserable, unfulfilled life terminating in our Lord removing you from this earth earlier than what He had initially planned.

> *No one can serve two masters; for either he will hate the one and love the other, or he will be devoted to one and despise the other. You cannot serve God and wealth. Matthew 6:24*

Since we are talking about greed, the lust for money, let us look at an Old Testament passage that describes the problem. It was not new in Jesus's day!

> *For the wicked boast of the desires of their heart, those greedy for gain curse and renounce the Lord. Psalm 10:3*

> *After all, a king who cultivates the field is an advantage to the land. He who loves money will not be satisfied with money, nor he who loves abundance with its income. This too is vanity. When good things increase, those who consume them increase. So what is the advantage to their owners except to look on? Ecclesiastes 5:9-11*

> *Better to be poor and walk in integrity than to be crooked in one's ways even though rich. Proverbs 28:6*

So far, in our study of following old sin nature lusts, such as greed, we have been ideological. It all seems theoretical. Let us make it more personal and say that you have been greedy. Even as a believer, the desire to acquire money motivates you, instead of the desire to serve God. In fact, you have been hooked on it to the degree that you cannot drive past a casino without dropping in to gamble. You have to experience the dopamine "high" of winning money. Of course, you do not always win! The house has to win more often; otherwise, it could not stay in business. Nevertheless, the logic that drives anyone to the conclusion, that you must lose more than you make over the long run, does not stop you. You are hooked on that winning feeling. This principle applies to many areas of lust: from gluttony to approbation lust, from greed to power lust, from sex lust to the lust to control.

> *Those conflicts and disputes among you, where do they come from? Do they not come from your cravings that are at war within you? James 4:1*

As you make decisions to pursue these old sin nature trends, your body actually changes chemically to give you physical pleasure from these things. You do become physically addicted to over-eating. You do become physically addicted to the rush of winning, and so on. The pleasure is of course, fleeting, causing you pain and misery in the end. The purpose of these things is to distract you from the real purpose in your life that is to "grow in grace and in knowledge of our Lord and Savior, Jesus Christ." We, as carnal human beings, or unbelieving human beings, do not have the power to resolve these resultant physical issues much less mental ones. Our bodies, even the neurotransmitters of our brains, change from constant bad choices! The one solution is the acquisition of divine power, first gained at salvation, then reacquired from confession of sin and renovation of our thinking through studying and applying the Word of God.

PART VIII

THE LOGISTICAL GRACE RATIONALE
MATTHEW 6:25-34

A. Matthew 6:25—The Application and Principle of Logistical Grace

For this reason I say to you, do not be worried about your life, as to what you will eat or what you will drink; nor for your body, as to what you will put on. Is not life more than food, and the body more than clothing?

Why do people become greedy, as in the case of this illustration of following one's old sin nature trends? You follow your greed temptations and envy, converting them to sin by pursing ill-gotten gain because you do not think you have enough. You are discontented! Perhaps you begin to fulfill this trend because you are actually short on cash to provide certain desired accouterments even perceived necessities of life. You think that gaining these things in the wrong manner is justified. Then you become hooked! Our Lord, in this next series of verses absolutely rejects that notion.

The theme that runs through these verses speaks of our Lord's perfect provision for each of us. Not only do we not need more than what our Lord provides; His provision feeds our bodies and soul what they need to survive, even to prosper. Learning and applying His Word through the empowering Spirit provides the capacity for right living, qualifying us for great blessing in this life continuing into eternity. These blessings, standing in direct contrast to our old sin nature pleasures, are real, eternal, and perfect. Why be deceived by Satanic promises? He is bound for the Lake of Fire, while we believers are bound for glory. This glory begins now, with your decision to live the life that God has provided, and lasts eternally. God has already provided for every exigency to see that you have the opportunity to land in glory complete with every blessing. You just need to make the right decisions and take advantage of the power He has provided.

This verse begins with a transition, a contrast, presenting the following verses as a much better choice than the greed of the previous verses.

For this reason, I say to you,
Διὰ τοῦτο λέγω ὑμῖν,

"For this reason" translates from the Greek preposition of causation, DIA (διά) with the nominative demonstrative pronoun OUTOs (οὗτος). We can expand the translation of these two words to, "this is why…" or "because of the things I just taught…" The next words, the present active indicative of LEGO (λέγω), "I say" with the second person plural personal pronoun, HUMIN (ὑμῖν) "to you-all," carry with them divine authority. We had better sit up and take note of what the Creator of the Universe is about to say to us! These things are going to stand in stark contrast to our natural magnetism toward doing the things of the flesh, or old sin nature.

… do not worry about your life …
… μὴ μεριμνᾶτε τῇ ψυχῇ ὑμῶν …

This command, if mastered by every believer, would diffuse most old sin nature temptations before we convert them to sin. We think we have deficits in our lives, so we follow either temptations from outside of us or inside through our sin natures, to fulfill them. That God has given to us everything we need in this life, and more in the form of blessings, embodies the principle of logistical grace. What can we infer, then, from this command? Our Lord implies by this that He has provided perfectly for us, in every possible way. To worry about your life is blasphemy! When you give into worry about your life, you are calling the God a liar, alleging that He has not provided for you as He has promised.

"Do not worry" is the negative adverb ME (μή) modifying the present active imperative of MERIMNAO (μεριμνάω). MERIMNAO has a range of meanings, such as "to care" or "to be anxious" or "to think about." This present tense verb means that the action is taking place presently. Worry characterizes your life, with no end in sight. The active voice means that you are the one producing the action. The imperative mood, coupled with the negative ME means that you should stop doing what you are doing. Stop worrying! Tension or anxiety should never characterize you when you think about fulfilling tomorrow's needs. "Worry" is a good translation in this context because the Lord is warning us not to commit that sin. Worry is one sin that distracts the believer from grace, from keeping his concentration on the Lord. The worried believer is preoccupied with himself whereas he should be concentrating upon God's provision for him. Anything less than worry, such as concern about making a living and being motivated to find a job is not sin. You should not be consumed by the sin of worry when you are looking for a job but should be relaxed knowing that God has already provided a job for you. You need to insure that you are following every doctrinal guideline you have learned while you look for that job, included being filled with the Spirit. This way you can relax and even enjoy looking for a job!

As an aside here, some earlier translations imply that we should not even give our logistics a second thought. This could be a translation from the verb MERIMNAO; however, a close look at the context causes us to translate it as "worry." The term "thought' in previous years really did imply worry.

"About your life" translates from TE (τῇ) PSUCHE (ψυχῇ) HUMON (ὑμῶν). PSUCHE has a range of meanings from "soul" to "life." In this context, the word refers to the material things that sustain one's life, for which our Lord has perfectly provided.

> *... as to what you will eat or what you will drink; nor for your body, as to what you will put on.*
> *τί φάγητε [ἢ τί πίητε], μηδὲ τῷ σώματι ὑμῶν τί ἐνδύσησθε.*

Those things listed above qualify as your logistical support. These things, what we eat or what we drink, comes from the present active subjunctive verb ESTHIO (ἐσθίω), which idiomatically refers to those things we consume to survive. Literally, it means, "to eat," but most translations take the idiomatic route. You also need clothes, which as we will see, God also provides for His saints.

> *Is not life more than food, and the body more than clothing?*
> *οὐχὶ ἡ ψυχὴ πλεῖόν ἐστιν τῆς τροφῆς καὶ τὸ σῶμα τοῦ ἐνδύματος;*

The first word in the Greek word order is OUCHI (οὐχί), translated, "not." It is in a position of great emphasis due to the fact of the word order. Because of this, we can take this as rhetorical, with the answer being positive, "absolutely yes!"[xlvii]

The point behind this rhetorical question is this: if you have to spend all of your time and thought to see that you have enough to eat and drink, much less to see that you are clothed, how are you going to see your way clear to spend time fulfilling the priorities of spiritual growth? God provides you with these things so that you can spend some time and thought in growing up spiritually, fulfilling the purpose for which God placed you upon this earth! Does this mean that you are not going to have to work for a living? Certainly not, work is a part of the curse we took on from Adam's sin. However, God provides a means for a living for every believer. It is a part of His logistical support.

Our Lord implied another principle with this statement as well. It follows a fortiori logic: If God provides us with the greater, those things which are more than food and clothing, and He does, will He not also provide you with the lesser, those things we need to live on this earth? You should know from other studies that God wants much more from you than just your day-to-day survival. He wants you to grow up spiritually. Spiritual growth requires more than church attendance for an hour or two a week. You need to spend at least an hour a day concentrating upon the Scripture, learning the whole realm of doctrine. Ideally, your local church supplies this. You also need to spend time in prayer and fulfilling other aspects of your spiritual life. Of course the arena in which you make a living often offers plenty of fodder for doctrinal application. Your family life also offers many areas for doctrinal application. God has provided everything you need to live and to grow up spiritually.

An interpretive translation of the verse reads this way:

Therefore I tell you, stop worrying about your life, what you will eat or drink, or about your body, what you will wear. Is not life more than food, and the body more than clothing? Absolutely!
Matthew 6:25

B. *Matthew 6:26-34, Luke 12:23-28—Illustrations of Logistical Grace*

So important is this lesson to every believer, that our Lord repeats it, illustrates it three times, and then repeats the command: Do not worry! Worry is probably one of the worst sins a believer commits. It is often so subtle that we do not catch it and deal with it, yet it evidences one of the greatest failures in our lives. In the following verse, our Lord illustrated logistical grace, the solution to worry. He brings to our attention how the Father provides for birds and flowers, which rank lower than we do, so we can logically conclude that the Father also provides for us. If we are confident of the Father's perfect provision, and we should be because He promises this all over the Scripture, then we should never worry!

Look at the birds of the air, that they do not sow, nor reap nor gather into barns, and yet your Heavenly Father feeds them. Are you not worth much more than they? And who of you by being worried can add a single hour to his life? And why are you worried about clothing? Observe how the lilies of the field grow; they do not toil nor do they spin, yet I say to you that not even Solomon in all his glory clothed himself like one of these. But if God so clothes the grass of the field, which is alive today and tomorrow is thrown into the furnace, will He not much more clothe you? You of little faith! Do not worry then, saying, 'What will we eat?' or 'What will we drink?' or 'What will we wear for clothing?' Matthew 6:26-31

For life is more than food, and the body more than clothing. Consider the ravens, for they neither sow nor reap; they have no storeroom nor barn, and yet God feeds them; how much more valuable you are than the birds! And which of you by worrying can add a single hour to his life's span? If then you cannot do even a very little thing, why do you worry about other matters? Consider the lilies, how they grow: they neither toil nor spin; but I tell you, not even Solomon in all his glory clothed himself like one of these.

ABIDING BY THE SERMON ON THE MOUNT

But if God so clothes the grass in the field, which is alive today and tomorrow is thrown into the furnace, how much more will He clothe you? You men of little faith! Luke 12:23-28

An outline of these verses clearly show how important a message this is:
A. God's provision for the birds illustrates how He provides for us.
B. God clothes insignificant, yet beautiful flowers and grasses, will He not do the same for us?
C. Conclusion: Do Not Worry!

1. Matthew 6:26

Look at the birds of the air ...
ἐμβλέψατε εἰς τὰ πετεινὰ τοῦ οὐρανοῦ ...

The word, "look" translated from the present active imperative of EMBLEPO (ἐμβλέπω), carries a stronger message than the simple word for "look," BLEPO (βλέπω). EMBLEPO is a compound word, combining the preposition EV and the verb BLEPO. Jesus could have used the simpler word, but the word He used includes applying some thought from what you are seeing. Do not just glance at it; look at it carefully to see what lesson you might learn from what you are looking at. When you look at the American flag, do you just see red, white and blue, the stars and stripes or do you think about what that flag symbolizes? Do you remember that God provides us freedom though military victory? Do you think about the countless men and women who have given their lives for our freedom? Do you draw the conclusion that freedom demands responsibility that you must discharge? If you think about these things when you see our flag, then you understand EMBLEPO! This verb is an imperative from our Lord. You must do this! Anytime you get a bit upset and even lean toward worrying about your logistical support, look at the birds! Remember how God has provided for them, remember that you have a greater purpose in God's plan than those birds, and draw the conclusion that God provides for you, for every day in your life!

Often, we respond to seemingly insignificant commands with a lackadaisical attitude, thinking that we know all of that. Wrong! If you find yourself overly concerned about what you are going to eat or wear, in other words, your logistics, go outside and look at the birds flying around! Get some fresh air! Breathe! Relax! God has provided for you! He did it, outside of space and time, in the distant past, as far as we are concerned!

The next word comes from the preposition of direction, EIS (εἰς), usually translated "at." "To" works better because it implies the necessity of something beyond a glance. Interpretively then, "Look to the birds of the air for your lesson…" works well.

... that they do not sow, nor reap, nor gather into barns,
... ὅτι οὐ σπείρουσιν οὐδὲ θερίζουσιν οὐδὲ συνάγουσιν εἰς ἀποθήκας,

This phrase contains three verbs, SPEIRO (σπείρω) "to sow," THERIZO (σπείρω) "to reap" and SUNAGO (συνάγω) "to gather" all in the present active indicative. These present tenses are gnomic presents, which mean that they continually and customarily occur. Negative particles also precede each verb. These birds do not sow, nor reap, nor build up supplies, as we do. In addition, the verbs are stacked, so to speak, in a row. All stand as a comparative unit forming a classical syntactical form that really heightens that sense.

> *... and yet your Heavenly Father feeds them. Are you not worth much more than they?*
> καὶ ὁ πατὴρ ὑμῶν ὁ οὐράνιος τρέφει αὐτά· οὐχ ὑμεῖς μᾶλλον διαφέρετε αὐτῶν;

The word MALLON (μᾶλλον) "more" is significant here. It is a clue that leads us to understand that this forms the classic *a fortiori* logic structure. If God provides for the lesser in importance, will He not provide for the greater in importance? Your answer to this rhetorical question should be a resounding "yes!" Then you should be confident that God has met all of your needs! On the other hand, however, you should not ignore that you need a job, that you need to provide for yourself and for your family. You should understand that birds constantly forage, as do all animals. The point here is that you do not go beyond normal concern and concentration upon your needs. Do not move into worry, because when you do, you grieve and quench the power of the Spirit in your life. You no longer fulfill the plan that God has prepared for you, the one from which you derive your happiness and satisfaction!

2. Matthew 6:27

> *And can any of you by worrying add a single hour to your span of life?*
> τίς δὲ ἐξ ὑμῶν μεριμνῶν δύναται προσθεῖναι ἐπὶ τὴν ἡλικίαν αὐτοῦ πῆχυν ἕνα;

Important words here include, "by worrying," the present active participle of means of PERIMNAW (μεριμνάω), once again, the word indicating anxiety, worry, and great concern. Can you add any time at all to your life by any means? That is addressed by the next word, the present middle indicative of DUNAMAI (δύναμαι), bringing attention to our abilities. We do not have the ability, or even the power to lengthen our lives. Our Lord determines the length of our lives. Worry, especially, will not add any time to your life. When you worry, you cause physiological changes to your body that may shorten your life. If you want to lengthen your life, living it to the maximum, obey God, applying every rationale presented in the Word of God. The middle voice of DUNAMAI—the power or ability word—would indicate our participating in extending our lives. We cannot even do that by eating right and exercising. We may keep our lives from necessarily being cut short by bad decisions, and we will live more comfortably being in shape and eating correctly, but God has our days numbered. If we follow His commands, growing up spiritually, those days will be full of happiness and divine comfort and blessing.

Another important phrase in this verse is "add a single hour to your span of life." Though the phrase is appropriately translated, it is an idiomatic translation from these Greek words:
1. The verb, PROSTITHEMI (προστίθημι) in the aorist active infinitive, translated, "to add."
2. The preposition EPI (ἐπί), translated, "to."
3. The articular accusative singular feminine noun, HALIKIA (ἡλικία), translated as a specific lifetime, stature or state of maturity.
4. The genitive singular third person personal pronoun AUTOS (αὐτός), translated, "of him" or "his."
5. The accusative singular masculine noun PECHUS (πῆχυς), translated as cubit, a unit of measure.
6. The numeral one, HEIS (εἷς).

As an interpretive translation, the NASB translators did well in communicating what our Lord said. We can add a bit of intensity to it: "…to add to his life, by a moment of worry, even a single moment of worry."

And can any of you by worrying add even a single moment to your life span? Matthew 6:27

3. Matthew 6:28

And why do you worry about clothing? Consider the lilies of the field, how they grow; they neither toil nor spin,

καὶ περὶ ἐνδύματος τί μεριμνᾶτε; καταμάθετε τὰ κρίνα τοῦ ἀγροῦ πῶς αὐξάνουσιν· οὐ κοπιῶσιν οὐδὲ νήθουσιν·

In this verse, our Lord used an agricultural illustration of the logistical need for clothes with the lily, one of the beautiful flowers that adorn nature. The word "consider" translates from the Greek compound word, KATAMANTHANO (καταμανθάνω) in the aorist active imperative. MANTHANO without the preposition means to come to an understanding from learning. Adding the preposition KATA intensifies the concept. Being in the imperative mood, this becomes a command from our Lord. If you are tempted to worry, go outside and do some reverse concentrating. Recall what you have learned about the Father's purpose for your life. He has provided so that you can fulfill that purpose. Does He repeatedly do the same for every flower, so that it can fulfill its purpose? He has done the same for you, so do not worry! This verb is not in the passive voice where the subject receives the action, but in the active voice, which means that you, the subject, must produce the action. You do the concentrating! You do the recalling and draw the correct conclusion. Believe it and act upon it.

4. Matthew 6:29

... yet I tell you, even Solomon in all his glory was not clothed like one of these.

... λέγω δὲ ὑμῖν ὅτι οὐδὲ Σολομὼν ἐν πάσῃ τῇ δόξῃ αὐτοῦ περιεβάλετο ὡς ἓν τούτων.

The meaning behind this verse is easy to understand. We all know about King Solomon; he was one of the wealthiest kings of that ancient time. Jesus considered even the best-clothed person in history not as well dressed as the beautiful flowers. We cannot even dress ourselves as well God does the flowers! The verb, "clothed" is the aorist middle indicative of PERIBALLO (περιβάλλω). As a constative aorist tense, it presents the action of Solomon being clothed as one event; "he was ever clothed." The middle voice indicates that he participated in the effect of being well dressed. Therefore, a good emphatic translation is this:

... yet I tell you, even Solomon in all his glory never clothed himself like one of these.

5. Matthew 6:30

But if God so clothes the grass of the field, which is alive today and tomorrow is thrown into the oven, will he not much more clothe you—you of little faith?

After the illustrations, our Lord sums up with a formal presentation of a fortiori logic, moving from the less, provision for the less, to the greater, provision for the greater. The key to that logical argument are the words, "much more." If God has provided for the lessor of value, grass whose purpose is to be incinerated for heat, will He not provide for the greater of value, with greater reason, human beings, especially His saints whose purpose it is to glorify Him and resolve the prehistoric angelic war? Do you not know God well enough to understand this foundational issue? The content of your knowledge of God, that which you believe and apply concerning Him, His plan and provision for you, is the very content of your faith.

.Looking at the overall purpose of this sermon, their training, our Lord's rebuke, "you of little faith," probably did not come across as such harsh as it sounds here. They were new in their faith. As one commentator noted in JFB, it was more of a gentle chide than a strong rebuke.

6. Matthew 6:31

Therefore do not worry, saying, 'What will we eat?' or 'What will we drink?' or 'What will we wear?'

These are panic words! Again, our Lord gives a direct order: Stop worrying!

7. Matthew 6:32

For it is the Gentiles who strive for all these things; and indeed your Heavenly Father knows that you need all these things.
παντα γαρ ταυτα τα εθνη επιζητουσιν οιδεν γαρ ο πατηρ υμων ο ουρανιος οτι χρηζετε τουτων απαντων

In the first phrase of this verse, our Lord presents a contrast between the unbeliever's position and the believer's. The word ETHNOS (ἔθνος) represents the unbeliever. Translated here as "Gentiles," it refers to the heathen and all of the other people. These people constantly pursue their logistical support, not understanding that God has even provided many aspects of logistics for them! The word translated as "strive" is the Greek verb EPIZETEO (ἐπιζητέω) in the present active indicative. It is the root ZETEO intensified by the added preposition EPI. That we live in a fallen world, governed for the most part by Satan, results in gross mismanagement of resources. Many people, then, do not see or understand the benefit of God's provision. Because they do not understand that God has provided life necessities, even for the unbeliever, they constantly stress about gaining these things. For the believer, He even overrides many aspects of our being fallen. God, then, has provided everything we need, even to a surplus. Even King David said that he had never seen the righteous forsaken. God's provides! So stop your worrying! What stands between your worry and comfort is your faith. Do you believe what our Lord has communicated to us so clearly?

8. Matthew 6:33

But strive first for the kingdom of God and his righteousness, and all these things will be given to you as well.
ζητεῖτε δὲ πρῶτον τὴν βασιλείαν [τοῦ θεοῦ] καὶ τὴν δικαιοσύνην αὐτοῦ, καὶ ταῦτα πάντα προστεθήσεται ὑμῖν.

In the above verses, our Lord told us to stop worrying. He knows that this is a sin we all involve ourselves in. He tells us how to stop worrying, to stop doing what we were doing. Stop that worrying! Then He told us why we should not worry. He knows that we do not, as fallen human beings, even as carnal believers have the ability or strength to stop our worrying, so He has provided us with a mechanic, a means to cease or worrying. This is how we stop worrying.

The first word in the Greek word order is ZETEO (ζητέω), in the present active imperative. The NASB correctly translates it as a command, meaning "to look for" or "to seek." This infers that instead of undue absorption with life's details, worry, we should supplant it by a different focus of concentration. That this change of concentration be made a matter of priority is inferred from, first, the adversative conjunction, DE (δέ) with adjective PROTOS (πρῶτος) translated, "but first." Our Lord commands that you change your worrying—undue concentration upon your logistics—to the subject the next few words introduce.

Our object of concentration, if we are to follow our Lord's imperative, is the articular Greek noun BASILEIA (βασιλεία), "the kingdom" with DIKAIOSUNE (δικαιοσύνη), "righteousness" with the 3rd person personal reflexive pronoun AUTOS (αὐτός), "his." The literal translation, reads as "His kingdom and righteousness." Though both of these, His kingdom and His righteousness, can be very technical in nature, our context demands simplicity. No one can be facing worry then expect to supplant it with a wall of technical information to digest and to apply. Because our Lord was training His disciples to present His Kingdom to Israel, their focus needed to be upon the job He had given to them. Their message to Israel had to be simple and direct to be effective.

To sum up His Kingdom: it is everything our Lord was offering to Israel. He was offering to usher in the Millennium after His sacrificial death. He was offering the Jews—His chosen people—the complete fulfillment of all Messianic prophecies presented in the Old Testament. It was a tremendous offering. All it required of the Jews was faith in Him by which they would receive His righteousness. For Israel to experience His Kingdom—His perfect authority over them—they needed to believe in Him, in every facet of His work for them to experience His perfect provision.

Though the ultimate definition of righteousness deals with God's perfect scale of values, in this context it deals with His imputation to us at salvation. His righteousness when combined with His kingdom is concentration upon who and what He is. In other words, learn Bible doctrine and then apply it. For Jews in our Lord's day, after faith in Him, it meant strict adherence to the Law. For you, Church Age believer, increase your knowledge to include every facet of His being and His plan for you, and then live it. Use the power that God has given you through His Spirit; combine it with the thought dynamics of the His Word, living the supernatural spiritual life He has provided. Concentration upon these things will supplant your worry. Paul wrote the same thing when he wrote to the Colossian believers, "… keep seeking the things above …" as recorded in Colossians 3:1.

> *Therefore if you have been raised up with Christ, keep seeking the things above, where Christ is, seated at the right hand of God.*
> *Colossians 3:1*

9. Matthew 6:34

> *So do not worry about tomorrow; for tomorrow will care for itself. Each day has enough trouble of its own.*

Some use this verse to justify laziness. However, we must understand it within its context of stopping worry, not stopping work! In it, our Lord drew the correct conclusion from the previous verses.

If you are constantly worrying about what lies beyond you tomorrow, not only are you not concentrating upon your present situation, upon our Lord's provision for it, but you are doubling your worry because you are thinking about today and tomorrow! Let tomorrow's concerns be tomorrow's. Understand that as our Lord has provided for you today, He will do so for you tomorrow.

PART IX

A WARNING, A REMINDER AND AN OFFER
MATTHEW 7:1-12

In keeping our interpretation in tune with the general context of this sermon—that our Lord was training His disciples to present the Kingdom to Israel through the announcement of His arrival—this part of the sermon served as general warnings, reminders and encouragements to them. At the same time, we must be aware that as Scripture, these warnings and encouragements to the disciples also apply to all believers, in all dispensations.

Applying the second principle of interpreting this passage, we need to make it directly applicable to our Church Age spiritual life. Our spiritual life relates directly to the empowering ministry of God the Holy Spirit. When we sin, we name our sin or sins to the Father, then regain fellowship with Him, and the Holy Spirit empowers us. The disciples did not receive the Spirit until Pentecost, so they did not have His empowerment as they went out to announce our Lord's advent. We, however, do. As we look at this passage, then, we are going to interpret the warnings keeping in mind the Spirit's power being available to us.

In the first few verses, our Lord teaches the disciples to guard against judging. From our standpoint, it results from carnality, from theirs, a malfunction in their spiritual life.

In the second paragraph of this last section, our Lord reminds them of the mechanics of their spiritual life: praying, learning doctrine, and the faith rest life. These mechanics apply to us today as well.

In the third section, our Lord presents the Gospel.

A. *Matthew 7:1-6—Stop Judging*

The first warning, concerning judging others, was to make them aware of the pitfalls of losing their objectivity when faced with people who did not meet their standards. What is judging? According to our Lord's brother, judging involves maligning a brother in Christ.

> *Do not speak against one another, brethren. He who speaks against a brother or judges his brother, speaks against the law and judges the law; but if you judge the law, you are not a doer of the law but a judge of it.*
> *James 4:11*

James also presents a relationship between maligning and the Law. At that time, because the Mosaic Law had been abrogated, the only Law he referred to was the greatest commandment, loving your neighbor as yourself.

We all have a tendency to judge those whom we do not think meet our level of whatever our pet area of righteousness or achievement may be. If you write, perhaps you may judge those who do not write as well as you, considering them less than yourself. On the other hand, you may feel threatened by someone you evaluate as better than you, then find an area that they do not measure up to your so-called high standard, then judge them for that! Both extremes indicate sin in the believer's life. Therefore, the danger enshrouded in judgment for the spiritual believer is carnality. Believers, to be effective in whatever ministry our Lord has directed, must not succumb to carnality. Carnality quenches the ministry and power of the Spirit in the believer's life, rendering him spiritually useless.

Another pitfall of judging deals with what it leads to. What do you do if you find someone who you think is lacking? You "set them right!" You try to run their life! As we will see, this leads to disaster.

> *Do not judge, so that you may not be judged. For with the judgment you make you will be judged, and the measure you give will be the measure you get. Why do you see the speck in your neighbor's eye, but do not notice the log in your own eye? Or how can you say to your neighbor, 'Let me take the speck out of your eye,' while the log is in your own eye? You hypocrite, first take the log out of your own eye, and then you will see clearly to take the speck out of your neighbor's eye. Do not give what is holy to dogs; and do not throw your pearls before swine, or they will trample them under foot and turn and maul you. Matthew 7:1-6*

1. Matthew 7:1

> *Do not judge, so that you may not be judged.*
> *Μὴ κρίνετε, ἵνα μὴ κριθῆτε.*

This verse, a very short one, is direct and to the point. Aside from its utter simplicity, it offers no exegetical surprises. The only block to our understanding of the verse is that word, "judge." In the Greek, the first use of it in this verse is the present active imperative of KRINO (κρίνω). It has a range of meanings. "To judge" serves as the most common one. In this context, you are condemning someone for not fulfilling your set of standards. The present tense indicates timelessness of the action of the verb. The active voice indicates that the subject, you, produces the verb's action. The imperative mood indicates that this is a command designed to change your direction in life. The negative adverb ME (μή) translated, "not" precedes the verb. The translation can read either "Do not judge" or "Stop judging."

Because this addresses all of us, we gain the sense that no one has a basis upon which to judge those with whom we come into contact. We have no reason to do so; furthermore, when we judge someone, we are taking God's prerogative of judgment. No person, any one of us, has all the facts about someone else. No one ever has the right to judge another without all the facts. Furthermore, when you judge, you compare yourself to another. You are saying, in a sense that they do not measure up to your standards. We humans only see a small slice of a person's being and when judging, compare it to a small slice of our being. We are not to compare ourselves with others. Invariably, it is like comparing apples and oranges. We never have the foundation of facts upon which to judge someone.

You can take part in this sin of judgment at the drop of a hat. It may even be a sub-trend of self-righteousness. You can do it mentally, thinking disdainfully toward someone, in a split second! The question to ask yourself is this: does the attitude you have taken toward someone reflect our Lord's love? When you take on a judgmental attitude, you cut off any hope of Gospel communication toward that one, because you subtly think that they are either not worthy of it or you assume that they would never believe!

Many verses teach this same message:

Therefore you have no excuse, whoever you are, when you judge others; for in passing judgment on another you condemn yourself, because you, the judge, are doing the very same things. Romans 2:1

This verse adds an additional penalty to judging. If you condemn someone for a sin, you are punished as if you are involved in that sin yourself, whether or not your victim is actually sinning. Furthermore, you receive discipline for your sin of judging. So, when you judge, you are disciplined twice, once for the judging, again for the sin you are judging. If you gossip all the while about this, add another layer of discipline to your account. Judging just is not worth it!

Who are you to pass judgment on servants of another? It is before their own lord that they stand or fall. And they will be upheld, for the Lord is able to make them stand. Romans 14:4

In this verse, Paul brings in the subject of chain of command. Are those you judge even responsible to you? No? Then why are you sticking your nose into their business? Why are you assuming that responsibility? Who is their Lord? Let the Lord, who is lord of us all, take care of the problem, not you.

This judging does not apply to the employer who must evaluate an employee's performance on the job. We must differentiate *bona fide* evaluation from judging.

A boss, for instance, is responsible for evaluating an employee's performance on the job. The employer is the expert, looking at a small part of the employee's life, how well he performs a certain task. This kind of evaluation is necessary if a company or organization is going to fulfill its role in the economy.

The verse continues with the adverbial conjunction, HINA (ἵνα), translated, "so that." Our Lord is giving us a reason to follow this command. Note that our Lord does not treat us like the sheep we are! He respects our volition, giving us a good reason to follow this command. This is followed by the aorist passive subjunctive second person plural of KRINO (κρίνω), again, the verb, "to judge." The aorist indicates that if you judge, at some point in time, you will be judged. The passive voice indicates that you will receive this judgment. The subjunctive mood, always used in this type of clause, indicates that there is a probability that you will judge.

Judging is a particularly harsh sin to commit. You take God's prerogative, stepping on His toes as it were, getting in the way of His perfect administration of justice. In judging, you are also infringing upon the right of the person to grow up spiritually. Your judging interferes with this person's spiritual growth by causing him to focus upon himself. That self-absorption is the easiest pathway to arrogance, to carnality. You, in effect, tempt an immature believer to become arrogant—carnal—himself. Furthermore, such judging, whether representing truth or not, interferes with a person's right to resolve his or her own issues before the Lord without peer interference. If they fall short of God's righteousness, He will deal with the offender. There are some limited situations, with Church discipline, for example, where God has delegated certain functions of judgment to the Church administration. The same holds true for law enforcement and the judge on the bench.

Note also, that even though our Lord was addressing His disciples, He was also addressing the religious establishment because this was one of their major failings.

2. Matthew 7:2

For with the judgment you make you will be judged, and the measure you give will be the measure you get.

For the believer who usurps God's right to judge, the punishment matches the sin. To both the degree that you judge and in the given area of judging, you will receive the same judgment. This is a great reason to treat judging like a hot potato. Do not get involved with it!

For with the judgment you make you will be judged,
ἐν ᾧ γὰρ κρίματι κρίνετε κριθήσεσθε,

This verse begins with the instrumental of means of the preposition EN (ἐν), translated as "with." The next word is "which," from the Greek relative pronoun HOS (ὅς). The next word in Greek is the postpositive conjunction GAR (γάρ), "for" which begins the sentence in the English. These words are translated, "For with which." Because this is built upon that instrumental of means, this sentence is going to tell us how we are going to be judged.

The dative neuter singular noun, KRIMA (κρίμα) follows, translated as judgment. This does not refer to an evaluation you may make of an employee or child for whom you are responsible, but of a peer of whom you do not approve, over whom you have no responsibility. You simply do not approve because he or she does not measure up to your standards. Even if your standards reach the lofty heights of perfect righteousness, as a believer you are to extend grace and virtue love to those who have not reached your level of spiritual growth. Chances are, though, your evaluation of this person, whom you do not even have a right to evaluate, does not come close to accuracy. You do not have all of the facts. Furthermore, this person, most likely, is not even under your authority, so you have no right to judge them! This noun, then, refers to the facts you find that do not measure up to your standards. You can visualize it as a written document, if you will. One column has your standards listed, and the other, the other person's shortcomings. It is meaningless. That this is a dative noun means that it is the object of the following verb.

The next word is the verb KRINO (κρίνω) in the present active indicative second person plural, which means, "you judge." The translation is "For with which judgment you judge..." In other words, to the degree you judge this person, to the degree of harshness you judge, to that degree, you will be judged. Of course, no one comes even close to God's perfect righteousness! If you condemn someone for failing to excel to your alleged or even real standard, God can judge you to the degree that you do not measure up to His perfect standard. I would rather be treated graciously than harshly!

The next word, derived from the same root as the previous two words, KRINO (κρίνω), only here it is the future passive indicative verb form. It is translated, "you will be judged." The passive voice indicates that you receive this judgment. From the context, we understand that this judgment will come from the Father. The indicative mood means that our Lord spoke this from the standpoint of it being a dogmatic reality. There are no ifs, ands, and buts here. It is an undeniable fact. A good translation then is this:

For with which judgment you judge, you will be judged...

I like using the three "judge" words here because all three appear in the Greek, only they read as an alliteration on steroids, KRINE KRINETE KRESISTHE!

The verse continues with words that give a bit more detail about the issue:

... and the measure you give will be the measure you get.
... καὶ ἐν ᾧ μέτρῳ μετρεῖτε μετρηθήσεται ὑμῖν.

This line begins with the conjunction KAI (καί) with the preposition of means, EN (ἐν), as above, with the relative pronoun HOS (ὅς). The words translate as, "and by which..." The next word is METRON (μέτρον), translated, "standard of measure." Any musician should be familiar with this word because a metronome measures time increments as dictated by written music. This raises the question, upon what are your standards based? You should base them upon our Lord's standards of ultimate righteousness! The first standard, the one carrying the highest priority, related to judging others, should be virtue love. When you are tempted to judge, recall how our Lord treated us when we all deserved to be condemned because of our spiritual death and resultant wickedness and self-righteousness. He died as our substitute fulfilling the ultimate virtue love dynamic.

The word METRO, "standard of measure" begins another alliteration: METRO METREITE METRETHESETAI. Perhaps our Lord's listeners groaned when hearing puns or alliterations as listeners today do, but He was certainly in top form here! Perhaps it was more of an attention getting device more than a form of humor as it is for us! These words translate this way:

> *... and by which standard of measure you measure, it will be measured to you.*

The message is clear! If you judge others, stop it! You only open up great liability for punishment for yourself from the Father. An awful lot of judging is contained in gossip. At least the two seem to relate closely. If you gossip habitually, you might want to consider seriously retiring that category of sin! Since this is an issue of sin, remember the solution to all sins: Name it to the Father. He forgives you because of our Lord's work on the Cross. Once the Father has forgiven you, the Holy Spirit empowers you with virtue love. That love enables you to be relaxed around those less mature than you, giving them the opportunity to grow up spiritually without your interference.

The next issue is resistance to that sin. If it is one of your pet sins or sin trends, you need to strengthen yourself against it. This is a matter of your own continued spiritual growth, enlightening you about the biblical subject of hamartiology. The result of spiritual growth is your love for and occupation with our Lord. If you become occupied with Him, you will not be preoccupied with your peers to the degree that you want to control their lives!

> *For with which judgment you judge, you will be judged and by which standard of measure you measure, it will be measured to you.*

3. Matthew 7:3

> *Why do you see the speck in your neighbor's eye, but do not notice the log in your own eye?*
> *τί δὲ βλέπεις τὸ κάρφος τὸ ἐν τῷ ὀφθαλμῷ τοῦ ἀδελφοῦ σου, τὴν δὲ ἐν τῷ σῷ ὀφθαλμῷ δοκὸν οὐ κατανοεῖς;*

The word "see" is the verb BLEPO (βλέπω) in the present active indicative, one of three words the Greeks used to express the concept of seeing. This one leans toward the visual sense of seeing, though sometimes it refers to comprehension. In this context, visual seeing makes sense. The speck is KARPHOS (κάρφος), also translated as splinter. A splinter in your eye keeps you from seeing. Though small, it still functionally presents a problem, a fault of the eye. We can infer from this statement that your neighbor does have some kind of fault, though small. It is comparably insignificant.

The word translated, "notice," is the Greek verb, KATANOEO (κατανοέω), in the present active indicative. Our Lord could have used the word NOEO (νοέω) instead of the intensified KATANOEO. It goes beyond simply noticing your own fault, hyperbolically called a log in your eye, but infers consideration and concentration upon that log. The word, "log" is DOKOS (δοκός). In contrast to the small speck, it is a beam used in construction. You do not have a small problem but a significant one, probably noticeable by everyone around you. You ignore your problem in favor of concentrating upon your neighbor's fault. Why, your own problem or fault is so glaring that it even prevents you seeing your neighbor's fault objectively! Your neighbor, by the way, is anyone with whom you are acquainted. You are close enough to them to want to judge them, putting your nose into their business. Your long nose is probably one aspect of your eye-bound log! We can restate this question this way. "Why do you make an issue of your neighbor's small fault while totally disregarding your own massive problem?" The person who does this judges his neighbor. He is finding small faults, when he should be looking at his own life. He needs to compare his own life to the Scripture then seek to take care of his own problems.

4. Matthew 7:4

Or how can you say to your neighbor, 'Let me take the speck out of your eye,' while the log is in your own eye?

With this next sentence, our Lord confirms that you are going beyond just noticing your neighbor's problem but trying to control his or her life.

'Let me take the speck out of your eye,
Ἄφες ἐκβάλω τὸ κάρφος ἐκ τοῦ ὀφθαλμοῦ σου,

The two words, "let me take" consist of two Greek words. The future imperative of APHEIMI (ἀφίημι) and the future subjunctive of EKBALLO (ἐκβάλλω) form a hortatory, an imperatival idiom. The above NASB translation is a good one, especially if you are a pushy person! Visualize yourself pushing your friend down so that you can operate with your speck-removing tweezers while you are saying this! You are more or less forcing yourself upon your neighbor but being polite by asking, even asking imperatively! "You let me do this!" Can you really focus on removing your neighbor's speck—his insignificant fault—if you have to look through your own two by four-impeding vision—your significant problem?

... while the log is in your own eye?
... καὶ ἰδοὺ ἡ δοκὸς ἐν τῷ ὀφθαλμῷ σοῦ;

You are not qualified to involve yourself in that person's life, especially if you are blind to your own problem! None of us is qualified! This clause begins with the conjunction KAI (καὶ), "and" "while," or "then." The interjection IDOU (ἰδοὺ), follows, translated, "behold" or, more emphatically, "look see now!" An interpretive translation can read this way:

> Or how can you say to your neighbor, 'You let me take the speck out of your eye,' but look see now, you have a log in your own eye!

Remember, that when you involve yourself with your neighbor's life, judging and trying to control him, you open yourself up to the measures our Lord may use to bring that person back into the fold of fellowship. It may include discipline for which you are now liable!

5. Matthew 7:5

> **You hypocrite, first take the log out of your own eye, and then you will see clearly to take the speck out of your neighbor's eye.**
> ὑποκριτά, ἔκβαλε πρῶτον ἐκ τοῦ ὀφθαλμοῦ σοῦ τὴν δοκόν, καὶ τότε διαβλέψεις ἐκβαλεῖν τὸ κάρφος ἐκ τοῦ ὀφθαλμοῦ τοῦ ἀδελφοῦ σου.

Is this verse hyperbole? On the surface it seems as if there will be a time when you will be able to see clearly enough to bring you neighbor into line, as you see it anyway. This entire series of verses has the ring of self-righteousness about it. That is, the person who ever assumes that he has arrived at the point in his life when he does not have some sort of log in his own eye is self-righteous. We may not be facing the same challenges as our neighbor, but we all have an old sin nature giving us each areas of weakness and vulnerabilities to sin; perhaps yours is not as visible as your neighbor's fault!

"You hypocrite" is the vocative noun, HUPOKRITES (ὑποκριτής) meaning that you assume that you have the clarity of vision from your faultlessness that you can resolve your neighbor's issues. You pretend to be qualified to judge then to correct, but you are not because you have faults of your own with which you need to deal. You pretend, but even though you may have "good intentions," and may be very well meaning, you cannot solve your neighbor's problems.

The next phrase begins with aorist active imperative of EKBALLO (ἐκβάλλω), meaning "to drive out," or "to exorcise," or "to remove." The aorist tense presents the action as a snapshot of the event, but not the time of it. The active voice combined with the imperative mood indicates that you must do this. Furthermore, because God commands it, you can do this! God never commands us to do something we cannot! So, you can take the log out of your eye! How do you go about removing that proverbial log? The first issue is spirituality. Does God the Holy Spirit fill you? Does He empower you? Do you keep short account of your sins by naming them to the Father when you commit them? To do this you need to understand thoroughly the doctrine of sin. You need to be able to identify your own temptations to sin and sins to be able to avoid sinning and resolve sins you do commit. This involves continually learning doctrine, with a concentration upon hamartiology.

Looking at the final phrase in this verse, we wonder if there is a situation where you do need to point out someone else's faults. Reserve this for two occasions. When someone asks for advice and you have the necessary knowledge of Scripture, then give it. However, what you advise had better be scriptural. Secondly, a pastor who detects any heresy circulating through his congregation needs to issue corrective advice as it comes up in the Scripture. He does this from the pulpit or through the protocol of church discipline. Paul also calls upon mature women both to council and to teach younger women. Otherwise, leave all judgment in the hands of the Lord.

6. Matthew 7:6

Do not give what is holy to dogs; and do not throw your pearls before swine, or they will trample them under foot and turn and maul you.

This verse, at first glance, seems to address a very different subject, but it serves to be a corollary to the judgment issue. To fulfill it, you actually need to be contemplating issuing corrective advice based upon correct evaluation of a situation. Of course, you have to fulfill two criteria in your life to be doing this. First, you have to be spiritually mature, having enough divine viewpoint to understand the situation as well as to advise upon it. Secondly, you need to have some kind of authority, either real or *de facto*, over the person you advise. A pastor has real spiritual authority over his congregation by virtue of that congregation having chosen him to lead. However, even he has to adhere to proper procedure to give advice. That advice must come from the pulpit. A councilor has *de facto* authority over those he's counseling; the one being counseled gives authority to the one counseling. What happens when you force your advice, either good or bad, upon those who have not asked for it? They may react, sometimes even violently. Satan is violently against divine righteousness. Those to whom you may want to give correctional advice may not have the capacity to accept it, and then react to the message with violence.

Do not give what is holy to dogs ...
Μὴ δῶτε τὸ ἅγιον τοῖς κυσὶν ...

This verse begins with the strong negative ME (μή) with the verb of giving, DIDOMI (δίδωμι) in the aorist active imperative. "Don't ever give" works as a good translation. The next word, the articular dative noun HAGIOS (ἅγιος), defined as "sanctified" or "set apart to God," serves as the direct object of the verb, "to give." In this context, what is holy or sanctified is the scriptural advice you are about to give. The only category of advice you ever want to give the unbeliever is the Gospel. Some local churches encourage their members to demonstrate against the homosexual community, abortion clinics or other evils with all kinds of invective. How wrong of the believers! How arrogant of them! Believers should never criticize anyone whose sins fall in certain categories, especially unbelievers; treat them with love. The believer has only one thing to communicate to unbelievers: the Gospel, the message of God's reconciliation. Moreover, it should be communicated because of your virtue love, either verbally or by your lifestyle.

To whom should believers not give doctrinal advice? Who are the dogs? This command, even from the mouth of our Lord, seems extreme! A category of human being exists that we should not give our nuggets of holy divine viewpoint to. The next word is the articular dative noun, KUON (κύων), translated, "dog." As always, a word's context determines what it means. In this case, even though people revere dogs for their loyalty and companionship, this use refers to a wild animal, a scavenger that would as soon eat you as to look at you. Being dangerous, we should avoid these dogs at all costs. How do you determine if a person fits that category of dog? The Holy Spirit, through His filling and empowerment will help you maintain your sensitivity to these situations. Three additional passages give us better insight as to what this verse means by "dogs."

For dogs are all around me; a company of evildoers encircles me. My hands and feet have shriveled; Psalm 22:16

This is one of David's Psalms in which he prophesied about our Lord's crucifixion. The dogs, in this case, are those who crucified and mocked Him.

He said to her, "Let the children be fed first, for it is not fair to take the children's food and throw it to the dogs." But she answered him, "Sir, even the dogs under the table eat the children's crumbs." Mark 7:27-28

In this context, dogs represent Gentile unbelievers. Our Lord is speaking to a Syrophoenician woman, a Gentile, who was imploring our Lord to cast a demon out of her daughter. He had replied that the Jews should have these privileges, not Gentiles. She replied that even Gentiles, dogs, should receive leftover crumbs. This demonstrated the faith this woman had in our Lord.

Outside are the dogs and sorcerers and fornicators and murderers and idolaters, and everyone who loves and practices falsehood. Revelation 22:15

Dogs, in this context, are evil unbelievers. Those ensnared in evil, especially in a mob-like group, react to corrective advice.

Beware of the dogs, beware of the evil workers, beware of those who mutilate the flesh! Philippians 3:2

We may be tempted to apply this verse, especially the phrase, "those who mutilate the flesh" to those who sport body art. However, Paul was referring to the Judaizers, those who insisted new Gentile believers apply circumcision as per the Mosaic Law. These dogs taught a false Gospel, misleading the Philippian believers.

Remember that the disciples were preparing to go out into legalistic Israel. Many of those living in Israel, having been steeped in legalism, fit this category of dog. Being legalistic, whether or not they knew it, they were, "the most despicable, insolent and miserable of creatures."[xlviii]

History has demonstrated, from the earliest times to the modern, that many people react, sometimes violently, to the Gospel and anything pertaining to righteousness. Avoid them, for, as the rest of this verse indicates, your life may be in danger. There is no shame in walking away from these types of people.

The next phrase repeats the message of the first phrase, only using a different analogy.

> *... and do not throw your pearls before swine.*
> *... μηδὲ βάλητε τοὺς μαργαρίτας ὑμῶν ἔμπροσθεν τῶν χοίρων,*

The "swine" CHOIROS (χοῖρος) refers to those who have believed in our Lord, have experienced some spiritual growth, and then return to their previous lifestyle. The Apostle Peter so designates that:

> **It has happened to them according to the true proverb, "A dog returns to its own vomit," and, "A sow, after washing, returns to wallowing in the mire." 2 Peter 2:22**

Do not throw to animals—that eat pretty much anything, that usually wallow in filth—your pearls of wisdom. Pearls, MAGARITAS (μαργαρίτης) were not unheard of in those days of antiquity. Those items of rare value were harvested from the Red Sea, the Indian Ocean, and Persian Gulf. After Alexander, they also came from the Orient. The Jews used the term for a valuable saying; pearls of wisdom. The idea: Do not communicate divine viewpoint to those who do not want it, to those locked into satanic control. From personal observation of those antagonistic to the Gospel or any form of the Word, it is often better to do your communication in a one to one situation, instead of to a group which may turn into an out of control mob of murderous antagonism. The point in both phrases is this: do not give your nuggets of divine viewpoint to unbelievers or those locked-in to reversionism. The only message the unbeliever can understand, thanks to the Holy Spirit, is the Gospel. The believer needs to understand sin recovery mechanics so that he can resume his spiritual life.

The next phrase, while issuing a warning to us, warns us of those who are antagonistic to divine power and viewpoint:

> *... or they will trample them under foot and turn and maul you.*
> *... μήποτε καταπατήσουσιν αὐτοὺς ἐν τοῖς ποσὶν αὐτῶν καὶ στραφέντες ῥήξωσιν ὑμᾶς.*

The conjunction MEPOTE (μήποτε) begins this final purpose clause. This conjunction emphasizes that this is something to fear. It introduces a warning!

The future active indicative of ΚΑΤΑΡΑΤΕΟ (καταπατέω), follows, translated, "they will trample," or "they will despise." The combination of these two words is from the Attic Greek, which emphasizes the concept to a greater degree. This antagonism can only come from one place, from Satan, himself. The third person personal pronoun serves as the direct object of the verb for a translation of "they will trample them…" The next words translated as, "under their feet" further emphasizes the trampling. The next words, "turn, and tear you to pieces" further emphasize the degree of antagonism and hatred these people have for God's righteousness. We do not need much more explanation. The message is clear.

The difficulty in applying this instruction lies in being able to identify dogs over those who possess a glimmer of desire for the Gospel of our Lord. Sometimes it may be completely obvious to you that you need to leave that area, as Paul did on several occasions. There is no shame in this. Stay alive and evangelize another day!

The visual image this evokes would not be lost to the Jews of the day. According to Marvin Vincent in his Word Studies book, wild boars haunt the land to this day. If a farmer threw seed pearls that resemble small grains to them, they would soon see the deception, trample them, then turn upon the feeder and rip him to shreds with their tusks.[xlix]

At least two other passages teach this same message:

Whoever corrects a scoffer wins abuse; whoever rebukes the wicked gets hurt. A scoffer who is rebuked will only hate you; the wise, when rebuked, will love you. Proverbs 9:7-8

Do not speak in the hearing of a fool, who will only despise the wisdom of your words. Proverbs 23:9

B. Reminder of Spiritual Life Functions—Matthew 7:7-10

Ask, and it will be given you; search, and you will find; knock, and the door will be opened for you. For everyone who asks receives, and everyone who searches finds, and for everyone who knocks, the door will be opened. Is there anyone among you who, if your child asks for bread, will give a stone? Or if the child asks for a fish, will give a snake? If you then, who are evil, know how to give good gifts to your children, how much more will your Father in heaven give good things to those who ask Him! In everything do to others as you would have them do to you; for this is the Law and the Prophets. Matthew 7:7-12

So I say to you, ask, and it will be given to you; seek, and you will find; knock, and it will be opened to you. For everyone who asks, receives; and he who seeks, finds; and to him who knocks, it will be opened. Now suppose one of you fathers is asked by his son for a fish; he will not give him a snake instead of a fish, will he? Or if he is asked for an egg, he will not give him a scorpion, will he? "If you then, being evil, know how to give good gifts to your children, how much more will your heavenly Father give the Holy Spirit to those who ask Him? Luke 11:9-13

In this section of the Sermon on the Mount, our Lord reminded His disciples about the mechanics of the spiritual life. He reduces it to three basic functions: to ask, to search, and to knock. He develops these in verses 7 and 8, and then illustrates them in the subsequent verses.

We need to pay careful attention to the Greek grammar and syntax especially in the first two verses because that understanding is crucial to the flow of the spiritual life as our Lord presented it. Note again, that the disciples did not have the Spirit's empowerment, though our Lord told them to ask for it. None did, but remember that as long as you keep short account of your sins, you do have the power of the Spirit to empower your spiritual life. You do not have to ask for the Spirit.

1. Matthew 7:7—Ask, Search, Knock

Ask, and it will be given you; search, and you will find; knock, and the door will be opened for you.

Ask, and it will be given you;
Αἰτεῖτε καὶ δοθήσεται ὑμῖν,

Verse 7 begins with a command for His disciples to follow as they present Him to Israel. This was the first time that they were to be away from our Lord's daily teaching; they were leaving home! With this reminder, He gave them specific mechanics to utilize so that they would keep their spiritual strength. We can reduce our spiritual life to this level of simplicity as well. The first word is AITEO (αἰτέω) in the present active imperative, translated, "ask." The present tense indicates that this action should always be in progress with no completion in sight. In other words, you should be asking continually, repeatedly. The active voice indicates that you should be the one doing the asking. No one else can ask on your behalf! The imperative mood tells you to do this. Our Lord makes this command to you. You may resist, you may be lazy, but that is no excuse. Our Lord tells you to ask, so do it! A good translation reads, "Keep asking…"

What does this asking consist of? It is prayer to the Father. Apply every principle of prayer the Scripture teaches. Note how our Lord has simplified this command: you need to pray. However, He did not take the time to review every principle of prayer at that time to His disciples. He had taught that before. This was to serve as only a reminder. We have noted that you must be "on praying ground," that is filled with the Spirit so that that Father hears your prayer. You need to address every prayer to the Father. These are two very important principles and mechanics of prayer.

The next word, the conjunction KAI (καί), translated, "and," connects the two clauses. That second clause consists of two words, DIDOMI (δίδωμι) in the future passive indicative, and the second personal dative pronoun, UMIN (ὑμῖν). These words are translated, "and it will be given to you." Not only does this future tense indicate that the action will happen future to the action of the previous verb, pray, but it also indicates a logical progression. Receiving logically follows asking in prayer. This passive voice is a divine passive, meaning that the one who asks will receive what he asks for. Because God is gracious, you will receive, not having earned or worked for it. The indicative mood indicates that our Lord taught this from the viewpoint of reality. The word UMIN, "to you," is in the dative of advantage. It is to your advantage to pray, which logically means that you are going to receive what you pray for. You will receive an answer to your prayers, including those for yourself and others. Remember that prayer is a complex matter. In order to pray correctly, you need to master that doctrine. This sentence then should be interpretively translated as, "Keep on asking (by means of prayer) and it will be given to you."

... search, and you will find,
... ζητεῖτε καὶ εὑρήσετε,

In this next sentence, our Lord continues reminding His disciples about the functions of the spiritual life. The first word, expressing another command, "search" comes from ZETEO (ζητέω), which carries the nuance of looking for or desiring information. As a believer, what kind of information should you desire and therefore, seek after? All believers should seek after knowledge of the Scripture, Bible doctrine. In this dispensation, God speaks to us through His Word, the completed Canon of Scripture. He does not need to take up the slack for an incomplete Canon with dreams, direct revelation, or angelic communication. These things belonged to an earlier time before the Canon was complete. Search, ZETEO (ζητέω) is in the present active imperative, just as the command "to ask." The active voice means that you, a Church Age believer, should do this continually. Our Lord has told all of us to keep on searching the Word.

This sentence continues with the conjunction KAI (καί), "and," with the future active indicative verb, HEURISKO (εὑρίσκω), "find." Note that this verb, "find," which logically follows "search," is in the active voice, instead of the passive voice we found in "receive," above. This means that you do not passively receive this but that you do the finding because of your searching. This requires some work, some effort. God is not going magically to put this doctrine in your thinking. You need to learn it by putting some effort in to it. In this Church Age, the Spirit's teaching ministry greatly assists us, but we still need to put forth the effort. The indicative mood, just as above, indicates the truth of the matter. You seek doctrine in His Word and you will find it.

Jim Oliver
... knock, and the door will be opened for you.
... κρούετε καὶ ἀνοιγήσεται ὑμῖν.

The last command in this verse, knock, is once again a present active imperative, from the verb KROUO (κρούω). Our Lord commanded His disciples, and us, to knock, as the present tense indicates, to keep on knocking, continuously. This refers to continually using spiritual life mechanics in your day-to-day life. Be persistently ensuring that the Spirit fills you, empowering you. Also, be persistently looking for the right doctrinal rationales to apply as you face situations in life. Continual knocking is an apt picture for this because the glorious function of the spiritual life is closed, like a door, to everyone except for the believer who confidently understands that on the other side of that closed door God has provided the solution to every problem in life. You as a spiritual believer have opened that door by virtue of your spirituality.

Our Lord also used the image of knocking on a door, as recorded by John in Revelation 3:20. He pictures Himself knocking on the door of a believer's volition, awaiting his choosing to open the door to fellowship with the Lord. In this image, the believer uses his volition to regain fellowship with the Lord, regaining his spiritual life.

Listen! I am standing at the door, knocking; if you hear my voice and open the door, I will come in to you and eat with you, and you with me.
Revelation 3:20

Returning to our passage, the believer uses his volition—expressed by the active voice—to do the knocking to gain entry into the spiritual life. When spiritual, the believer fellowships with the Father and Son as well as with the Spirit. Furthermore, the Spirit provides empowerment to both learn and apply our Lord's thinking for spiritual living for this believer. Our Lord's thinking is the Scripture. So knocking includes two concepts for the Church Age believer: First, insuring spirituality, and second leaning and applying our Lord's thinking. Once you express your desire to live your life spiritually, by a moment-by-moment decision by means of knocking, what then? The last phrase in this verse answers that question.

The phrase consists of three words, a conjunction, a verb, and its object. The conjunction KAI (καί), as before, connects the two clauses together, translated, "and." The verb ANOIGO (ἀνοίγω), "open," is in the future passive indicative mood. Note the importance of the passive voice. You receive this without merit. This is a picture of grace. You keep knocking, and God, having provided everything "pertaining to life and godliness," opens the door of the spiritual life to you. You only need to use the mechanics, pictured by the knocking, and God does the rest. It is a logical progression, as indicated by the future tense. The indicative mood presents this as completely real from the viewpoint of the speaker, our Lord. To whom does this door open? Our Lord opens it to you, as indicated by the second person dative pronoun, HUMIN (ὑμῖν).

Keep asking, and it will be given you; keep searching, and you will find; keep on knocking, and the door will be opened for you. Matthew 7:7

2. Matthew 7:8—Ask, Search, Knock

For everyone who asks receives, and everyone who searches finds, and for everyone who knocks, the door will be opened. Matthew 7:8

At first glance, this verse looks like a repetition of the previous verse, only perhaps a more general presentation. The previous verse presented three commands: ask, search and knock, then presents the results from obedience to those commands. This verse seems to present a general presentation of those same truths, moving from the specific, "you" to the general, "everyone." However, we need to look at the Greek source words and syntactical structure to see if there is a progression to this message. Structurally, the Greek presentation is concise, exact, and entertaining to look at!

For everyone who asks receives ...
πᾶς γὰρ ὁ αἰτῶν λαμβάνει ...

The first two words, PAS (πᾶς), "all," with the postpositive explanatory conjunction, GAR (γάρ), "for" read as "For all..." Since we are talking about people here, "everyone" works as a good translation. In this context, though, we are speaking about only one category of human being, that is, the spiritual believer in Jesus Christ. The unbeliever can utter only one prayer that our Father will hear, that which expresses his faith in our Lord Jesus Christ. The only heard prayer a carnal believer can offer is that of sin confession. Therefore, the message in both of these verses applies, in our dispensation, only to the spiritual believer while in the previous dispensation, to the righteous Law-abiding believer.

The next three words establish a syntactical pattern that our Lord repeats for each phrase of this verse, that pattern being a definite article + a substantive participle + a finite verb. The Greek reads like a steam-driven pile driver, really hitting the message home! Bam, bam, bam! The last "bam" drives the message home with a great crescendo!

The first word, the definite article in the nominative singular masculine, HO (ὁ), usually translated "the," causes the following participle to read as a substantive, as the subject of the phrase. This definite article precedes the first two participles. The first participle, present active, nominative masculine singular of AITEO (αἰτέω), "ask," reminds us of the importance of prayer in our spiritual lives. The two words can be understood as "praying ones," or, with the adjective PAS, "all," "all praying ones" or "all who pray." The present active participles, the form being repeated three times, indicate habitual action on the part of the believer. It is a hard-hitting way of communicating this necessity. Those first two participles, then would read this way: "all praying ones...all searching ones..."

The finite verb in the present active indicative, LAMBANO (λαμβάνω), reads as "they receive." Interestingly enough, this present tense verb, indicating repeated timelessness, is in the active voice, meaning that the subject produces the action! Asking ones keep on producing the action resulting in their receiving. One would think that this verb would be in the passive voice indicating receiving, undeservedly, under grace. This, when coupled with the preceding participle emphasizes the volition, the choice, of the believer. You ask in prayer then you will receive. It is a dogmatic reality as indicated by the indicative mood. Look at the Greek word structure to see how hard hitting the words would sound: HO AITON LAMBANEI, meaning, "asking ones receive!"

Again, as emphasized in the previous paragraph, only the spiritual believer asking in prayer receives. Believers should address all prayer to the Father, be empowered by the Holy Spirit, and pray in the Son's name. Furthermore, believers must pray according to His will, which he or she can only understand by means of His Word.

... and everyone who searches finds ...
... καὶ ὁ ζητῶν εὑρίσκει ...

The next phrase follows the same pattern. Connected to the previous phrase with the coordinating conjunction KAI (καί) and, it continues with the same definite article, HO (ὁ), but with the present active participle, nominative singular masculine ZETEO (ζητέω), to seek. It can be translated, "the seeking one." The concept is still plural, as in, "everyone who seeks." This again, has to be restricted to the spiritual or righteous believer. As above, the object of searching is the Word of God, seeking through Bible study.

But he answered, "It is written, 'One does not live by bread alone, but by every word that comes from the mouth of God.' " Matthew 4:4

The blessing the believer receives by searching the Scripture or seeking is described in the next verb, the present active indicative of HEURISKO, "to find," or even stronger, "to discover." What is this blessing? You will find the will of God and the power to live it resulting in a blessed, fulfilling, and happy life. There is no greater blessing than to have the Father share His perfect happiness with you! Look again at this hard-hitting syntactical structure: HO ZETON HEURISKEI, "...the seeking one finds or discovers!" Bible study is indeed a wonderful discovery!

... and for everyone who knocks, the door will be opened.
... καὶ τῷ κρούοντι ἀνοιγήσεται.

The last phrase, the crescendo, begins with the connective conjunction, KAI (καί), "and," it continues with the same definite article, HO (ὁ), but with the substantival nominative singular masculine present active participle, KROUO (κρούω), translated, "knock." As with the participles above, this conjugation presents the concept of one who continually knocks. The continual knocking refers to the continued use of God's total provision to live your spiritual life. As indicated by the present active, your volition must be involved. The one who continually knocks will receive the blessing indicated by the last word in the verse.

The verb, because of its form, the future passive indicative, presents the last concept—the last blessing in this verse—as a crescendo! This finite verb, ANOIGO (ἀνοίγω) translates as "will be opened." The concept here? God does the opening! You have established a pattern in your life from the three commands of verse 7. You receive the blessings from those activities, so you continue with your new set of priorities. Then God opens the door to your fantastic spiritual life, a life which over flows to your temporal life then to everyone around you. We can interpretively translate this verse as this:

Asking ones receive, searching ones find, for knocking ones, God opens the door. Matthew 7:8

But if any of you lacks wisdom, let him ask of God, who gives to all generously and without reproach, and it will be given to him. But he must ask in faith without any doubting, for the one who doubts is like the surf of the sea, driven and tossed by the wind. For that man ought not to expect that he will receive anything from the Lord, James 1:5-7

3. Matthew 7:9—Illustration of the Father's Love: Bread and Stone

Is there anyone among you who, if your child asks for bread, will give a stone? Matthew 7:9

Our Lord's message of grace becomes exceedingly clear in the next two verses as He illustrates the reality of the Father's grace towards His family. This illustration shows that we can understand the Father's love by looking at parental attitudes toward their children.

This verse does not offer us any exegetical surprises, aside from the fact that the syntax demands a negative answer. If your child asks for a necessity, such as bread, which, during that era was a main stay of life, would you give him something that looks like bread but wasn't? It would be cruel to give someone who needed food, especially one in your family, whom you begot, a worthless substitute.

Bread, in that part of the world, usually cooked in a pan, looked like a stone. Bread and stones were also considered opposites, though similar in appearance. Note the following verse:

The devil said to him, "If you are the Son of God, command this stone to become a loaf of bread." Luke 4:3

4. Matthew 7:10—Illustration of the Father's Love: Fish and Snake

Or if the child asks for a fish, will give a snake? Matthew 7:10

Our Lord continued with another illustration involving a snake given instead of the requested fish. Again, this is a deception since snakes look somewhat like fish, especially eels that are considered a delicacy in that land. The answer to both questions is obvious. No parent would do this to his or her child. The Father obviously would not, will not do this to us. Both questions lead us to an inescapable conclusion based upon a lesser to greater logic.

C. Matthew 7:11—Offer of the Holy Spirit to the Disciples

If you then, who are evil, know how to give good gifts to your children, how much more will your Father in heaven give good things to those who ask him! Matthew 7:11

If you then, who are evil
εἰ οὖν ὑμεῖς πονηροὶ ὄντες

This verse begins with the first class condition conjunction, EI (εἰ), translated, "if and it is true," which confirms the veracity of this clause. The next word, translated, "then" or "therefore," coming from the inferential conjunction OUN (οὖν), means that this sentence draws a conclusion from the previous two verses. You, as a parent, love your child to the degree that you will not give him a stone for bread or a snake instead of a fish to eat. No matter how the child has behaved, you are not going to deny him these things to eat. So, if this is true for you, what conclusion can we derive about our Heavenly Father from that truth? The next word is translated, "you," from SU (σύ). The next word, PONEROS (πονηρός), translated, "evil' combined with the present active participle of the verb of being EIMI (εἰμί) describes each one of us! These words, together, translate as "If then, you being evil ..." Our Lord calls each one of us evil! Without going into the entire doctrine of evil here, understand that this refers to the fact that each of us, most of time, reflect that we are fallen, corrupt. No matter how hard we try, we will never be perfect parents. However, even not being perfect, we will still give our children the food they need and ask for.

... know how to give good gifts to your children,
... οἴδατε δόματα ἀγαθὰ διδόναι τοῖς τέκνοις ὑμῶν,

The word, translated, "you know," comes from the perfect active indicative second person plural of OIDA (οἶδα). In this context, this word is not infused with any spiritual knowledge connotation or value as in other New Testament passages. The perfect tense emphasizes this understanding as a current state of affairs. It is a part of your foundational, inherent knowledge as a parent; you know how to give to your children.

The next three words, following the Greek word order translate as "to give good gifts." The word, "to give," the verbal infinitive in the present indicative of

DIDOMI (δίδωμι) is an expression of grace, underserved and unearned. Your children do not earn the food you give them. You give to them because you love them, no matter what their behavior. Moreover, you do this even though imperfect, having an old sin nature! The word AGATHOS (ἀγαθός), good carries with it the implication of intrinsic value. So we have moved from the giving of necessities, bread, and fish, to gift giving; even giving gifts of intrinsic value. In addition, you do receive joy when giving gifts to your children!

> *... how much more will your Father in heaven give good things to those who ask him!*
> *... πόσῳ μᾶλλον ὁ πατὴρ ὑμῶν ὁ ἐν τοῖς οὐρανοῖς δώσει ἀγαθὰ τοῖς αἰτοῦσιν αὐτόν.*

The next two words present the key to the logic in this verse, going from the lesser, you, as imperfect, even evil, giving gifts to your children, to the Father's perfect provision to each of us! What a beautiful picture of the Father's loving personality! Those words are POSAS (πόσος) MALLON (μᾶλλον), the interrogative pronoun with the comparative adverb: "how much more!" The next words complete the thought: "How much more will your Heavenly Father give to those asking Him? Do you understand the grandeur of this promise? Luke quoted our Lord with these words, which qualifies this promise with the greatest gift, aside from eternal life, which He was to bestow upon His disciples:

> *If you then, who are evil, know how to give good gifts to your children, how much more will the heavenly Father give the Holy Spirit to those who ask Him! Luke 11:13 HCB*

Interpretively, Luke's quote of our Lord's words limit, as if the empowerment of the Spirit were a limitation, this promise presented by Matthew! Remember that our Lord gave this entire sermon to His disciples before they were to go out and evangelize Israel. They needed the Holy Spirit's power in their ministry, as we do. Therefore, a strict interpretation of this verse precludes it as a "007-license-to-pray-for-everything-you-want-and-you'll-receive-it" promise. Our Lord promised the empowerment of the Spirit, either through filling or enduement, to those disciples who asked. None did, as far as we know, but they were to receive Him on the Day of Pentecost. So where does this lead us Church Age believers who receive the Spirit's empowerment automatically upon salvation, lose it at the first blush of sin, then regain Him upon confession of sin? This is a prayer promise to us, but with qualifications. After having interpreted this verse, how do we, as Church Age believers, apply this it?

Those qualifications include these factors. First, the Church Age believer must ask in prayer, while empowered by God the Holy Spirit and adhering to strict prayer protocol. Secondly, the believer must have searched the Scripture in the form of consistent Bible study to gain the knowledge of His will so that he always prayers within His will. This requires much spiritual growth. Then, having fulfilled those factors, the believer will receive from the Father, positive answers to his prayers. Furthermore, even when we do pray erroneously, even outside of His empowerment, the Spirit graciously intercedes for us.

> *Likewise the Spirit helps us in our weakness; for we do not know how to pray as we ought, but that very Spirit intercedes with sighs too deep for words. Romans 8:26*

D. Matthew 7:12—The Golden Rule: The Limits of the Mosaic Law

> *In everything do to others as you would have them do to you; for this is the law and the prophets. Matthew 7:12*

Understand that the Scripture does not call these words of our Lord the "Golden Rule." Nor does this verse have anything to do with the spiritual life of the Church Age believer.

The meaning of the first phrase of the verse is clear; the original Greek words, though difficult to translate, offer us no exegetical surprises.

The last phrase, though, needs some explanation. The Law and the Prophets refers to the entirety of the Scripture, as it then existed: to the Old Testament, the Mosaic Law. The main purpose of the Law was to demonstrate that people could not hope to attain to God's standard of righteousness. People need a Savior. The Law and the Prophets also teach Christology, presenting the gospel of our Lord, faith in Whom is the only means of salvation. The first phrase then belongs to the previous dispensation because it teaches something that a person cannot fulfill without the empowerment of the Holy Spirit, which our Lord had just offered His disciples.

Because they did not ask for the Spirit, Who would have given them freedom from the Law, this so-called Golden Rule was the highest function for which they could hope. Church Age believers, reaping freedom from the Law by virtue of the Son's substitutionary sacrificial death, need not only to not ask for the Spirit, but enjoy His filling and empowerment automatically by keeping short accounts of sin. This grace provision, however, we should never construe as license to sin! Church Age believers, then, live by a higher principle; we are to do to others as Christ has done, and continually does for us! We are to treat others with the same grace He has treated us, not with the legalism of the Law. No one earns or deserves anything from God; He has given us everything because of His grace.

> *Bear with one another and, if anyone has a complaint against another, forgive each other; just as the Lord has forgiven you, so you also must forgive. Colossians 3:13*

> *A new commandment I give to you, that you love one another, even as I have loved you, that you also love one another. John 13:34.*

PART X

ENTERING THE GATE OF SALVATION: THE GOSPEL MATTHEW 7:13-14

Enter through the narrow gate. For the gate is wide and the road is broad that leads to destruction, and there are many who go through it. How narrow is the gate and difficult the road that leads to life, and few find it. Matthew 7:13-14

Strive to enter through the narrow door; for many, I tell you, will seek to enter and will not be able. Luke 13:24

These two verses comprise the command to believe the Gospel of our Lord, to receive salvation. Entering the narrow gate is a metaphor for faith.

A. Matthew 7:13—The Narrow Gate

Enter through the narrow gate; for the gate is wide and the way is broad that leads to destruction, and there are many who enter through it.

Enter through the narrow gate.
Εἰσέλθατε διὰ τῆς στενῆς πύλης.

This verse begins with "enter," the aorist active imperative verb, EISERCHOMAI (εἰσέρχομαι). Its meaning is as translated, "to enter." The New Testament uses different words for varied kinds of entering, but the most common one relates to God. It refers to entering into His Kingdom, presence or will. As an imperative, it is a command to the entire human race to believe the Gospel of our Lord, entering into His will. Obviously, not every human being will obey this command. God built freedom of choice, at least in the spiritual arena into every human being giving the opportunity to accept or to refuse this great gift of salvation. The aorist tense indicates action of entry. At some point preceding belief, you had to have heard the Gospel. Then you made the decision to believe it. The active voice indicates that you made that decision to believe.

The next word, "through" is the preposition DIA (διά) which when combined with the genitive indicates an instrument of means. The next three words include that instrument: HO (ὁ) with STENOS (στενός) and PULE (πύλη), the narrow gate. The narrow gate is the Gospel of our Lord, to include His deaths, both physical from which He was resurrected and substitutionary spiritual by which He paid for our sins. When you heard the Gospel, you stood before that gate. When you believed it, you entered the Kingdom through that gate. Note that the gate is narrow. Only one way exists through that gate, faith in our Lord Jesus Christ. Only one road leads to salvation, that of faith in Him.

Jesus said to him, "I am the way, and the truth, and the life; no one comes to the Father but through Me." John 14:6

And there is salvation in no one else; for there is no other name under heaven that has been given among men by which we must be saved. Acts 4:12

Our Lord continued His message with the antithesis, referring to those who refuse the narrow gate leading to salvation.

For the gate is wide and the road is broad that leads to destruction, and there are many who go through it.
ὅτι πλατεῖα ἡ πύλη καὶ εὐρύχωρος ἡ ὁδὸς ἡ ἀπάγουσα εἰς τὴν ἀπώλειαν καὶ πολλοί εἰσιν οἱ εἰσερχόμενοι δι' αὐτῆς.

That the gate is wide and road broad means that many paths exist that will result in a person sharing his or her destination with Satan. While only faith in Christ results in salvation, every religion and so-called life philosophies lead to the Lake of Fire. Because of our having been born into spiritual death, retaining our old sin natures even after salvation, we all default to the wide path leading to destruction.

Though believers avoid judgment leading to the Lake of Fire because they possess eternal life, they remain vulnerable to that broad road leading to temporal destruction. This destruction does not refer to the Lake of Fire but to the destruction of one's spiritual life. Often believers become focused upon the temporal success unbeliever's seemingly enjoy. Though evil, they appear to prosper to the greater degree than most believers do. As taught in the Doctrine of Happiness, their prosperity is not only temporary, being limited to this life, but also deceptive, being a substitute of God's perfect happiness. Satan's so-called happiness leads only to destruction, both temporal and eternal.

Another factor believers need to consider when facing temptations from the worldly system of thinking deals with Satanic rewards. Though Satan rewards his minions, those living in his system, he does not reward believers who enter his system. When it comes to believers, Satan designed his system to discredit and to destroy them. You as a believer will not prosper in the satanic system because you are its enemy. He designed it to destroy and to discredit your spiritual life and your ministry. Do not fall for lies from the satanic system. Your spiritual life road is narrow, yet full of happiness and divinely given prosperity, often undetectable by the world.

B. Matthew 7:14—The Small Gate

For the gate is small and the way is narrow that leads to life, and there are few who find it.
τί στενὴ ἡ πύλη καὶ τεθλιμμένη ἡ ὁδὸς ἡ ἀπάγουσα εἰς τὴν ζωὴν καὶ ὀλίγοι εἰσὶν οἱ εὑρίσκοντες αὐτήν.

In this verse, our Lord expands the gate concept. The word, "narrow" in verse 13 and the word "small" in this verse both come from the Greek word, STENOS (στενός), meaning either narrow or small. Our Lord further expanded this concept in His conversation with the rich young ruler.

Again I say to you, it is easier for a camel to go through the eye of a needle, than for a rich man to enter the kingdom of God.
Matthew 19:24

The "eye of the needle" refers to the small gate leading into a walled town or city that gives access to it after the main gates are closed. The gate is so small that a camel has difficulty going through it. The rich man has a problem with this gate because he has baggage that will not fit through it. That baggage is his temporal priorities that distract from the eternal.

Why is the gate leading to life, eternal life, said to be small and narrow? Entering this gate is contrary to the human's natural tendency that comes from spiritual death. Entering that gate begins with God consciousness, a factor that He built into every person. This is an awareness that an entity greater than humans must exist. If a person seeks that entity, then God sees to it that this person will receive the Gospel of our Lord. Not many people seek God; things of this world distract them. These things include self, entertainment, and religion. Even those seekers become distracted upon hearing the Gospel then refuse to believe. These distractions involve believing satanic deceptions and lies resulting in human arrogance and evil.

On a different occasion, our Lord used entering the gate as an analogy for faith as well. He was asked if many were being saved. He replied in the form of a command:

Strive to enter through the narrow door; for many, I tell you, will seek to enter and will not be able. Luke 13:24

The word, "strive" is AGONIZMAI (ἀγωνίζομαι) in the imperative. This word, reminiscent of the English word, agonize, places great emphasis on the effort required to enter through the narrow gate leading to salvation. It is not difficult in terms of divine provision. God has provided everything we need for salvation, but our arrogance, self-centeredness and tendency to believe the lie serves to block our way. This block is completely self-induced and in no way attributable to God.

PART XI

FALSE PROPHETS
MATTHEW 7:15-23

A. Matthew 7:15-20—Warnings of False Prophets

Beware of the false prophets, who come to you in sheep's clothing, but inwardly are ravenous wolves. You will know them by their fruits. Grapes are not gathered from thorn bushes nor figs from thistles, are they? So every good tree bears good fruit, but the bad tree bears bad fruit. A good tree cannot produce bad fruit, nor can a bad tree produce good fruit. Every tree that does not bear good fruit is cut down and thrown into the fire. So then, you will know them by their fruits.

These verses address an area that all new believers are very vulnerable to: false teachers. False teaching may distract new believers who do not have a store of doctrine within their thinking to compare what a teacher disseminates with known true doctrine. Paul also addressed this problem to the Galatian believers. These five verses warn believers about false teachers. Generally, the way to recognize a false teacher is by what he produces. Our Lord used the tree along with its fruit or produce to make an analogy.

1. Matthew 7:15—Sheep's Clothing

Beware of the false prophets, who come to you in sheep's clothing, but inwardly are ravenous wolves.
Προσέχετε ἀπὸ τῶν ψευδοπροφητῶν, οἵτινες ἔρχονται πρὸς ὑμᾶς ἐν ἐνδύμασιν προβάτων, ἔσωθεν δέ εἰσιν λύκοι ἅρπαγες.

"Beware," the first word in this verse in both the Greek and English is the present active imperative of PROECHO (προσέχω). The imperative mood means that this is a command from our Lord, one we need to take seriously. We need to be alert to what our Lord taught as well as to a reservoir of correct doctrinal thinking with which to compare the teaching.

The term "false prophets," PSEUDOPROPHETES (ψευδοπροφήτης), along with their description, "in sheep's clothing" and "ravenous wolves," could lead one to believe that these false teachers are insincere, very aware that they are teaching satanic deceptions. Often these teachers, not necessarily forth-tellers only, are well meaning and sincere about their teaching, being deluded themselves. Even though they think they are teaching accurately, having been deceived, they take on the character of the master deceiver himself. These teachers have been exposed to the truth but have rejected it. They have assimilated and propagated the lie instead of the truth. So they are every bit as culpable for the falsehood and deceptions they teach as Satan, himself.

For the believer, either new or seasoned, alertness takes on certain characteristics. First, as mentioned earlier, every believer must have some content of doctrine in his thinking. For the new believer, this may mean only an accurate knowledge of the Gospel. The new believer will not be challenged in any doctrinal area to which he has not yet been exposed. God has promised that a believer will not be tested beyond the degree of his spiritual growth.

No temptation has overtaken you but such as is common to man; and God is faithful, who will not allow you to be tempted beyond what you are able, but with the temptation will provide the way of escape also, so that you will be able to endure it. 1 Corinthians 10:13

Being exposed to a false teacher is a test, a challenge to one's spiritual growth. More accurately, a believer will not be tested beyond the doctrine he has been taught. If the believer was not listening to the accurate teaching or has rejected it, he may still be tested on it. That testing may well come from a false prophet or teacher. The false prophet or teacher the seasoned, well-taught believer may hear will present persuasive arguments challenging doctrines that are more complex.

Not only is mastery of doctrines to which you have been exposed important but of utmost importance to your spiritual status. Are you empowered by God the Holy Spirit? He will bring to your thinking the doctrines you have been taught and believed so that you can be alert to falsehoods false teachers teach you.

These false prophets, characterized as wearing sheep's clothing, ENDOMA (ἔνδυμα) PROBATON (πρόβατον), means that they appear harmless, as sheep, but instead are dangerous. "Ravenous wolves" is derived from the Greek words LUKOS (λύκος) HARPAX (ἅρπαξ). HARPAX can be translated to include many forms of violence, but in this context, it refers to consuming an unaware victim. You can be devoured by believing false doctrine, becoming totally ineffective as a believer. Though speaking to their congregations as angels of light, they promulgate counterfeit doctrines.

> *But the Spirit explicitly says that in later times some will fall away from the faith, paying attention to deceitful spirits and doctrines of demons,*
> *1 Timothy 4:1*

An example of wolves in sheep's clothing in our Lord's day was the Pharisee, who taught a false spirituality by misapplying the Mosaic Law. In Paul's day, the Judaizers were teaching that believers needed to follow the Mosaic Law as a part of their Christian spirituality. The Gnostics continually challenged John's teaching.

> *Beloved, do not believe every spirit, but test the spirits to see whether they are from God, because many false prophets have gone out into the world. 1 John 4:1*

Today, the examples are impossible to count. Ignorant preachers populate pulpits who do not know the Word of God, teaching only liberal philosophies and satanic doctrines under the guise of good.

2. Matthew 7:16—Knowing by Fruit

> *You will know them by their fruits. Grapes are not gathered from thorn bushes nor figs from thistles, are they?*
> *ἀπὸ τῶν καρπῶν αὐτῶν ἐπιγνώσεσθε αὐτούς. μήτι συλλέγουσιν ἀπὸ ἀκανθῶν σταφυλὰς ἢ ἀπὸ τριβόλων σῦκα;*

In this verse, our Lord continued to educate His disciples, teaching them how to recognize false teachers. They did not have the written Word, so they needed to compare what the Pharisees were teaching with the Words of our Lord. Not only did they need to pay attention to their teaching but also to the results of their teaching. In your own life, when you learn and apply *bona fide* doctrine under the filling of the Holy Spirit, your life will change! At least, you have the opportunity to change your life. You will be cognizant of the power God has given to you to change. You just need to add your own volition to the mix, using His power to make right decisions. You will produce, by means of the empowering Spirit and doctrine the fruit of the Spirit.

> *But the fruit of the Spirit is love, joy, peace, patience, kindness, goodness, faithfulness, Galatians 5:22*

No such results come from false teaching. You may gain temporary stimulation from interacting with followers of false doctrine, but the long-term results will be misery.

The second line in this verse drives the principle home with an analogy. You cannot pick worthwhile fruit from plants that do not naturally produce them!

3. Matthew 7:17—Good Tree, Good Fruit

> *So every good tree bears good fruit, but the bad tree bears bad fruit.*

Jim Oliver

So every good tree bears good fruit.
οὕτως πᾶν δένδρον ἀγαθὸν καρποὺς καλοὺς ποιεῖ,

The two words "good" and "bad" are the key to understanding this verse. Actually, we need to understand four words, because the English word, "good" comes from two different Greek words, and the word "bad" comes from two different Greek words.

The "good" that describes the tree comes from the Greek word, AGATHOS (ἀγαθός) referring to good of intrinsic value. In other words, whenever this good is found, there is value to it. Gold carries intrinsic value because no matter where it is found or in what form it is, it still has value. So it is with the Divine. There is nothing related to His righteousness that is not good having intrinsic value.

And He said to him, "Why are you asking Me about what is good? There is only One who is good; but if you wish to enter into life, keep the commandments." Matthew 19:17

But when Christ appeared as a high priest of the good things to come, He entered through the greater and more perfect tabernacle, not made with hands, that is to say, not of this creation; Hebrews 9:11

This tree, then, is AGATHOS, good, because it is related to God. This good tree prophet is not a false prophet but a true one related to God. The fruit from this one is characterized by the second word translated as "good" in the English; KALOS (καλός). The prophet or Bible teacher characterized as AGATHOS good, being related to God, will produce KALOS good fruit or work.

The good work or fruit is a work that results from AGATHOS good. We can call good coming from God, divine good. Good produced by believers in this Church Age who are filled, empowered by the God the Holy Spirit has intrinsic value.

... but the bad tree bears bad fruit.
... τὸ δὲ σαπρὸν δένδρον καρποὺς πονηροὺς ποιεῖ.

The verse continues with the antithesis: a bad tree, referring to the false prophet, producing bad fruit. The "bad" characterizing the tree and the fruit comes two different Greek words. The bad tree is a SARPOS (σαπρός) one, meaning that it is rotten and decaying. This is a picture of spiritual death. If one does not change his thinking, remaining instead in a state of separation from God, then he is in a state of decay. The culmination of this rot is eternity in the Lake of Fire in a body designed to withstand continual pain. The fruit produced by this tree is characterized as PONEROS (πονηρός), evil, disadvantageous, worthless and of the evil one.

4. Matthew 7:18—Good Tree, Bad Fruit

A good tree cannot produce bad fruit, nor can a bad tree produce good fruit.

This sentence appears to be a "dumbing down" of the previous two verses. Perhaps when our Lord said this sentence, He was looking directly at Judas. He had been following our Lord from the beginning, yet he had not leaned even the simplest of lessons, how to be saved. He was still wallowing in sin and evil, though he thought he was doing the right thing. From his standpoint, the work he is most noted for, turning Jesus in for the shekels of silver, was a good act. Through it, he may have been trying to move Jesus to militarily resist arrest then take up arms against Rome. He was trying to move Jesus into the direction of freeing Israel from Roman domination. How far from the truth was he? Even had this been our Lord's goal, not being saved, Judas could not produce good fruit from an AGATHOS tree. He fit the category of a bad tree, even though well meaning, only able to produce bad fruit. Judas's work was evil! No matter how good his works appeared to be, there was no way he could ever produce good fruit because he was a bad tree. No matter how much he tried or how many "good" things he did, all he could ever produce was evil.

5. Matthew 7:19—Into the Fire

Every tree that does not bear good fruit is cut down and thrown into the fire.
πᾶν δένδρον μὴ ποιοῦν καρπὸν καλὸν ἐκκόπτεται καὶ εἰς πῦρ βάλλεται.

To make the matter as clear as possible, in the most simple language possible, our Lord concluded the lesson by revealing the final destination of not only the false prophet but also any evil fruit tree. That tree is EKKOPTO (ἐκκόπτω), cut down or done away with. It is then thrown into fire. If our Lord was addressing Judas, an unbeliever, then the fire He was referring to is unmistakable. He was referring to the Lake of Fire. Every tree or person that is not AGATHOS, not related to God, will be removed from this earth and at the end of the Millennium, being cast into the Lake of Fire. So many unbelievers take this news glibly saying that all their friends will be there so that it will be a party. One could only call eternity in the Lake of Fire a party if one's idea of a party is eternal darkness and interminable pain. That people choose to ignore our Lord's gracious work on the Cross is tragic. Judas, unless he were to change his thinking about our Lord was doomed to the Lake of Fire.

Even we as Church Age believers can take an application from this. Though we possess eternal life, having already passed through judgment, there is a fire we need to consider. Paul talked about this to the Corinthian believers.

If any man's work which he has built on it remains, he will receive a reward. If any man's work is burned up, he will suffer loss; but he himself will be saved, yet so as through fire.
1 Corinthians 3:14-15

The context of these two verses is the building up of spiritual assets upon the foundation of salvation that our Lord has provided us. The lesson is this: if the believer lives his life empowered by God the Holy Spirit, then his work will have value that the Father will reward. However, if the believer remains carnal throughout his life, his work, his deeds will all be burned, leaving nothing of value for the Father to reward.

6. Matthew 7:20—Knowing by Fruit

> *So then, you will know them by their fruits.*
> ἄρα γε ἀπὸ τῶν καρπῶν αὐτῶν ἐπιγνώσεσθε αὐτούς.

This verse wraps up the entire lesson concerning false prophets. Again, to interpret properly this verse, we need to understand its context: Jesus was delivering this lesson to His disciples during the Age of Israel, not during the Church Age. Secondly, we need to understand the words, "know" and "fruit."

The interpretive issue regarding the dispensation in which our Lord taught is important. Misapplying this verse, applying it literally during this age, can lead to legalism. During the Age of Israel, the spiritual life, though motivated by love for God, was manifested externally. One's adherence to the Mosaic Law was very visible because it required fulfilling outward rituals. The Church Age, however, is a horse of a different color. Spirituality is being filled with God the Holy Spirit, which often carries no outward manifestation at all. Certainly a spiritual believer fulfills standards of morality, makes Bible study a top life priority and manifests integrity in every area of life. Nevertheless, often such things are invisible even if that believer were to be continually observed by another believer. Therefore, this sentence does not strictly apply during this dispensation. One believer does not have the spiritual authority or knowledge of all the facts to evaluate the spiritual life of another.

Another point of context however, does allow for the evaluation of one's spiritual production. This entire passage deals with the doctrinal communicator, the prophet or priest, in the Age of Israel. Therefore, in this dispensation, this applies to the believer evaluating the ministry of the pastor-teacher or Bible teacher. The believer must make sure that the pastor he has chosen to lead him spiritually teaches orthodox doctrine and lives the life that the writers of the Scripture prescribe.

> **It is a trustworthy statement: if any man aspires to the office of overseer, it is a fine work he desires to do. An overseer, then, must be above reproach, the husband of one wife, temperate, prudent, respectable, hospitable, able to teach ... 1 Timothy 3:1-2**

Getting back to our passage, the word, "know," comes from the Greek word, EPIGNOSKO (ἐπιγινώσκω) in the future middle indicative. It is active in meaning, however, indicating that the subject carries out the action of the verb. This word often has a very technical meaning, when used by Paul, but in this case, the idea of recognition is strong. You, as a growing, spiritual believer will recognize orthodox doctrinal teaching when you hear it because you are able to line it up with doctrines which you have been taught, have believed, and have allowed the Holy Spirit to circulate throughout your thinking. The word, "fruit," KARPOS (Κάρπος) probably needs no further definition if you understand it as production. In this case, we are talking about the spiritual production of a doctrinal communicator, presumably his preparation and his teaching by which he cares for and guards his congregation.

B. Matthew 7:21-23—The Condemnation of the False Prophet

Not everyone who says to Me, 'Lord, Lord,' will enter the Kingdom of Heaven, but he who does the will of My Father who is in heaven will enter. Many will say to Me on that day, 'Lord, Lord, did we not prophesy in Your name, and in Your name cast out demons, and in Your name perform many miracles?' "And then I will declare to them, 'I never knew you; depart from Me, you who practice lawlessness.' Matthew 7:21-23

Jesus continued His lesson on the false teacher in the following verses by teaching about their destination.

1. Matthew 7:21

Not everyone who says to Me, 'Lord, Lord,' will enter the kingdom of heaven, but he who does the will of My Father who is in Heaven will enter.

Not everyone who says to Me, 'Lord, Lord,' ' will enter the kingdom of heaven,
Οὐ πᾶς ὁ λέγων μοι, Κύριε κύριε, εἰσελεύσεται εἰς τὴν βασιλείαν τῶν οὐρανῶν,

This verse begins with the two words OU PAS (οὐ πᾶς), meaning, "not all." Everyone will call our Lord, "Lord, Lord," KURIOS (κύριος), recognizing our Lord's ultimate authority. For many this recognition will come too late, occurring at the Great White Throne Judgment. However, that will not be enough to enter into His kingdom, to live with Him eternally.

... but he who does the will of My Father who is in Heaven will enter.
... ἀλλ' ὁ ποιῶν τὸ θέλημα τοῦ πατρός μου τοῦ ἐν τοῖς οὐρανοῖς.

Certainly, all those who in time do the Father's will, believing in His Son, will enter into His kingdom. The first thing a person can do to qualify as doing the Father's will is to believe in Christ. All those who believe in Jesus Christ will enter into the Kingdom. However, there is a category of those, though recognizing our Lord's authority, who will not, "at that time" enter.

2. Matthew 7:22

Many will say to Me on that day, 'Lord, Lord, did we not prophesy in

Your name, and in Your name cast out demons, and in Your name perform many miracles?'

Visualize those who only recognize His authority at the Great White Throne Judgment. At this point, it is too late. These failed to believe in our Lord in time and now, after time, they appear at His throne, trying to justify themselves, trying to get into Heaven because of their work. Their works, which do not get them into Heaven, are listed: prophecy, casting out demons and performing miracles. These, though seemingly *bona fide*, because they come from the unbeliever are satanic.

3. Matthew 7:23

And then I will declare to them, 'I never knew you; depart from Me, you who practice lawlessness.'
and He will say, 'I tell you, I do not know where you are from; depart from Me, all you evildoers.' Luke 13:27

And then I will declare to them ...
καὶ τότε ὁμολογήσω αὐτοῖς ...

The word, "declare" comes from the Greek HOMOLOGEO (ὁμολογέω) in the future active indicative, used in the sense of a public announcement. This word needs some further explanation, as its meaning has had some development over the centuries after its coinage. This discussion is probably deeper than its use in this context demands, but this word is so charged with meaning that a closer look at it is irresistible.

It is often true that one can discern the meaning of a compound word by looking at its parts. This was true of this word, being a combination of HOMO (ὁμο), "the same" and LOGEO (λογέω), "to say," as meaning "to say the same thing" or "to agree in statement" in the 5th century BC. However, even in the 5th century, its range of meanings varied according to context. This range of meanings included:

"to agree to the statement of another (or others)"
"to accept his affirmation" or specifically "to admit a charge,"
"to make a confession of guilt"
"to confirm the receipt of money"
"to agree to a proposal"
"to agree to a wish"
"to promise..."[1]

So, we can learn from all of these uses of the word, even when it was coined in the in the 5th century BC, that we need to study its context to nail down its given meaning.

Its use was significant in the Socratic debate method because those dialogs point was to bring people to a consensus through logic. Often that consensus directly conflicted with the current thinking. Because of the logic involved to reach the consensus it implied not just agreement but "definite resolve and action, by ready attachment to a cause. The aim in HOMOLOGEO (ὁμολογία) is not a theoretical agreement which does not commit us, but acceptance of a common cause..."[li] This word then becomes a definite call to action on the part of its user.

This call-to-action implication becomes very significant to one applying the word in 1 John 1:9. One does not simply name his sin to the Father as a confession of guilt, then carry on with his life with no intention of developing strength against that category of troublesome sin. Not to add works to sin confession, but the drive to spiritual growth is important to believers as they keep a clean slate of sin with the Father. A glib naming of one's sin to the Father may, for a short time, bring about the resumption of one's spiritual life. However, if one does not bring to bear all of his spiritual assets to resolve problem areas of sin, then that period of spirituality will be short lasting. Carnality from sin will overtake the believer. He may even become evil.

The word's continued development in the Old Testament included the concept of praise toward God, as in confessing God's greatness through the public confession of sin. The New Testament use intensifies the concept of confession in terms of both one's own sin and faith in Christ.

Returning to our verse, there, then, will be no mistaking this message. Unbelievers are to be totally excluded from God's Kingdom. This is a dynamic declaration with a call to action to include all those who do not confess the Deity of the Son during time.

'I never knew you.
ὅτι Οὐδέποτε ἔγνων ὑμᾶς.

The criterion of exclusion is our Lord's knowledge of that person. The word "knew" is the aorist active indicative of GINOSKO (γινώσκω), indicating intimate knowledge of that person. These whom He does not know are not of His family, as believers are. The aorist tense in the indicative mood refers to the past time, the time on earth before unbelievers are to be judged.

depart from Me, you who practice lawlessness.'
ἀποχωρεῖτε ἀπ' ἐμοῦ οἱ ἐργαζόμενοι τὴν ἀνομίαν.

Continuing this verse, He quoted from Psalm 6:8, beginning with the present active imperative of APOCHOREO (ἀποχωρέω). Applying the overall context of this section of the Sermon, those practicing lawlessness refers to those steeped-in-religion Pharisees. The Pharisaic teaching qualified as lawless because it misconstrued the Mosaic Law. It qualified as religion, as opposed to a saving relationship with Jesus Christ, because it taught working instead of receiving grace. Bringing this into our dispensation, it refers to all those who teach the Scripture erroneously. Obviously, no pastor's ministry—his Biblical interpretation and application—is perfect. However, all pastors should seek to teach from a consistent and systematic foundation that falls within the strict Biblical context. All religion is antithetical to Christianity. All those who are religious, evil doers in this contest, are enemies of the Cross of Christ.

Other passages teach this same theme.

> *"Then you will begin to say, 'We ate and drank in Your presence, and You taught in our streets'; Luke 13:26*

> *Depart from me, all you who do iniquity, For the Lord has heard the voice of my weeping. Psalm 6:8*

> *"Then He will also say to those on His left, 'Depart from Me, accursed ones, into the eternal fire which has been prepared for the devil and his angels; Matthew 25:41*

PART XII

ILLUSTRATION COMPARING THE BELIEVER WITH THE UNBELIEVER
MATTHEW 7:24-27

Therefore everyone who hears these words of Mine and acts on them, may be compared to a wise man who built his house on the rock. And the rain fell, and the floods came, and the winds blew and slammed against that house; and yet it did not fall, for it had been founded on the rock. Everyone who hears these words of Mine and does not act on them, will be like a foolish man who built his house on the sand. The rain fell, and the floods came, and the winds blew and slammed against that house; and it fell—and great was its fall. Matthew 7:24-27

Everyone who comes to Me and hears My words and acts on them, I will show you whom he is like: he is like a man building a house, who dug deep and laid a foundation on the rock; and when a flood occurred, the torrent burst against that house and could not shake it, because it had been well built. But the one who has heard and has not acted accordingly, is like a man who built a house on the ground without any foundation; and the torrent burst against it and immediately it collapsed, and the ruin of that house was great.
Luke 6:47-49

    Our Lord concluded the main body of this Sermon with a metaphor illustrating the difference between the one who believes in Him and the one who does not. The metaphor also applies to the Church Age believer, comparing the one who listens, believes and applies our Lord's doctrines with the one who does not. The person who hears these words, even now, becomes responsible for them. Only two choices exist: one either believes them and acts upon them or does not believe, then rejects them. There is no in-between. The unbeliever who listens and applies these words will believe in our Lord. From then on, his life would have been built upon the Rock, eternally.

The one who believes is likened to the one who builds upon the foundation of rock. When building any edifice, the foundation upon which it is built determines its ability to withstand adversity. The adversities with which our Lord illustrated included water from both above and below the earth, and wind. These illustrations would have resonated with His audience because they experienced these natural disasters being so close to the Sea of Galilee. For the Church Age believer, the one who continually studies the Word, believes it, and then applies it builds his life upon the thinking of the Rock. This one becomes unshakable when faced with any adversity in life.

In several passages, the Scripture characterizes our Lord as the Rock:

> *Let the words of my mouth and the meditation of my heart*
> *Be acceptable in Your sight, O Lord, my Rock and my Redeemer.*
> *Psalm 19:14*

> *To You, O Lord, I call; My Rock, do not be deaf to me,*
> *For if You are silent to me, I will become like those who go down to the pit. Psalm 28:1*

> *...and all drank the same spiritual drink, for they were drinking from a spiritual rock which followed them; and the rock was Christ.*
> *1 Corinthians 10:4*

PART XIII:

JESUS' AUTHORITY/CONCLUSION
MATTHEW 7:28-29

When Jesus had finished these words, the crowds were amazed at His teaching; for He was teaching them as one having authority, and not as their scribes. Matthew 7:28-29

When Jesus had finished these words ...
Καὶ ἐγένετο ὅτε ἐτέλεσεν ὁ Ἰησοῦς τοὺς λόγους τούτους ...

This verse begins with a Hebraism, generally not translated into the English. This consists of the conjunction KAI (καί), "and," with the aorist active indicative of the verb of being, GINOMAI (γίνομαι), which Matthew used frequently to complete a section in his book. These words could be translated as, "and it happened that..." The verse continues with the temporal adverb HOTE (ὅτε), "when," with the aorist active indicative of TELEW (τελέω) meaning, "to complete." The aorist tense, in this case, works to indicate a snapshot of the event.

The subject of the sentence, in the Greek word order, is next: the articular nominative noun IESOUS (Ἰησοῦς)—transliterated Jesus—the name of our Lord's humanity. The article is qualitative emphasizing our Lord's uniqueness. Next is the articular genitive noun, LOGOS (λόγος), "these words." The translation reads as, "And it happened that when Jesus had completed these words..."

As with many other words explored in this text, LOGOS carries great meaning with it. In this context, referring to the lessons our Lord had been teaching, goes beyond indicating the simple words He had spoken. Of the secular use of LOGOS, the TDNT has this to say: "...this λόγος is not taken to be something which is merely grasped theoretically. It claims a man. It determines his true life and conduct. The λόγος is thus the norm ..."[lii] Even in its secular use, LOGOS translated here as "word," indicates the gravity and importance we need to give the words our Lord spoke.

The aorist tense lends credence to His teaching these many things once, upon that mountain, but then perhaps He often repeated these many important lessons. One of the most dramatic and important uses of LOGOS refers to our Lord as the source of divine thought.

Matthew then recorded the crowd's response. He did not record if anyone believed because of this Sermon, only that they were amazed. Our Lord may have been focusing the Gospel presentation on Judas, who, at that time, was the only disciple who did not believe. So Matthew recorded that the crowd of people was amazed and astonished! Better than amazed, the Greek source word, EKPLESSOMAI (ἐκπλήσσομαι) expresses shock and total astonishment! "The verb means literally 'were struck out of themselves.'"[liii] The Greeks used THAUMAZO to express a milder amazement. EKPLESSOMAI expresses an intense shock! The reason for their shock was our Lord's expression of authority, not necessarily the content of His message. The crowd just was not used to anyone teaching with authority that resided within himself instead of relying upon an earlier teacher. Our Lord was the author of everything He taught so that His divine authority shone through everything He said. You remember how He had preceded His statements with, "but I say to you!" His authority resided in Himself, not on others previously published. "The consciousness of divine authority, as Lawgiver, Expounder, and Judge, so beamed through His teaching, that the scribes teaching could not but appear driveling in such a light."[liv]

Our Lord's teaching was in complete contrast to the scribes. "They had heard many sermons before from the regular rabbis in the synagogues. We have specimens of these discourses preserved in the Mishna and Gemara, the Jewish Talmud when both were completed, the driest, dullest collection of disjointed comments upon every conceivable problem in the history of humanity. The scribes quoted the rabbis before them and were afraid to express an idea without bolstering it up by some predecessor. Jesus spoke with the authority of truth, the reality and freshness of the morning light, and the power of God's Spirit."[lv]

When pastors teach from the pulpit, they should also teach with authority, understanding that they teach the Word of God. Pastors, who use the power of the Spirit during their study process then maintain spirituality while teaching, can be confident that what they teach carries divine authority as well.[lvi]

In the next couple of chapters, Matthew described how our Lord superseded His spoken authority with action, with miracles of further healings.

Author's Conclusion

Concluding an in-depth study of one of our Lord's foundational sermons presents a difficulty for a Bible teacher who does not usually conclude a study but simply moves on to the next! Like Jesus' listeners, I experienced astonishment, thrill and pure joy when exploring each sentence, delving into how Matthew and often Luke and Mark recorded what our Lord taught. Not only did He pack His lessons with content applicable to all generations but did so with language sure to thrill the translator! Yet the attempt to conclude such a collection of continually pertinent and applicable words leaves me with the desire to return to them to keep learning from them. There can be no end to the study of these or any of our Lord's words because just as He, Himself, has no limits, we can never completely fathom the depth of His words.

Returning to the thesis of this study, a look into each verse has demonstrated that our Lord prepared His disciples to announce His advent through it, yet He has also given Church Age believers lessons of vital importance. The most important distinction between His disciples' ability to gain from this series of lessons and how we Church Age believers gain lies in the means of increasing knowledge. While our Lord offered His disciples the empowerment of the Spirit to power their comprehension, they most likely did not understand its importance. Perhaps they would have understood Him to a greater degree had they accepted the Spirit's power. In this age, He has made His Spirit's power available to every believer. Church Age believers need only keep a short account of sins to the Father to access the Spirit's teaching ministry. For this reason, we should able to keep gaining from continually studying every word our Lord spoke and His apostles wrote for us. It is my prayer that every believer use the spiritual resource our Heavenly Father has uniquely provided us to understand and apply His Word.

ABOUT THE AUTHOR

Jim Oliver graduated from Western Conservative Baptist Seminary in Portland Oregon in 1996 with a Masters of Exegetical Theology. He was ordained by Berachah Church in Houston, Texas. He pastored Teleios Bible Church in Salem, Oregon for 3 years. He has also authored blogs on various Biblical subjects including the Dispensations, Building Your Faith, Exegesis of the Book of Philippians, The Life of Christ, and other subjects.

Jim now resides in Keizer, Oregon with his wife and six children.

LINKS TO OTHER STUDIES

Slide Presentations on **AuthorStream.com** include:
Happiness, Logistical Grace, Dispensations, Prayer and Sanctification.
Studies on **Wordpress.com** (oliverministries.wordpress.com) include:
Building Your Faith, Dispensations, Philippians

Other Versions Available
Audio and an Abridged Versions Available at:
Amazon.com/author/jim_oliver

[i] Thieme, R. B. Class Notes from Berachah Church

[ii] http://www.culturewars.com/CultureWars/1999/kerouac.html

[iii] See link to *Happiness* above.

[iv] See *Sanctification* above.

[v] Newman, B. M., & Stine, P. C. (1992). *A handbook on the Gospel of Matthew* (p. 111). New York: United Bible Societies.

[vi] "Scar tissue of the soul" is a term coined by R. B. Thieme, Jr. who used it to describe what is tantamount to the inability to recall and apply the truths of the Word of God. He used the term through-out his teaching ministry.

[vii] Vincent, M. R. (1887). *Word studies in the New Testament* (Vol. 1, p. 38). New York: Charles Scribner's Sons.

[viii] Kittel, G., Bromiley, G. W., & Friedrich, G. (Eds.). (1964–). *Theological dictionary of the New Testament* (Vol. 4, p.316). Grand Rapids, MI: Eerdmans.

[ix] "Divine Establishment" is a term R. B. Thieme, which refers to those institutions God designed to protect human freedom. These include the sanctity of marriage and family, the preservation of individual volition, the importance of bona fide authority within organizations and independence of nations.

[x] [Zerwick, M., & Grosvenor, M. (1974). *A grammatical analysis of the Greek New Testament*. Originally published under title: Analysis philologica Novi Testamenti Graeci; translated, revised and adapted by Mary Grosvenor in collaboration with the author. (10). Rome: Biblical Institute Press.]

[xi] [Newman, B. M., & Stine, P. C. (1992). *A handbook on the Gospel of Matthew*. Originally published: A translator's handbook on the Gospel of Matthew, c1988. UBS helps for translators; UBS handbook series (113). New York: United Bible Societies.]

[xii] *Theological dictionary of the New Testament*. (Vol. II, p. 174)

[xiii] Thieme, R. B., Unpublished Notes from Lectures on *The Gospel of Matthew*. Berachah Church, Houston, TX.

[xiv] TDNT, Vol. IV, p. 832.

[xv] Vincent, M. R. (2002). *Word studies in the New Testament* (1:38—39). Bellingham, WA: Logos Research Systems, Inc.

[xvi] TDNT, Vol. III, p. 958

[xvii] TDNT, Vol. I, p. 336.

[xviii] Lukaszewski, A. L. (2007). In *The Lexham Syntactic Greek New Testament Glossary*. Logos Bible Software.

[xix] Gary Glenny, Notes from Lectures on 2 Peter to Portland Bible Church.

[xx] Fruchtenbaum, A. G. (2003). *The footsteps of the Messiah : a study of the sequence of prophetic*

[xx] *events* (Rev. ed.). Tustin, CA: Ariel Ministries, p. 135.

[xxi] Porter, S. E. (1999). *Idioms of the Greek New Testament* (p. 59). Sheffield: JSOT.

[xxii] Ibid. Thieme.

[xxiii] Thieme, R. B., *Rebound and Keep Moving,* Berachah Church, Houston, Tx.

[xxiv] Harris, R. L., Harris, R. L., Archer, G. L., & Waltke, B. K. (1999, c1980). *Theological Wordbook of the Old Testament* (electronic ed.) (662). Chicago: Moody Press.

[xxv] Ibid. Thieme, R.B. *Unpublished Notes on Matthew.*

[xxvi] Harris, R. L., Harris, R. L., Archer, G. L., & Waltke, B. K. (1999, c1980). *Theological Wordbook of the Old Testament* (electronic ed.) (662). Chicago: Moody Press.

[xxvii] TDNT Vol. IV, p. 971

[xxviii] Freeman, J. M., & Chadwick, H. J. (1998). *Manners & customs of the Bible* (pp. 410–411). North Brunswick, NJ: Bridge—Logos Publishers.

[xxix] Ibid. Thieme, R. B. *Unpublished Notes on Matthew.*

[xxx] Freeman, J. M., & Chadwick, H. J. (1998). *Manners & customs of the Bible* (pp. 410–411). North Brunswick, NJ: Bridge—Logos Publishers.

[xxxi] Wallace, D. B. (1999). *Greek Grammar Beyond the Basics - Exegetical Syntax of the New Testament* (p. 569). Zondervan Publishing House and Galaxie Software.

[xxxii] TDNT, Vol. 3, p. 973.

[xxxiii] For rich Rabb. material cf. Str.—B., I, 388; IV, 536 ff. Schl. Mt. on 6:2 thinks that we are perhaps to take the trumpets lit.

[xxxiv] TDNT, Vol. 2, p. 477.

[xxxv] Grace Seminary. (1987; 2002). *Vol. 8: Grace Theological Journal Volume 8* (41). Grace Seminary.

[xxxvi] Ibid. TDNT

[xxxvii] TDNT Vol. 3, p. 974

[xxxviii] Friberg, T., Friberg, B., & Miller, N. F. (2000). *Vol. 4: Analytical lexicon of the Greek New Testament.* Baker's Greek New Testament library (286). Grand Rapids, Mich.: Baker Books.

[xxxix] Friberg, T., Friberg, B., & Miller, N. F. (2000). *Vol. 4: Analytical lexicon of the Greek New Testament.* Baker's Greek New Testament library (286). Grand Rapids, Mich.: Baker Books.

[xl] (1999). *Chafer Theological Seminary Journal Volume 5.* p.54

[xli] TDNT Vol. VI, p. 1002.

[xlii] Trench, R. C. (1880). *Synonyms of the New Testament.* London: Macmillan and Co., p. 240.

[xliii] TDNT Vol. IV, p. 926

[xliv] Vincent, M. R. (1887). *Word studies in the New Testament* (Vol. 1, p. 50). New York:

Charles Scribner's Sons.

[xlv] TDNT Vol. III. p. 974

[xlvi] TDNT Vol. IV. p. 325.

[xlvii] (Porter, S. E. (1999). *Idioms of the Greek New Testament* (278). Sheffield: JSOT.)

[xlviii] TDNT Vol. III, p. 1101

[xlix] Vincent, M. R. (1887). *Word studies in the New Testament* (Vol. 1, p. 50). New York: Charles Scribner's Sons.

[l] TDNT Vol. V. p. 200.

[li] Ibid.

[lii] Kittel, G., Bromiley, G. W., & Friedrich, G. (Eds.). (1964–). *Theological dictionary of the New Testament* (electronic ed., Vol. 4, p. 81). Grand Rapids, MI: Eerdmans.

[liii] Robertson, A. T. (1933). *Word Pictures in the New Testament* (Mt 7:28–29). Nashville, TN: Broadman Press.

[liv] Robertson, A. T. (1933). *Word Pictures in the New Testament* (Mt 7:28–29). Nashville, TN: Broadman Press.

[lv] Robertson, A. T. (1933). *Word Pictures in the New Testament* (Mt 7:28–29). Nashville, TN: Broadman Press.

[lvi] Ibid.

PERMISSIONS:

Scripture quotations taken from the New American Standard Bible®, Copyright © 1960, 1962, 1963, 1968, 1971, 1972, 1973, 1975, 1977, 1995 by The Lockman Foundation are used by permission." (www.Lockman.org)

The Greek Text is quoted from the UBS4: The Greek New Testament, Fourth Revised Edition, edited by Barbara Aland, Kurt Aland, Johannes Karavidopoulos, Carlo M. Martini, and Bruce M. Metzger in cooperation with the Institute for New Testament Textual Research, Münster/Westphalia, © 1993 Deutsche Bibelgesellschaft, Stuttgart. Used by permission.

Made in the USA
San Bernardino, CA
11 March 2017